Learn
Microsoft®
Visual J++™ 6.0
Now

Kevin Ingalls and Daniel Jinguji

PUBLISHED BY
Microsoft Press
A Division of Microsoft Corporation
One Microsoft Way
Redmond,Washington 98052-6399

Library of Congress Cataloging-in-Publication Data
Jinguji, Daniel J., 1956-
    Learn Microsoft Visual J++ 6.0 Now / Daniel J. Jinguji, Kevin L. Ingalls.
       p. cm.
    Includes index.
    ISBN 1-57231-923-2
    1. Java (Computer program language)   2. Microsoft Visual J++.
  I. Ingalls, Kevin L. II. Title.
  QA76.73.J38J56   1998
  005.13'3--dc21   98-26270
                                        CIP

Printed and bound in the United States of America.

1 2 3 4 5 6 7 8 9 WCWC   3 2 1 0 9 8

Distributed in Canada by ITP Nelson, a division of Thomson Canada Limited.

A CIP catalogue record for this book is available from the British Library.

Microsoft Press books are available through booksellers and distributors worldwide. For further information about international editions, contact your local Microsoft Corporation office or contact Microsoft Press International directly at fax (425) 936-7329. Visit our Web site at mspress.microsoft.com.

For Microsoft Press
Acquisitions Editor: Eric Stroo
Project Editor: Melinda A. Faulkner

For WASSER*Studios*
Content Services Manager: Marcelle Amelia
Print Production Services Manager: Mary C. Gutierrez
Desktop Publishers: Kim Tapia, Ismael Marrero
Manuscript Editors: Jennifer Jurcik, Pm Weizenbaum
Technical Editors: Lisa Camire, Beryl Doane

*To my family and friends who help me to make the possible happen,
and to my mom and dad without whom I would not have been possible.*
Kevin Ingalls

*To my friends and family whose quiet and constant encouragement
made this possible.*
Dan Jinguji

Acknowledgments

I'd like to thank the academy…You must have noticed by now that book acknowledgments read like the author accepting an Academy Award. Well, this one's no different. You can't win an Oscar for acting without having an excellent producer, director, cast, and crew. The guy who wins the Oscar is really just the front man for a whole gaggle of talent. Thanks to Dan Jinguji for inviting me on to the project. Dan knows how to find great adventures, and this one did not disappoint. Thanks to Lisa Camire and Jennifer Jurcik, the technical and manuscript editors, respectively, for phase one of the project. They made the process of stepping my work up to the next level enjoyable (we sensitive artists can be hard to deal with). Thanks to Beryl Doane and Pm Weizenbaum, the technical and manuscript editors for phase two of the project. They stepped in and went from zero to 100 miles an hour in no time flat. A great deal of credit goes to Lisa, Jennifer, Beryl, and Pm for making the book what it is (but I'll take the blame for any bad stuff).

Wayne Beardsley, who has been my manager at Boeing for years, is the kind of manager whom people dream of (rather than have nightmares about). Wayne is that rarest of managers who lead by example, and a good example he is. While he wasn't involved in the creation of this book, it certainly would not have been possible without him. Thanks, Wayne.

I'd like to thank my wife, Misa, and my girls, Linnea and Megan, for making everything worth doing (in fact, for making anything worth doing). Misa was the first editor of both the text and the code examples, and her suggestions made for a better book. As I was writing this book, Linnea (six years old) was writing a few books of her own. Printing out the pages on the laser printer and stapling them together, she acted as her own publisher. I look forward to the day that she is a published author in the more traditional sense. And to Amelia, our dog, for curling up at my feet while I was working on the book late into the night. Never once did she ask what I was doing, but she must have wondered: "He stares at that box with the colored lights and paws at that thing for *hours*! He is so easily entertained."

Kevin Ingalls
July 1998

There are so many people I need to thank. Thanks to Kevin Ingalls who joined me in this escapade. Like all journeys, it had its rocky times and its smooth times, but it's always the company you keep that makes the trek enjoyable. Thanks to Lisa Camire, Jennifer Jurcik, Beryl Doane, and Pm Weizenbaum, the editors who guided us on our way. Theirs is the voice of clarity and consistency in these pages; mine is the quirky one off on a tangent.

Thanks to Brian Engler, Niall McDonnell, Lars Mohr, and Fay Tanagi, who kept asking how well it was going. Thanks to Jordan, James, and Philip Fleming who helped bring joy to the long days of writing and revising. Thanks to the supportive community at St. James Cathedral who kept everything in perspective, especially to Marianne Coté, the McCabe-Schmeltzers, Alison Warp, David Brazier, and Joe Adam.

And special thanks to my family: Dorothy, Beth, Teresa, Todd, Mayumi, Rebecca, Tom, and LeeAnn. It's incredible; you're always there for me.

Dan Jinguji
July 1998

TABLE OF CONTENTS

Introduction

Welcome to *Learn Visual J++ Now*. You are on the threshold of a big adventure: an adventure in Windows Java programming. What probably drew you to Java, and to this book about Java programming in Windows, is the explosion of interest in the World Wide Web. The World Wide Web represents a huge step toward the electronic global village that we've been hearing about over the last few years. And Visual J++ 6.0 is right there to help us, as programmers, move into that future. Using Visual J++ you will be able to develop both Windows applications and Web applets quickly and easily.

This book is geared toward the programmer. Java is a powerful, expressive programming language, and things can get a little hairy for the raw recruit. Although you don't have to be an expert programmer to use Java, it's definitely a good idea to be well grounded in the fundamentals of computer programming.

To get the most out of this book, you should be able to find your way around Windows as a user, but no prior Windows programming experience is required. If you haven't had the chance to use Microsoft's programming software before, you are going to enjoy the power and benefits of programming for Windows using Visual Studio and Visual J++.

This book takes you step by step though the Visual J++ environment. We'll start with Windows applications and the basics of the Java language, and then we'll switch over to Java applets embedded in Web pages. Then we'll move on to creating and using reusable components in Java for Windows.

As you progress through the material in the book, you will have the chance to use the Visual J++ environment to create Windows applications and Web applets based on the projects described in the text and the follow-on lab exercises at the end of each section. A CD-ROM is included in the back of this book. It includes all of the sample code and lab projects found in this book and the Publisher's Edition of Microsoft Visual J++. You can use these projects to help you learn about Visual J++. As you work through the laboratory exercises in the book, follow along with the provided code.

This book is not a catalog of Java methods. Just documenting the standard Java libraries would take hundreds, if not thousands, of pages. An important part of using the Java programming language is finding your way around the huge library of existing routines. As we often hear when writing programs: don't reinvent the wheel. This goes double for Java. While we use a number of important Java library methods in introducing you to the language, we have by no means covered the vast majority of them. On the other hand, this book is self-contained: you won't need another Java reference as you read the examples and work through the exercises. At some point in your Java career, you will want to find a good reference manual to keep by your side as you progress in using the language.

This book describes the functionality of the Visual J++ Standard Edition. Features unique to the Professional Edition or the Enterprise Edition are not covered.

Here's a description of what you will find in each chapter.

Chapter	Contents
1: Getting Started	This is a quick overview of the Java language and Visual J++. We talk about the features of the language and the major features of Visual J++We also use the Application Wizard to create our first Java application, a Notepad-style editor.

Chapter	Contents
2: Writing an Application from Scratch	We discuss some basics of Windows applications: forms, events, and event handlers. We use WFC controls to interact with the user. On the Java side, we create methods using Java syntax to handle user events. Java program comments and JavaDoc comments are discussed in this chapter.
3: Classes and Forms	Classes are at the heart of Java programming, and forms are at the heart of creating Windows applications using Visual J++. This chapter introduces both. We define and use classes, objects, references, and constructor methods here. Methods and member variables are also introduced in this chapter.
4: Menus, Types, and Methods	This chapter fleshes out more Java syntax details, and introduces the Visual J++ Menu Designer. We discuss the built-in data types of the Java language, and extend our knowledge of the basic building block of a Java class: the method. Having introduced member variables in Chapter 3, here we look at ways to modify their behavior using Java syntax.
5: Inheritance	Inheritance is a key feature of any object-oriented programming language, and Java provides plenty of support for inheritance. In this chapter, we examine inheritance as the Java programmer uses it. We extend classes and override methods. It's here that we see how class modifiers affect class behavior and inheritance. The Visual J++ Class Outline window helps us build our code and get a handle on what we've got to work with.
6: Creating an Applet	This chapter sees our first switch from talking about Windows applications to talking about Java Web applets. We start using Java's built-in library methods to create applets that run inside an Internet browser. We discuss Web pages, HTML, the Visual J++ applet template, and the Java Abstract Window Toolkit (AWT) drawing package.
7: Enhancing Your Applet	Adding sound and images to applets is discussed here. We also explore two ways to allow others to customize the behavior of our applets: the <PARAM> tag and JScript function calls. We show how to bind together HTML controls and JScript code to communicate with an applet.

(continued)

Chapter	Contents
8: Saving Information	So far, our applications have had relatively limited capacity to process and store information. This chapter talks about a number of different ways to store information in our application: arrays, files, and lists. We also learn about sorting and interfaces, a class-like construct in Java.
9: Animation in Applets	One of the first uses of Java was in applets. Here we learn about creating animated images in applets. In order to do this, we also learn about two very powerful features of Java: exceptions and multithreading.
10: Packages in Java	As you now know, there are zillions of methods in thousands of classes in Java. Packages help manage all these classes by arranging logically related groups of classes. In this chapter, we explore the classes in the standard Java and WFC packages. We also create our own package and learn how to use it.
11: Console Applications	Here we learn what makes a Java class an application. We find out how to run Java applications and how to pass parameters to those applications. We also learn how to read and write to an MS-DOS prompt.
12: Using External Components in WFC	One of the exciting areas of software development is component technology—building and using reusable pieces. In this chapter, we use ActiveX controls and a new WFC component. We also use J/Direct to gain direct access to the Win32 application programming interface (API).
13: Portable I/O	Here, we access the Internet from our application. The standard Java libraries include packages for connecting to a URL and accessing the resources there.
Appendix A	*Quick Syntax Comparison*—A comparison is made of Java, C, C++, and Visual Basic code modules.
Appendix B	*Quick Reference to Java Syntax*—Java syntax and Java language keywords are provided.
Appendix C	*Programming: What's Going On?*—This is a short description of the development lifecycle of a software project.
Appendix D	*Event-Driven Programming*—A perspective on the difference between event-driven and sequential programming is offered.

Java is a language with its own personality and is fast developing its own culture. We think Java is a good tool and find Visual J++ to be the best way to develop Java applications. We hope that you enjoy the experience of learning Java and that you find this book helpful, interesting, and fun.

In addition, the following learning resources will help you take your next steps with Microsoft Visual J++ 6.0:

For more information about programming in Microsoft Visual J++ 6.0, see *Programming Microsoft Visual J++ 6.0* (Microsoft Press, 1998).

For information about using and extending network APIs using Microsoft Visual J++ 6.0, check out *Network Programming with Microsoft Visual J++ 6.0* (Microsoft Press, 1998).

Intermediate-level programmers can try the task-oriented approach to developing Windows-based applications found in *Microsoft Visual J++ 6.0 Developer's Workshop* (Microsoft Press, 1998).

For comprehensive reference information for the Windows Foundation Class libraries, turn to the two-volume *Microsoft Visual J++ 6.0 Reference Library* (Microsoft Press, 1998).

About the Companion CD-ROM

A CD-ROM is included in the back of this book. It includes all of the sample code and lab projects found in this book and the Publisher's Edition of Microsoft Visual J++. You can use the sample projects to help you learn about Visual J++. As you work through the laboratory exercises in the book, follow along with the provided code.

Installing the Sample Projects on Your Computer

The install program copies the sample project folders and files to a folder named LearnVJ on your hard disk.

To install the samples

1. Close any currently running programs.

2. Insert the Learn Visual J++ Now compact disc into your CD-ROM drive.

3. On the taskbar at the bottom of your screen, click the Start button, and then click Run. The Run dialog box appears.

4. In the Open box, type D:\setup. (If your CD-ROM drive is associated with a different drive letter, such as e, type it instead.)

5. Click OK, and then follow the directions on the screen.

Visual J++ Code Projects

Each chapter of the book includes laboratory exercises designed to reinforce the concepts presented. As you come across each lab, you will be directed to start Visual J++ and open the appropriate file.

Visual J++ organizes Java source code and other resources into "solution" files (filename extension .sln) and "project" files (extension .vjp). A Visual J++ project is analogous to a Windows application, and each solution can contain one or more of these projects. While it is possible for any solution to contain multiple projects, the example code in the book contains only one project per solution. Each solution/project installed from the CD-ROM will be contained in its own Windows directory.

The CD-ROM includes example projects, lab projects, and solution projects. The files follow this naming convention:

Project type	Filename
Example project	Chapter04\BuiltIn\BuiltIn.sln
Lab project	Chapter03\Lab3-1\BidMaker.sln
Solution project	Chapter02\Sol2-2\Hello.sln

Example projects

Each example project illustrates a concept of the Java programming language. Example projects are described in the text of the book as you come to them, and you can open and examine them at any time. No modification of the Java code is required, although the curious reader may do so. Not all sections have example projects.

Lab projects

The lab project is the starting point of each laboratory exercise. It gives you a quick start, by providing Java code to be modified in some way. Usually you will practice using a new feature of the Java language or the Visual J++ environment. The lab concept is discussed in the section preceding the exercise. Exercises do not necessarily have starter projects; you will create some projects from scratch.

Solution projects

A solution project represents a possible solution to a laboratory exercise. Use the solution projects to check your work on an exercise. Every laboratory exercise has a solution project.

Installing Visual J++ on Your Computer

The Learn Visual J++ Now CD includes the Publisher's Edition of Microsoft Visual J++. This is a 90-day trial version of the Standard Edition of Microsoft Visual J++. You can create, build, run, debug, and edit your Java programs with the included version of Visual J++.

If you already have another version of Microsoft Visual J++ installed on your computer, you do not need to install the Publisher's Edition.

Visual J++ requires Internet Explorer 4.01 Service Pack 1 and Microsoft Windows 95, Microsoft Windows 98, or Microsoft Windows NT.

The Visual J++ setup files are located in the VJ98 folder on the CD.

To install Visual J++

1. Close any currently running programs.

2. Insert the Learn Visual J++ Now compact disc into your CD-ROM drive.

3. On the taskbar at the bottom of your screen, click the Start button, and then click Run. The Run dialog box appears.

4. In the Open box, type D:\VJ98\setup.exe. (If your CD-ROM drive is associated with a different drive letter, such as e, type it instead.) Then follow the instructions on the screen.

5. Click OK, and then follow the directions on the screen.

System Requirements

Computer/ Processor	PC with a Pentium-class processor. Pentium 90 or higher processor recommended.
Memory (RAM)	24 MB for Windows 95 or later (48 MB recommended); 32 MB for Windows NT 4.0 (48 MB recommended).
Hard Disk	Typical: 107 MB. Maximum: 157 MB. IE 4.01: 43 MB (typical). MSDN: 57 MB (typical). NT 4.0 Option Pack: 20 MB (Windows 95+), 200 MB (Windows NT 4.0).
Drive	CD-ROM drive.
Display	VGA or higher-resolution; Super VGA recommended.
Operating System	Microsoft Windows 95 or later operating system or Microsoft Windows NT operating system version 4.0 with Service Pack 3 or later.
Peripheral/ Miscellaneous	Microsoft Mouse or compatible pointing device.

Internet Explorer 4.01 SP1 is required for proper operation.

Getting Started

Welcome to *Learn Visual J++ Now*. This book is designed to get you
started creating applications using the Microsoft Visual J++ development
system for Java and the Java programming language.

In this chapter, you will get a quick overview of:

■ The Java language

■ Microsoft Visual J++ version 6.0

You will create:

■ A simple text-editor application using the Application Wizard

The Java Language

The Java programming language has captured a lot of attention. One of
the chief reasons so many people are talking about Java is that Java is one
of the best choices for programming on the World Wide Web (also known
as the Web or the Internet). People are talking about a number of things
when they talk about Java, but particularly about the way the language
is designed.

In this section, we present some basic information about Java. It's not necessary to understand the concepts presented in this section to program in Java, but it's good background material to have.

Java is, first and foremost, a programming language. Here are some of the important features of the Java language:

- It's an object-oriented programming (OOP) language.
- It has a syntax similar to that of the C and C++ programming languages.
- It uses simplified grammar.
- It's portable.

Let's look at each of these features more closely.

Object-Oriented

Computer programs are typically too large and complex to write as a single piece. Because of this, programs are broken into smaller pieces or *modules*. Modules can be created using several different schemes. The aim is for each module to be relatively independent so that different people can work on different modules at the same time.

How modules are structured is even more important when a programmer needs to change the program later, an activity referred to as *maintenance* programming. Maintenance generally means that someone wants the program to do something differently or more optimally, or to use a new feature of the operating system, or to correct how some function of the program is working. If the modules aren't relatively independent, maintaining an application might mean going into several modules to make associated changes. Those changes, in turn, might mean going into other modules to make more associated changes. The ripple effect can be far-reaching.

A number of books and papers suggest that object-oriented programming is a good technique for both modularizing an application and resolving maintenance issues. In OOP, the modules are based on the *objects* that the application handles, as compared to a common technique for creating modules called *functional decomposition.* In functional decomposition, the modules are based on the functions that the application performs.

Let's take a look at an example, an inventory control application. In OOP, the objects would probably include inventory items, part numbers, packing lists, store locations, and so forth. In functional decomposition, the functions would include receiving, tagging, packaging, shipping, and such. Now, what happens when there is a change in the format for part numbers, say from a 6-digit number to a 6-character alphanumeric string? In a well-designed OOP solution, the part number manipulation is only handled within the part number module. The other modules use part number objects, but they treat them as "black box" entities. That is, the other modules do not have any information about the structure or implementation of a part number. In a standard functional decomposition solution, a fundamental entity like a part number is probably manipulated directly by every module in the application. So, the change in format for part numbers means every module that uses part numbers (probably all of them) needs to be updated to accommodate the new format.

Again, this emphasizes the benefit of having modules that are self-contained as well as distinct. A well-structured object-oriented program should be easier to write and easier to maintain than one based on functional decomposition.

Libraries of books have been written about objects and OOP; a full discussion of OOP is well beyond the scope of this book. However, we'll introduce objects and programming with objects in subsequent chapters.

Syntax Similar to C and C++

The *syntax* of a programming language describes how the pieces of the language are put together to create programs. At first glance, a Java module looks like a C or C++ module. (Appendix A gives some simple comparisons of some of the grammar of C, C++, Java, and Visual Basic.)

C is a very powerful and flexible language. A good percentage of commercial software is written in C. However, it doesn't have built-in support for OOP. C++ uses C-like syntax, but does have built-in support for OOP. A considerable amount of software on the market is written in C++. Both C and C++ are popular languages. This means that a lot of folks know how to program in C or C++. Because the syntax of Java is similar to that of C and C++, these people can easily transition to programming in Java.

Simplified Grammar

The creators of Java had experience with C and C++. They took the best features of C++ for use in Java, and they eliminated some of the chronic pitfalls of the C++ language. (Unfortunately, they didn't get all of the problems, but they did get most of them.)

Both C and C++ use devices called *pointers*. Pointers are the basis for some of the most elegant things that C and C++ can do. Pointers, however, can be tricky. A good number of bugs in C and C++ programs can be traced to the inappropriate use of pointers. One can liken a pointer to an extremely sharp chef's knife. In the hands of the right person, it can work wonders. But, if it's not used with care, it can create disaster.

It's also difficult to add OOP elements to a language that wasn't designed for them. Java doesn't use pointers; Java uses *references*. With references, the creators removed many of the tricky aspects of pointers, but kept much of the flexibility. The primary building block of a C program is the function. This fit well with functional decomposition. The creators of Java made the primary building block of Java the class. Classes are well suited to handle objects, and hence they fit well with object-oriented programming. The shift removed much of the ambiguity in the syntax of C++.

These two factors make Java a simpler language to learn than either C or C++.

Portable

One reason Java is getting so much acclaim is that it's designed for portability. Portability is attractive because creating a program that can be downloaded from a Web site requires flexibility.

How the user gets a program: the traditional scenario

When someone creates a program, he or she creates it for a specific machine and operating system; the program will work only on that specific system. So, a program written for a PC will work only on a PC. It won't work on another kind of computer, such as an engineering workstation using UNIX or a mainframe that an accounting company uses to do its books. This is just fine when the user goes shopping at a computer store to buy programs; the user simply buys a program to fit his or her particular computer.

How the user gets a program: the Web scenario

On the Web, it doesn't work this way. When a user visits a Web site, the files from that Web site are downloaded to the user's computer from the Web server. The HTML, the images, the sounds—they all get downloaded. The browser then takes the pieces and puts together the Web page for the user to see.

What happens if the Web page has a program that needs to run? You can't assume that every person who's going to visit your Web site will have the same kind of computer. So, if you want to have a program running on a Web page, you need to make sure it will run on any computer that visits that page. Java is designed to do exactly this.

Compilers

The popular languages of today use English words to help make it easier for the programmer to develop applications. Because the computer doesn't understand words such as "if" or "public" or "return," this code is translated into *machine code* for the computer by the compiler. Different kinds of computers, however, use different machine code. Java is designed to resolve the issues that arise when applications for different computers are being created.

Bytecode and the Virtual Machine for Java

The Java compiler translates Java source code into something that a machine can understand. However, the machine code that it generates isn't specific to a PC or a workstation or a mainframe. Instead, the machine code is for a "fake" machine; that is, the Java compiler creates machine code for the *Virtual Machine for Java*, or VM for Java. The machine code for the VM for Java is called *bytecode*.

So, what good is it to have machine code for a machine that doesn't exist? Although the VM for Java doesn't exist in the form of transistors, diodes, and integrated circuits, it *does* exist. The VM for Java is a program that translates the bytecode for the real machine. This might sound peculiar—until you remember the challenge of programming for the Web.

On the Web, you don't know what kind of machine the user is going to use to get to your Web site. With a traditional programming language, you'd need to create a version of the program you want to use for each kind of machine that a user might have. Then, somehow, you'd need to make sure that the right one got downloaded to the user's machine. It's difficult enough for visitors to your Web page to respond to options like, "Click here to view this page without frames" or "Click here to see this page in Spanish" without needing to tell you what kind of computer they are using. This is one of the chief reasons that Java has generated the interest it has.

Implications of portability

While Java's portability makes it possible to create nifty applets to provide animation and user interaction on Web sites, it does have some drawbacks.

First, it can be slow. With other programming languages, the machine code is already in place. With Java, the bytecode has to be processed again to create real machine code.

Second, Java is dependent on the VM for Java. You're probably familiar with the issues raised by trying to run newer versions of software on older operating systems; the difference in versions is extremely important. Well, the VM for Java has versions too—dozens of versions of the VM for Java for Windows 95 alone. So, something that runs just fine on one machine might run poorly or not at all on the same machine with a different version of the VM for Java.

Third, portability itself is a hassle. On one system you might have a mouse with only one button; on another, two mouse buttons; on yet another, five mouse buttons. (The X Window System is designed to support five mouse buttons.) To make sure your program behaves properly every-where, you have to write it for the simplest possible system, the lowest common denominator. If all the other programs are using two mouse buttons, but a Java program (for portability's sake) is using only one, the Java program seems rather lame.

Fourth, technical issues have prevented people from using the Web as a primary delivery vehicle. The chief issue is the time required to download software of any complexity. As with any large program, size can outweigh the attractiveness of Java's portability.

Fifth, many people who are writing "Internet software" are not writing it for the World Wide Web, but rather for a smaller network within their own company. This is sometimes called a *corporate web* or an *intranet*. And, within a company, the kinds of machines people are using and the versions of software that are on those machines are often standardized, so there are fewer concerns about having completely portable software. Internal networks typically have sufficient bandwidth to make the concerns around download times moot.

So, portability isn't always the most important concern. Download technology does, however, provide a very exciting feature: automatic updates.

Automatic updates

As you know, every time you visit a Web site, you get a new copy of the content on that site. So, if someone updates a site every day, each new day you visit that Web site you get the new content. The same thing happens with the Java bytecode. If you put new Java bytecode on a corporate Web site, then the next time someone visits that Web site, the new bytecode will be downloaded to the user's machine.

This is very cool. Putting out software maintenance updates for the folks that come to the site is painless. The next time they visit the Web site, they will get the most recent version of the site software.

Java packages

Back in the earliest days of computer programming, everything that an application could do was either provided by the language itself or was something you wrote for yourself. FORTRAN is an example of this. The commands for reading data from a disk or tape (storage) or writing things to storage are inherent in the FORTRAN language.

Most modern programming languages come with a library of useful subprograms. These subprograms handle functions like reading from and writing to storage. Libraries provide two benefits:

■ The language is simpler and smaller, because the libraries are external to the language.

■ The libraries can be replaced with newer ones without the need to change the language.

Java is no exception. Java has libraries for drawing, handling storage, even for creating applets. The libraries in Java are arranged into *packages*. These packages are an integral part of using the language. In fact, almost all the code that makes portability possible is in the libraries.

Some of these packages are intimately tied to the Java language. For instance, you can't write Java programs without using the java.lang package. The java.lang package includes the *String* and *Object* classes. It is particularly difficult to write a Java application without using *String*. It is impossible to write one without using *Object*.

Other packages, such as the Abstract Window Toolkit (AWT), are much more specialized. This package handles graphical user interface (GUI, pronounced "gooey") elements, such as displaying windows, menus, and buttons. The AWT is written to support the portable Java GUI. Other packages also handle GUI elements. The WFC (Windows Foundation Class) library, contained in the com.ms.wfc.ui package, that comes with Visual J++ 6.0 can replace the AWT for displaying windows, menus, buttons, and the like. The goal of WFC is to take advantage of the power and flexibility of the Win32 graphics library. (More on this in the next section.)

The use of external libraries gives you, the programmer, the ability to choose the AWT or WFC for your GUI package.

The Visual J++ Development System for Java

Microsoft Visual J++ is a development tool for creating applications using the Java language. Visual J++ is part of the Microsoft Visual Studio suite of tools for creating applications. Other development tools in Visual Studio include the Microsoft Visual C++ and Visual Basic development systems.

Visual C++ provides a development environment for creating robust applications in C++. It includes a sophisticated debugger, a flexible project build system, and a highly optimized compiler. Visual Basic is a Rapid Application Development (RAD) environment. It is a very popular tool because it facilitates the creation of Windows-based applications. Visual J++ shares features of both of these tools.

Earlier versions of Visual J++ had a development environment similar to that of Visual C++. Version 6.0 of Visual J++ adopts many features of the Visual Basic development environment. These include a visual form designer and the Properties window.

In Visual J++, many of the high-productivity features that have made Visual Basic one of the most successful programming languages are combined with a powerful environment for designing, coding, building, and debugging applications. This is referred to as the Integrated Development Environment (IDE).

Solutions and Projects

The IDE works through a system of projects and solutions. A *solution* consists of a project or collection of projects that solves a problem. Each *project* contains the specific elements that address all or some parts of the problem. Here's an example that will make this concept clearer.

Let's say you want to create an application to track the orders people phone in to a TV shopping network. You can break up the application into simpler components, such as a control to handle dates, a control to handle currency, and the form that uses these two controls.

In Visual J++, you create this application as three separate projects:

- A project to create the control for dates
- A project to create the control for money
- A project to create the form that uses these two controls

Creating three separate projects gives you the flexibility to use them independently.

Now let's say you want to create a diary. You could create it totally from scratch, or you could reuse your control for dates. Including the project for the date control lets you update that control if necessary.

Of course, the simplest case is when a solution contains only one project. Most of the labs and examples in this book have only one project per solution. The chapters that discuss creating and using new components contain multiple projects per solution.

Java and Windows: WFC and J/Direct

Lots of computers out there are running the Windows operating system. With Visual J++, it's easy to write applications that take advantage of the features of Windows, thanks to the new Windows Foundation Class (WFC) for Java.

WFC

As noted earlier in this chapter, Java relies on packages to handle most functions. To compare the standard Java packages and WFC, let's consider a specific example: windowing.

The standard Java windowing packages is the Abstract Window Toolkit. The AWT package supports simple controls and is contained in the java.awt package. It consists of drawing code that is designed to be portable.

The WFC windowing library is contained in the com.ms.wfc.ui package. Its drawing code is optimized for Win32, the application programming interface (API) for the Windows 95, Windows 98, and Windows NT operating systems. It supports all the Win32 controls, including the tree view, the list view, and rich-text edit controls.

AWT Controls	WFC Controls
Button	Animation
Checkbox	Button
Choice	CheckBox
Label	ComboBox
List	Edit
Menu	ImageList
Scrollbar	Label
TextArea	ListBox
TextField	ListView
	PictureBox
	RichEdit
	StatusBar
	TabStrip
	ToolBar
	TrackBar
	TreeView

WFC also gives you a way to manipulate dynamic HTML (DHTML). DHTML allows Internet developers to create Web pages and server-side applications that interactively make changes to client-side HTML after it has been downloaded to the user's machine.

J/Direct

J/Direct is an application programming interface for native methods in Java. In places where WFC doesn't provide enough functionality, you can use the J/Direct API to access Microsoft Windows dynamic-link libraries (DLLs), including the Win32 API.

Native methods are non-Java methods. They are called "native" because they access the native machine instead of the VM for Java. Native methods are used when the VM for Java does not supply support for a given operation. For example, you can use J/Direct to call the Win32 API for accessing the Windows registry.

Using the J/Direct Call Builder in Visual J++ 6.0, you can take advantage of—and quickly build—applications that include J/Direct. J/Direct Call Builder makes it easier for you to write Java programs for Windows that use all of the features of Win32. Previously, you might have written these programs in C or C++.

Portable Java and Visual J++

Visual J++ supports portable Java creation. The compiler has full support for version 1.1 of the Java language, including Java Beans. So, any program for fully portable Java—whether for Java applets, Java Beans, or Java applications—will compile and run in Visual J++.

As noted in the "Portable" section earlier in this chapter, portability is based upon machine-independent bytecode. The bytecode that Visual J++ generates will run anywhere there is an appropriate VM. Here, "appropriate" means that it supports the same version of the language. Some Virtual Machines for Java out there support version 1.0 of the language. Others support version 1.1. It's important to remember that code written using language features defined in version 1.1 of the language won't run on a VM for version 1.0 of the language.

Java applications that use WFC won't be portable, however. WFC is specifically designed to use the Win32 API. Java applications that use WFC will run on Windows 95, Windows 98, Windows NT, and other Win32-based operating systems.

Editions of Visual J++

Microsoft Visual J++ development system version 6.0 comes in three editions:

- Standard Edition
- Professional Edition
- Enterprise Edition

The Standard Edition is available as a stand-alone product. The Standard Edition is designed for users learning Java and for competent rogramming aficionados. It has full support for the Java language and J/Direct. You can use it to create full-featured Windows-based applications, applets for the Web, and new WFC components; it supports the creating of executable (EXE) files for your applications; and it contains all of the WFC library. It does not include tools to support database access or the installation of data providers or database drivers. This book is based on the Standard Edition.

The Professional Edition of Visual J++ is designed for the professional programmer using Java. It has everything that the Standard Edition has, plus added support for building, packaging, and deploying COM and MTS server components, DLLs, CABs, and ZIPs, as well as for direct data access. It is included as a component of the Microsoft Visual Studio Professional Edition along with Visual Basic, Visual C++, Visual InterDev, Visual FoxPro, and the Microsoft Developer Network (MSDN) library.

The Enterprise Edition of Visual J++ is available only as a component in the Visual Studio Enterprise Edition. The Visual Studio Enterprise Edition is designed for people working on a programming team where multiple languages and tools are needed to create the solution. It includes everything in the Visual Studio Professional Edition, plus Visual SourceSafe and Microsoft BackOffice tools such as SQL Server, Microsoft Transaction Server, Internet Information Server, and SNA Server.

A Quick Tour of Visual J++

The next section is a quick tour of the product. If you haven't yet installed Visual J++, this would be a good time to do so.

To start Visual J++

■ From the Start menu, choose Programs, and then select Microsoft Visual J++ 6.0.

The Visual J++ splash screen appears briefly, followed by the Visual J++ IDE, and then, typically, the New Project dialog box. You can use the New Project dialog box to create a new Visual J++ project or to open an existing project or solution. For the sake of this walk-through, click Cancel to dismiss this dialog box. You will now see the IDE for Visual J++. This is the initial configuration for the windows.

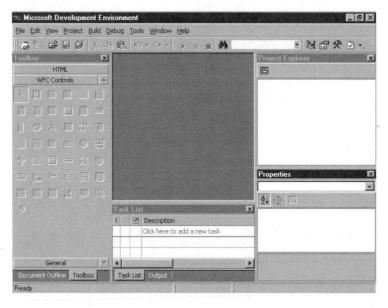

Figure 1-1.   *The Visual J++ IDE.*

The icons in the toolbar at the top of the IDE handle these tasks:

New project

New project item

Open project

Save

Save all

Cut

Copy

Paste

Undo

Redo

Start (with debugging)

Break

End

Search

Search text

Project Explorer

Properties window

Toolbox

Task List

View Other Windows

In the upper right portion of the IDE, you see the Project Explorer window, which displays the files in the current project. Use it to open files in your projects. You can also use the Project Explorer to add new files to your projects or remove files from your projects.

Below the Project Explorer window is the Properties window, which displays information about the form or control that is selected in the form designer (View Design mode).

On the left side of the IDE are two tabbed tool windows, shown in layers. To view either one, click its respective tab. The Document Outline displays information about the active Java or HTML file. The Toolbox gives you access to the controls you can place on your forms.

At the bottom center of the IDE is the Task List window, which displays different kinds of messages. These messages include syntax errors, compilation errors, TODO comments, and user-defined tasks. (The Output tab is discussed in Chapter 2.)

All six of these windows are tool windows that are docked to the sides of the main window. You can adjust the size and position of any of the tool windows. You can also dock and undock the tool windows.

To adjust the size of a tool window

■ Drag the thick border of the tool window to the desired size.

To change the location of a tool window

■ Drag the title bar of the tool window to the desired location.

While you are dragging the window, an outline of the window shows the location of the window.

To dock a tool window

■ Drag the tool window near the edge of the main window.

The outline indicates where the tool window will dock. When docking a window, you can control only its location. After the window has been docked, you can adjust the size of the docked window.

To prevent a tool window from docking

■ Hold down the Ctrl key as you drag the tool window.

Recall that in Figure 1-1 the Document Outline and Toolbox windows appear together. Any tool window can be tabbed together with another tool window.

To tab two tool windows together

1. Position one tool window where you want it to be.
2. Drag the second window onto the title bar of the first window.

   The outline will change from a rectangle to a tabbed shape.
3. Release the mouse.

To rearrange tabbed tool windows

■ Drag the tool window by the tab to the desired location.

   The tabs will rearrange themselves as you drag them.

To remove a tabbed window

■ Drag the tool window by the tab to the desired location.

To hide a tool window

■ Click the Close button in the upper right corner of the tool window.

To show a tool window

■ From the View menu, choose the window you want to show.

   It's also possible to configure tool windows for particular preferences. Let's define a window layout so that we can easily return to this window configuration.

To define a window layout

1. From the View menu, choose Define Window Layout.
2. In the Define Window Layout dialog box, enter the name for the window layout.
3. Click Add to define the layout.
4. Click Close to close the dialog box.

To apply a defined window layout

1. From the View menu, choose Define Window Layout.

2. In the Define Window Layout dialog box, select the desired window layout.

3. Click Apply to apply the saved window layout.

4. Click Close to close the dialog box.

   A number of other tool windows and toolbars are also available for your use.

To see a list of the available tool windows and toolbars

■ Browse the View menu.

   We will use many of these tool windows as we continue through this book. Each tool window will be explained when we first use it.

Lab 1-1: Creating an Application with the Visual J++ Application Wizard

Let's use Visual J++ to create an application.

Lab overview

In this lab, you will practice:

■ Creating a Visual J++ project in a new solution.

■ Using the Application Wizard.

■ Running a project from the IDE, with and without debugging support.

To help you get started creating applications, Visual J++ has templates and wizards. *Templates* are simple skeletons for a project or project item. *Wizards* are step-by-step guides.

In this lab, you will create your first application using the Visual J++ Application Wizard to create a simple text editor. Your application will use many of the features of the WFC library that you will learn about in this book.

Lab setup

1. From the File menu, choose New Project.

   The New Project dialog box appears.

2. In the New Project dialog box, select the New tab.

3. On the New page, select Visual J++ Projects/Applications.

   In the right pane, the templates and wizards for applications appear.

4. Select Application Wizard.

5. Enter a name for the new project. For this exercise, type *SimpleEditor*.

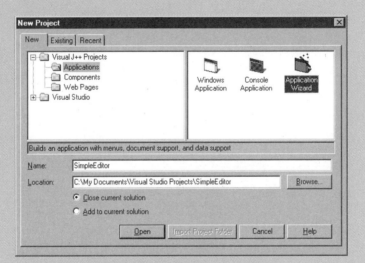

6. Click Open to start the Application Wizard.

   The Application Wizard displays an introductory screen on which you can select a profile. A profile is a stored set of answers to the questions the wizard asks. At the end of running a wizard, you are asked if you'd like to save the response you gave as a profile. Since this is the first time you have used the wizard, no profiles are available.

(continued)

Lab setup *continued*

7. To use a profile, select the profile file from the drop-down list, or click the button with the ellipsis points (...) to find a profile file.

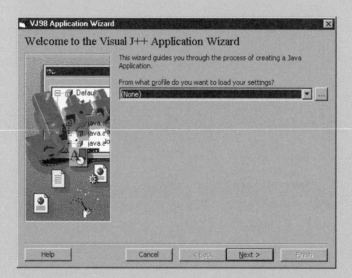

8. Click the Next button to move to the next step of the Application Wizard.

Lab instructions

1. Add features to your application.

   The next step of the Application Wizard asks for the features that you want to include in the application.

   > **OTE** If you have the Professional or Enterprise Edition, you will first be asked for the type of application: Form-Based or Form-Based with Data. The Standard Edition does not include database support. If you get this screen, select Form-Based Application. Click Next to move to the Add Features To Your Application step.

Specifically, the Add Features To Your Application step asks which of the following feature capabilities you want to include in your application:

- *Menu*—When this is selected, your application includes a menu.

- *Edit*—When this is selected, your application includes an edit control; this is similar to a Notepad application.

- *Tool Bar*—When this is selected, your application includes a standard toolbar for common commands.

- *Status Bar*—When this is selected, your application includes a status bar with panes that report whether the Num Lock or Caps Lock key is set.

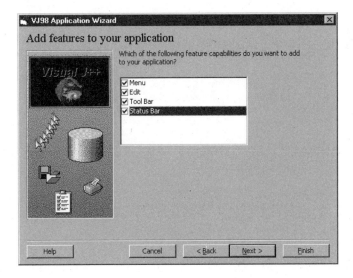

For this lab, select all four features. Click Next.

2. Choose the kind of comments you want.

The next step of the Application Wizard asks for the type of comments you want in the generated code. Specifically, the Choose The Kind of Comments You Want step asks you which of the following types of comments you want to include in your application:

■ *JavaDoc comments*—When this is selected, the generated code includes JavaDoc comments describing the classes and methods in the application.

■ *TODO comments*—When this is selected, the generated code includes TODO comments that appear in the task list.

■ *Sample Functionality comments*—When this is selected, the generated code includes other comments explaining the functionality provided by the code.

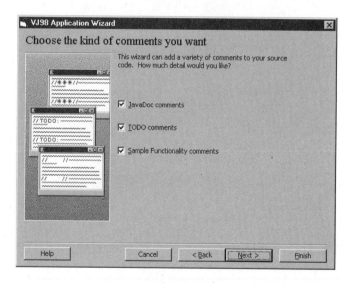

For this lab, select all three types of comments. Click Next.

3. Save and review your settings in the Application Wizard Summary, and create the application project.

   The next step of the Application Wizard gives you the opportunity to do all this.

 OTE If you have the Professional or Enterprise Edition, you will be asked about program packaging. The Standard Edition does not include program packaging support. Click Next to move to the Application Wizard Summary step.

■ To save settings to an existing profile, select a profile from the drop-down list.

■ To save settings to a new profile, click the button with the ellipsis points (...) to specify a name for the new profile file.

   The new profile filename appears in the drop-down list. For this exercise, do not specify a profile to save the settings.

■ To view the settings, click View Report.

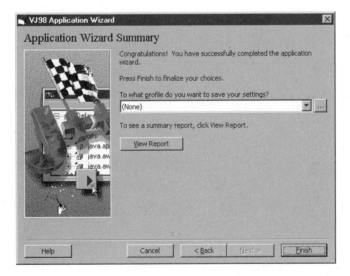

You can save this report as an HTML file in your project.

■ To create the application, click Finish.

For this lab, view the report and create the application.

4. Run the application.

Congratulations! You have an application. Let's see what you created.

■ To run an application with debugging, click the Start button on the toolbar.

■ To run an application without debugging, from the Debug menu, choose Start Without Debugging.

Debugging is the process of fixing errors in a program. This often involves figuring out exactly what the program is doing. The debugger is a part of the IDE that helps you follow the program as it performs each line of code. To find out more about debugging, see Chapter 2.

Debugging requires a lot of information from the program, so starting an application with debugging can be somewhat slower than starting the application without debugging. On the Debug toolbar is a button for running the application without debugging.

■ To display the Debug toolbar, from the View menu, point to Toolbars and choose Debug. Or, right-click in the menu or toolbar and, from the pop-up menu, choose Debug.

The Start Without Debugging button is the dark-red exclamation point. The other Debug toolbar buttons are discussed in Chapter 2 and in Help.

Getting Help

Visual J++ features integrated Help. The Help topics can be grouped as follows:

■ Help about the IDE

■ Conceptual material about programming using Visual J++

■ Reference materials for the Java language and WFC

To access Help in a dialog box

■ Click the Help button in that dialog box.

To access Help for a Java keyword or WFC construct

1. Select the term for which you want help.

   If the term is a single word, it is sufficient to place the cursor within the word.

2. Press the F1 key.

All this Help information is stored on the MSDN compact disc. You have the option to move these files to your hard disk.

If you install the Help files on your hard disk, you will be able to use Help at any time. Otherwise, any requests for Help will look for the Help topic on the compact disc. If the disc is not in the CD-ROM drive, the IDE will prompt you to insert it.

To install Help files on your hard disk

1. From Control Panel, open Add/Remove Programs.

2. In the list of programs, select MSDN Library - Visual Studio 6.0.

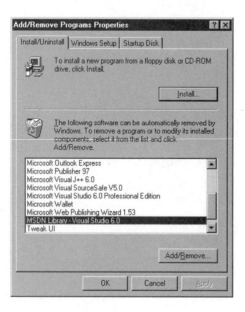

3. Click Add/Remove.

4. In MSDN Library - Visual Studio 6.0 Setup, click Add/Remove.

5. In MSDN Library - Visual Studio 6.0 - Custom, select Master Index File, VJ++ 6.0 Documentation, and VJ++ 6.0 Product Samples (optional).

6. Click Continue to install the Help files.

7. Click OK to exit Add/Remove Programs.

Writing an Application from Scratch

We've introduced you to the development environment for Java and defined a few key terms. You've gotten your first look at version 6.0 of the Microsoft Visual J++ development system for Java, and even used Visual J++ to create a simple application for the Windows operating system. Now you're ready to explore some of the features that make Visual J++ a powerful and easy development tool.

In this chapter, you'll learn about:

- Designing and creating an application

- Handling events and writing event procedures

- Displaying pictures in your application

- Adding colors to your application

- Using comments in Visual J++ programs for Java

You will get practice using:

- Properties

- Event handlers

- *if* statements
- Comments and TODO tokens
- The Visual J++ debugger

Creating a Simple Form

In the previous chapter, you created a simple application using the Application Wizard. Let's perform a hands-on exercise this time and create a basic form using a Form template. A Form template allows us a little more control over what our application looks like, and we'll only have to think about the pieces that we need for our application.

If it isn't already running, start Visual J++ as you did in the last chapter, and follow along.

Using a Form Template

When you start Visual J++ the first time, it displays the New Project dialog box, as shown in Figure 2-1. If this dialog box does not appear when you start Visual J++, just go to the File menu and choose New Project.

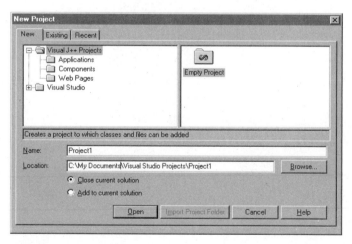

Figure 2-1.   *The New Project dialog box that appears when you start Visual J++.*

In the left pane, you should see the Visual J++ Projects folder and, underneath that, the Applications, Components, and Web Pages subfolders. (If you don't see these, expand the list by clicking the plus sign (+) to the left of the Visual J++ Projects folder.) Select the Applications subfolder.

In the right pane are three icons labeled Windows Application, Console Application, and Application Wizard. In Chapter 1 we selected Application Wizard. This time, select Windows Application. When you do, the message in the status box in the middle of the window reads:

```
Creates an application which uses the Win32 user-interface and hosts
controls
```

In the box labeled Name, you can enter any legal Windows filename as the name of the project. Let's call this project "Hello" (without the quotation marks). In the box labeled Location, enter a Windows path where you want your project files kept. You can place the project wherever you like. Here we'll use the My Documents folder. Once you've entered the project filename and location, you can click the Open button.

 OTE Clicking the Open button creates a folder and three files on your hard disk. The folder has the same name as the name of your project (Hello). Inside the Hello folder is the project file itself (Hello.vjp), a default Java source code file (Form1.Java), and a data file that Visual J++ uses internally (codebase.dat). The Java source code file is where the Visual J++ Forms Designer is going to put the code required to support the form that we are about to create.

Now that you have clicked Open, your screen looks something like Figure 2-2.

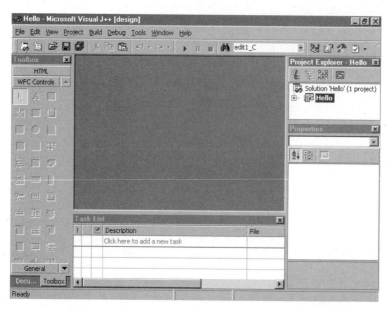

Figure 2-2.   *Visual J++, ready to help you build your Windows-based application.*

Let's start with the Project Explorer window. We see a solution, Solution 'Hello', and a project, Hello. When we save our work, our solution will be saved in a file called Hello.sln, in the same folder as the project file (which has an extension of .vjp). In the Project Explorer view, we don't see these filename extensions.

Expand the Hello project list. Select the source code file called Form1.java. On the Project Explorer toolbar are several buttons for viewing information about items listed in the Project Explorer. Click View Designer, which is the second button from the left. (Notice the ToolTip text describing the button as you move your mouse over the button.) The View Designer shows you the blank form Visual J++ created (by applying a default Form template) when we selected Windows Application to build our current application (see Figure 2-3).

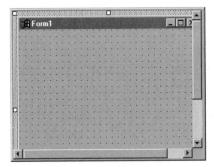

Figure 2-3.   *The View Designer view of Form1.java.*

Now click the View Code button. A window appears that displays the Java code in Form1.java that produces this blank form. As you can see, a fair amount of code is involved in creating a form that Visual J++ handles for you.

Adding Controls to a Form

Now we can start using Visual J++ to modify our form.

Before we start adding to the form, we should verify that a number of crucial windows are visible to help us develop our application. Check the development environment for these windows:

- Project Explorer
- Properties
- Toolbox
- Task List

If any one of them is not visible, bring it up now. To do this, simply go to the View menu and select the appropriate window name. (The Task List window can be found on the Other Window submenu.)

Click View Designer. Notice the Properties window. This window shows the properties, or settings, of *Form1* (the name of our blank form based on the Form template). Whenever a form is the active window, the form's properties are visible here.

In the Toolbox window, click the WFC Controls button to display a list of controls you can add to your form (see Figure 2-4). Use the up and down arrow keys to scroll through the list.

Figure 2-4. *Toolbox with WFC Controls selected.*

We are going to place two labels, an edit box, and a button on our form. Let's start with a Label control. Drag the Label control from the Toolbox onto the form. A label appears on the form with an outline around it. Notice the change in the Properties window. Now, instead of displaying the properties of *Form1*, we see the properties of *label1*. All new controls that we drag onto the form will be named this way (that is, with the name of the control followed by a number) unless we change the names. For now, we'll use the default names that Visual J++ supplies.

Drag another Label control onto the form above *label1*. This Label control is automatically named *label2*. Add an Edit control and a Button control so that your form looks like Figure 2-5. Notice that the Properties window changes to match the last added WFC control.

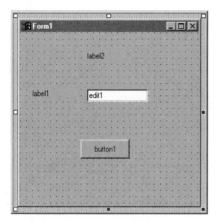

Figure 2-5.   *Our form with the controls in place.*

Setting Properties

We have seen how the Properties window reacts every time we put a
new control on our form. This window shows us the properties, or
characteristics, associated with all of the components in our project. If
the last control that you added to the form was an Edit control, then the
Properties window is showing the properties of that control: *edit1*.

button1

In the View Designer (the window currently titled Form1.java), click
(don't double-click) the button called *button1*. Use the scroll bar in the
Properties window to view all the properties of this button. All buttons
have the same properties, but of course each button's values will be
distinct for that button, and no other button on this form can be called
button1.

The property for the name of a Button control is called Name. You can
give *button1* a new name here, but for now we'll continue to use the
default. Instead, let's change the caption of the button. The property for
the caption of a Button control is called Text. You change the property

33

of a control by clicking in the field to the right of the name of the property. Change the Text property of *button1* to *OK*. Notice that the caption of the button changes instantly on the form.

 IP   If you want a quick description of what a property is for, you can read the description at the bottom of the Properties window while the property is selected.

---

label1 and *edit1*

The Properties window shows the properties of all the controls on a form, one control at a time. To go to another control and change the properties there, simply click the down arrow at the top of the Properties window. A drop-down menu appears with the names of all the controls on your form and the form itself.

Select *label1*. Find the property called Text and change its value from *label1* to *Name:*. Go back to the drop-down menu and select *edit1*. Change the Text property of *edit1* to be empty by selecting the value of the field and pressing the Delete key.

label2

Click the *label2* control on *Form1*. Set the Text property to *Enter Your Name Below* and then expand the Font property by clicking the plus sign. A list of format options appears below the Font property. Set Size to be *24*. Click the pull-down arrow in the Weight field to see the values for this field. Set Weight to *Extrabold*.

Since the text for *label2* is longer than before, and bigger too, it doesn't fit in the original space that we provided for it. Go to the View Designer and drag the handles of the label outline outward until all the text of the label is visible on the form.

Your form should now resemble Figure 2-6.

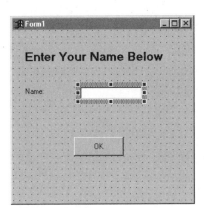

Figure 2-6. *Our form with the controls in place and the properties set.*

Adding Event Handlers

Now that our form is set up, we can add some action! Just as every form has a predetermined set of properties that we can modify as we see fit, every form also has a predetermined set of events to which it can respond. When a control is first placed on the form, the control's response to all events is to do nothing. We must decide what should be done as the result of an event taking place while our program is running.

In order for a control on a form to respond to an event, such as a user moving a mouse, we need to add an *event handler* (also called an *event procedure*) to our code. Visual J++ makes it easy to add an event handler for the most common events associated with a control.

button1

We can add an event handler to *button1* by simply double-clicking the button in the View Designer. When you do this, Visual J++ takes you to the form's code window and a skeleton of an event handler for the control. The code looks like this:

```
private void button1_click(Object source, Event e)
{

}
```

Your cursor's insertion point will be between the curly braces ({, }), ready for you to type the code that will execute when the button is clicked in a running application. The name of the event handler that is executed when the user clicks *button1* is *button1_click*. Visual J++ uses this naming scheme whenever it creates a skeleton of an event handler: the name of the control, followed by an underscore (_), followed by the name of the event.

What happens when the user clicks *button1*? Let's add some code that takes the name that the user types and displays it on the form:

```
private void button1_click(Object source, Event e)
{
    String name = edit1.getText();
    label2.setText("Hello " + name);
}
```

 IP   As you type this code, list and Java statement boxes appear. This is the Statement Completion feature of the Visual J++ environment and the way Visual J++ advises you on Java syntax and your options for a particular statement. This feature is extremely handy and will often save you time previously spent looking at documentation. If you see red wavy lines under any of the code, you need to check your typing.

Saving and Running Your Application

Saving project files

Now is a good time to save your work. To do this, click the Save button on the toolbar or select Save Form1.java on the File menu. You can also use the Save All command, which saves all files related to the project. If we wanted to save our form using a different name, we would choose Save As from the File menu. For now, we'll continue to use Form1.java.

Running the application

Everything is now ready to go. Let's run the application. Click the Start button on the toolbar, or select Start Without Debugging from the Debug menu. Figure 2-7 demonstrates the Hello program window that appears when the application is running.

Figure 2-7.   *The Hello application running and waiting for input.*

Type your name into the box labeled Name, and then click the OK button. You should see the title at the top of the form change to

`Hello` *`Yourname`*

Congratulations! You've just completed your first Java application from scratch!

To stop the application, just click the Close button in the title bar of the program window. This takes you back to Visual J++.

What's Going On?

Writing computer programs is really a matter of solving problems for users. Solving problems, in our case, means answering two basic questions: what problem are we trying to solve, and how can we get the necessary information from the user in order to solve that problem? This means designing an application to address users' needs and designing forms to communicate with users. Once we have designed our application and forms, we must attach event handlers to the controls on our forms to enable users to interact with the application.

Designing the Application

First, let's determine the problem to be solved. For this example, we want to greet the user by name. To do this we need to somehow get the user's name, add a greeting to it, and then display the result. Not surprisingly, we decide to use a Visual J++ form with controls to communicate with the user. A *form* is a visually oriented approach to designing and creating a user interface and functionality for your application. Behind all forms is source code, so it is possible to create an application without using forms. However, the capability to build an application through forms is a major feature of the development environment for Visual J++.

Designing the Form

Now that we have decided what problem we are solving, we turn our attention to how we might solve that problem. What information will we need from the user? How will we indicate to the user that we need that information? How will we provide an answer back to the user? What do we need, in terms of controls, to solve this problem?

This is what we need to achieve, and these are the basic controls that we will use to achieve it:

- A way to tell the user what information we require (For this we use a Label control.)

- A way to get the text that we require from the user (For this we use an Edit control.)

- A way to identify the field in which the user types information (For this we use another Label control.)

- A way for the user to tell us that he or she has finished typing (For this we use a Button control.)

After we have dragged these controls onto the form and arranged them attractively, we set their properties so that they appear as we want when the application is started. Then, by adding event handlers, we manipulate our controls in a running application.

Handling Events

So far, we have added only one event handler, *button1_click*. This event handler will execute whenever a particular event (called Click) happens to the button *button1*. How does this event happen to *button1*? Every time the user clicks *button1*, the Click event is passed to your program, and (because you wrote an event handler to deal with just such an eventuality) your code, *button1_click*, runs.

Here's the *button1_click* event handler again:

```
private void button1_click(Object source, Event e)
{
    String name = edit1.getText();
    label2.setText("Hello " + name);
}
```

Now that you have seen the application run, let's see what is going on in the code. The *button1_click* event handler modifies *label2*. The Text property of *edit1* is the string that the user typed. The Java *getText* method gets the Text value of the *edit1* control and saves it in the local *String* variable called *name*. We then set the Text property of *label2* (using the method *setText*) to the word *Hello* appended by the *String* value of *name*. We'll be seeing more examples of Java methods as we go along, and we'll really delve into them in Chapter 4.

Lab 2-1: Revising the Hello Code

In this lab, you get a chance to put code into another event handler and see how it affects the behavior of the application.

Lab overview

You will practice creating event handlers using the View Designer. In the Hello application, a user must click the OK button to see a change in the greeting at the top of the form. Adding an event handler to the Edit control causes the application to update the greeting immediately, without waiting for further input from the user.

Lab setup

1. If you have been following the code example in this chapter, you are ready to go. Skip to the lab instructions.

2. If you have not been following the code example in this chapter, start Visual J++ now.

3. Open the Lab2-1 starter project (Chapter02\Lab2-1\Hello.sln).

4. Look in the Project Explorer window. If nothing appears under the project icon (called Hello), click the plus sign next to it to display the files associated with this project.

5. Select Form1.java, and at the top of the Project Explorer window, click the View Code button.

Lab instructions

1. In the View Designer, double-click the Edit control. This should take you to the code window for the form and create the skeleton of an event handler for the Edit control, called *edit1_textChanged*. The code should look like this:

```
private void edit1_textChanged (Object source, Event e)
{
}
```

This event handler is called every time any change is made to the *edit1* properties. Add the following lines for *edit1_textChanged*:

```
String name = edit1.getText();
label2.setText("Hello " + name);
```

2. Run the application again. Does it behave differently? How? Do we still need an OK button?

3. Check your work against the solution in Chapter02\Sol2-1\Hello1.

Next steps

Now we have the basic application laid out. We designed an application to solve a problem. We designed a form to help us communicate with the user. We attached event handlers to specific events that occur in our application. The foundation is complete. From here, we spruce things up a bit with decision logic, colors, and pictures.

Enhancing Your Application

This is cool! We have a basic application written from scratch using the Visual J++ environment. Still, a few more features would be an improvement. Let's start by making the application a little smarter with an *if* statement.

Adding Decision Logic

What happens to the application if you click the OK button without typing a name? If you do this, you will see that the welcome message simply says "Hello." It would be more useful, however, if the application could detect whether or not a name was typed, and then take some appropriate action. In our application, the code for handling this with an *if* statement would look like the following:

```
private void button1_click(Object source, Event e)
{
    String name = edit1.getText();
    if (name.equals(""))
    {
        label2.setText("You Must Enter a Name");
    }
    else
    {
        label2.setText("Hello " + name);
    }
}
```

This new code, if translated into English, would read, "If the user has not typed anything, then prompt the user for a name; otherwise, change the value of the Text property of *label2*." Modify your *button1_click* event handler to include this new piece of code. Now, let's discuss the statements you've added to the code.

if statements and Boolean expressions

The *if* statement in Java lets the programmer test some condition or *Boolean expression*. A Boolean expression can have only one of two possible values: *true* or *false*. If the expression is true, then the code between the first set of curly braces ({ }) is executed; if the expression is not true, then the code after the word *else* and between the second set of braces is executed. We'll discuss Boolean values more in the next chapter.

In this example, the Boolean expression is

```
name.equals("")
```

This Boolean expression compares the value of *name* with the "nothing" value for *String* variables. The nothing value for *String* variables is usually called the *null string*, and it is represented by a set of empty quotation marks. The *equals* term in this expression is a method that compares the value of *name* with the null string. The bottom line is that if the user has not typed anything in the Edit control, the code in the braces warns the user of that fact by changing the Text property of *label2*.

See the appendixes for a quick summary of Java syntax, including the *if* statement.

Using Color

The use of color in a user interface is a powerful tool, and it can make quite a difference in the appearance of an application. Most of the Visual J++ controls have a Color property that can be set using the Properties window while we're building our application (design time), and can also be modified when the application is executing (run time). Here, we will change the background of the form at both design time and run time.

Go to the Properties window, select the form *Form1*, and find the property called backColor. Click the pull-down arrow to the right of the current value of the property. A window with two tabs (System and Palette) appears. Click the Palette tab and select a color (say, one of the shades of green). You'll see that the background color of the window changes to reflect your selection.

Go back to the code window and add the *setBackColor* line as you see it in the following code:

```
private void button1_click(Object source, Event e)
{
    String name = edit1.getText();
    if (name.equals(""))
    {
        label2.setText("You Must Enter a Name");
    }
    else
    {
        label2.setText("Hello " + name);
        setBackColor(Color.BLUE);
    }
}
```

IP If you want to see all the color names available, just wait a moment after typing the period (.) after Color. A Statement Completion list box of color choices appears. If you select BLUE and press the Tab key, that value will be placed in the code for you.

When you run the application now, the form starts out gray. When you type something in the *edit1* edit box and then click the OK button, the form background color changes to blue.

Showing a Picture

The PictureBox control allows us to place a graphic on the application form. As with the other controls, it is simply a matter of dragging a PictureBox control onto the form. To resize the picture box, drag the PictureBox control's handles.

IP To remove a control you no longer want or don't like, simply select that control and press the Delete key.

When you have placed and sized the picture box to your satisfaction, go to the Properties window and find the Image property for *pictureBox1*. The value field for Image will be blank. Click the box to the right of the blank field with the ellipsis points (...) on it. From the Open dialog box, locate and select any graphics file to place in your picture box. Then go to the PictureBox property sizeMode, and click the pull-down arrow. Select StretchImage.

When you are finished, your form will look something like Figure 2-8.

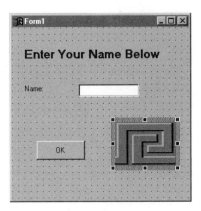

Figure 2-8.   *Our form with a PictureBox control.*

Inserting Comments

Comments are lines of text in a Java source code file (a .java file) that are ignored by the Java compiler, but are nonetheless important to the programmer, or programmers, working on the application. They allow us to document the application right in the source code itself. No programming language produces self-documenting code, and a well-placed comment helps the reader understand what is going on in a program. You might be surprised at how quickly you can forget why you placed a particular line or two of code in a Java program.

In the next three sections we will explore Java and Visual J++ comments in detail.

Creating Comments in Java

All comments appear as green text in the Visual J++ Code View window.

- *Single-line comments* start with two forward slash marks (//) and continue until the end of the line of code. Single-line comments are the most commonly used and are sometimes called "C++ style" comments. Here are a couple of examples:

```
int count = 0; // represents the number of entries
count = count + 1;   // increment the entry count
```

- *Multiline comments* start with slash mark-asterisk (/*) and end with asterisk-slash mark (*/). Since they start and end explicitly (unlike single-line comments, which end because the line ends), multiline comments can be used to easily comment out a whole section of code. However, multiline comments look a lot like JavaDoc comments, and might be confusing to the reader. Multiline comments are sometimes called "C-style" comments. Here is an example:

```
private void button1_click(Object source, Event e)
{
    /* this event procedure will blah, blah, blah.
    Notice that C-style comments can continue for
    any number of lines. */
}
```

■ *JavaDoc comments* are like multiline comments, and are very useful for documentation purposes. They start with slash mark-double asterisk (/**) and end with asterisk-slash mark (*/). We will talk more about JavaDoc comments shortly.

TODO Comments

TODO is a special Microsoft Visual Studio *token* (that is, an indicator that the Visual J++ environment recognizes and to which it will react) that you can use within all three types (single-line, multiline, and JavaDoc) of comments. Any comment in a Java program with the TODO token in it shows up automatically in the Task List window, and if you double-click the Task List entry with a TODO token in it, you are taken directly to that line of code. TODO tokens let you know that a piece of the code is needed and will eventually require completion. Microsoft uses the TODO token in code templates (such as the Form template that we used at the beginning of the chapter). But take note! The TODO token must be the first thing after the comment marker, and it must be in uppercase letters; otherwise, it will not show up in the Task List.

In the following example, the text of the TODO comment will appear in the Task List window:

```
private void button2_click(Object source, Event e)
{
    // TODO: button2's event procedure still not done
}
```

JavaDoc Comments

JavaDoc comments are a special form of comment designed to allow some types of documentation to be generated directly from the source code. We won't go into the details of creating JavaDoc comments here, as they are not part of Visual J++. It is important, however, to understand that some of the code generated on your behalf by the Visual J++ environment uses this form of comment, and, until you have more experience with JavaDoc comments, you should not delete any JavaDoc comments that you might encounter.

One special ability of JavaDoc comments of which you might want to take advantage uses the Class Outline feature of Visual J++. If you place a JavaDoc comment just before a class, method, or data member, you can see the first line of the JavaDoc comment when you select the class, method, or data member in the Class Outline. Here's an example:

```
/**
 * This class can take a variable number of parameters on the command
 * line. Program execution begins with the main() method. The class
 * constructor is not invoked unless an object of type 'Application1'
 * is created in the main() method.
 */
public class Form1 extends Form
{

/** "OK" button event procedure
    (user-added JavaDoc comment)
 */
    private void button1_click(Object source, Event e)
    {
        String name = edit1.getText();
        // the code continues …
```

There are two JavaDoc comments in the above code. The first one is part of the code of the Form template, and the second one represents a JavaDoc comment that you might add. To see the first line of each in the Class Outline window, make the Class Outline window visible. If you can't find it on the screen, go to the View menu and choose Other Windows, and then choose Document Outline. This should bring the Class Outline window to the front. If a message similar to "There are no items to show for the selected document" appears, go to the Project Explorer window and click the View Code button. Find *Form1* in the Class Outline window and select it. At the bottom of the window is the first line of the JavaDoc comment associated with *Form1*. Expand the list to the left of *Form1*. Find the entry for *button1_click* and select it. Again, at the bottom of the window you will see the first line of the JavaDoc comment. This is illustrated in Figure 2-9.

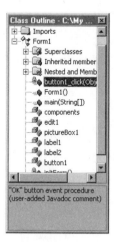

Figure 2-9. *Viewing JavaDoc comments in the Class Outline window.*

Class Outline is a powerful navigation tool that we will look at in more detail in Chapter 5.

Lab 2-2: Typing the Secret Word

Let's add some more behaviors to our application by watching what the user types and responding to it.

Lab overview

In this lab exercise, you will practice using:

- *if* statements.
- Colors.
- PictureBox visibility.

You will use some of the tools that we have been discussing to provide your application with a secret word. If the user types the secret word, your application will notice, make the picture box invisible, and change the label text and the color of the label text.

Lab setup

1. If you have been following the code example in this chapter, you are ready to go. Skip to the lab instructions.

2. If you have not been following the code example in this chapter, start Visual J++ now.

3. Open the Lab2-2 starter project (Chapter02\Lab2-2\Hello.sln).

4. Look in the Project Explorer window. If nothing appears under the project icon (called Hello), click the plus sign next to it to display the files associated with this project.

5. Select Form1.java, and at the top of the Project Explorer window, click the View Code button.

Lab instructions

1. Find the event handler called *edit1_textChanged* and add an *if* statement that will test the current value of the Text property of *edit1*.

2. If the value of the *edit1_textChanged* Text property is *secret*, add code to make the application:

   ▪ Change the foreColor property of *label2* to *Color.RED*.

   ▪ Change the Text property of *label2* to *That's the Secret Word!*

   ▪ Change the Visible property of *pictureBox1* to *false*.

3. Add this Boolean expression to test the Text property of the Edit control:

   ```
   edit1.getText().equals("secret")
   ```

   Whenever you want to determine the value of a control property, use "get" with the property name. Whenever you want to change a property value, use "set" with the property name.

4. Now make the *else* part of the *if* statement do what the event handler did before this modification:

```
else
{
    String name = edit1.getText();
    label2.setText("Hello " + name);
}
```

5. Take the application for a spin. Type the secret word and see how it behaves.

6. Check your work against the solution in Chapter02\Sol2-2\Hello.sln.

Next steps

You can now write an application using the Form template that allows the user to interact with a form. Your application can sense what is going on and it behaves accordingly. Not bad. Occasionally, though, we might find that our code does not perform exactly as we like. For those times, the debugger is our best friend. We step into it in the next section.

Debugging Code

For those really tricky chunks of code, we'll pull out the programmer's ultimate weapon: the debugger. The Visual J++ debugger allows you to observe your program as it is running. Using it, you can step through your code one line at a time, set breakpoints, and watch variables. Let's take a look.

First, we need to get the Visual J++ environment set up for debugging. To do this, we use the Debug toolbar. If the Debug toolbar is not visible, right-click in the toolbar area away from any toolbar buttons and select Debug in the pop-up menu. (You can get the same list of toolbars by using the Toolbars menu item on the View menu.) The commands associated with the Debug Toolbar buttons correspond to the commands in the View menu. See Figure 2-10 for a picture of the Debug toolbar.

Figure 2-10. *The Debug toolbar.*

Up to this point, we have been running our applications by clicking the Start Without Debugging button. Now we will use the Start button on the Debug toolbar, which begins executing the code in *debug mode*—that is, with all of the debug functions enabled.

Breakpoints

In order to examine our code as it is running, we need to be able to stop the code in midstride. For this we set *breakpoints*. A breakpoint is a mark that you put on a line of your code that tells the debugger to stop at that line when executing the code.

Breakpoints can be set four ways:

- Select the line of code and click the Insert Breakpoint button (the button with the little hand on it).

- Select the line of code and select Insert Breakpoint from the Debug menu.

- Right-click in any line and select Insert Breakpoint from the pop-up menu.

- Click the gray area in the margin of the code window.

When the application is started, the code runs until the line with the breakpoint on it. You can see which lines have breakpoints on them by looking for the stop sign symbol that appears in the left margin of the code window, as illustrated in Figure 2-11.

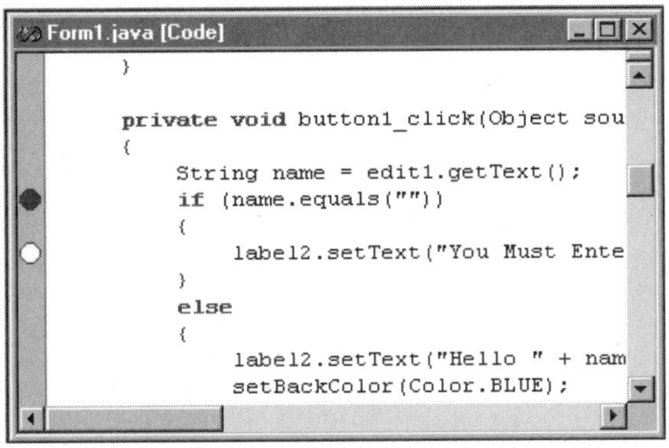

```
Form1.java [Code]                              _ □ X
      }                                              ▲

      private void button1_click(Object sou
      {
          String name = edit1.getText();
          if (name.equals(""))
          {
              label2.setText("You Must Ente
          }
          else
          {
              label2.setText("Hello " + nam
              setBackColor(Color.BLUE);          ▼
◄                                            ►
```

Figure 2-11.   *Breakpoints indicated by using stop sign icons in the left margin of a code window.*

Clearing, or removing, breakpoints is pretty much a matter of reversing what you did to set them. You can select Remove Breakpoint from the pop-up menu you get when you right-click on any line, or you can click the Remove Breakpoint button on the Debug toolbar. Probably the easiest way to clear breakpoints is to click the stop sign in the left margin of the code window. To remove all breakpoints with one click, use the Clear All Breakpoints button.

Visual J++ also provides us with a way to ignore breakpoints but leave them otherwise intact. This is known as *disabling* a breakpoint. There are Disable Breakpoint commands in each of the areas with a Remove Breakpoint command. In the code window, a disabled breakpoint shows up as a clear stop sign (see Figure 2-11).

If you want to see all your breakpoints at a glance, use the Breakpoints button. This brings up the window shown in Figure 2-12.

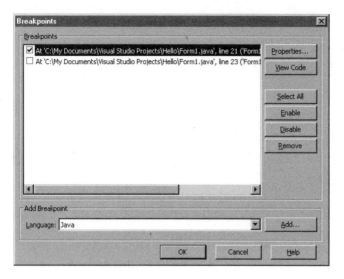

Figure 2-12. *The Breakpoints window.*

Using this window, you can see all the breakpoints in your project. This includes the name of the source code file, the line in that file, the name of the method that the breakpoint is in, and the line of that method. If the breakpoint's check box is selected, then the breakpoint is enabled (that is, it will cause the debugger to stop at this line). If the check box is not selected, then the breakpoint is disabled. You can also remove breakpoints completely by selecting the breakpoint and clicking the Remove button in this window.

Breakpoints can also be added from this window, but it is easier to simply select them in the source code.

Stepping Through the Code

When you have added your breakpoints to the code, click the Start button. The Watch window appears (see Figure 2-13), and the debugger begins executing your code. We'll get back to the Watch window momentarily. First, let's discuss how you can move through your code.

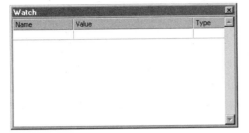

Figure 2-13. *The Watch window.*

 OTE The Visual J++ environment often displays a different set of windows when in design mode than when in debug mode. It doesn't make a lot of sense to display the Watch window when you are in design mode, for example. Don't be surprised if a particular window does not appear at any given time. You can always make it visible by selecting the appropriate menu item from the View menu. Make sure, however, that you are in the proper mode for that window.

Depending on where you placed the breakpoints, you might have to execute either more or less of the program to get to the breakpoint. For example, if you place the breakpoint in the event handler of a Button control, then you will have to click the button to see the application stop at that line.

When the debugger encounters the breakpoint that you added to the code, the code window marks the location of the line of code with an arrow in the left margin (see Figure 2-14).

```
Form1.java [Code]

        }

    private void button1_click(Object source,
    {
        String name = edit1.getText();
        if (name.equals(""))
        {
            label2.setText("You Must Enter a
        }
        else
        {
            label2.setText("Hello " + name);
```

Figure 2-14. *The code window in debug mode, stopped at a breakpoint.*

You're now ready to examine the current state of the application, or to step through the code. All Debug toolbar buttons have unique behaviors where methods are concerned.

You have several toolbar button options for stepping through your program when the current line contains a method whose source code you have access to:

- Step Into—The debugger jumps to that method and sets the current line to be the first line of the method.

- Step Over—The debugger immediately executes the code for the method on the current line without showing you any of that code.

- Step Out—The debugger executes the remainder of the code for the method that is currently being executed, and the next line shown is the line in the calling method after the line with the call.

If the current line is not a method, or you don't have the source code for that method, then the Step Into and Step Over toolbar buttons behave identically. Note that breakpoints are still in effect even when stepping out of a method. If you step out of a method, but a breakpoint occurs before the end of the method, execution still stops at that breakpoint.

 OTE   There might be times when you're stepping through code and there is nothing for your application to display. Don't worry. Debugger values appear as the program's state changes. In any case, you might find yourself clicking back and forth on the taskbar between your running application and the Visual J++ project environment button until you get used to the process of debugging.

Watching Variables

When you start an application using the debugger, a Watch window appears with a lot of blank fields in it. This window holds space for those variables whose values are of interest to you. To place a variable in the Watch window, you can right-click the variable and select Add Watch from the pop-up menu. This places the variable in the column labeled Name in the window. The variable's value and a short description of the variable's type appear as well. If the value changes as a result of the execution of a line of code, then the variable's value appears red. When you step to the next line, the color of the value goes back to black.

For example, consider these three variables:

```
int count = 5;
int maximum = 10;
boolean maximumReached = false;
```

Figure 2-15 shows these variables in the Watch window.

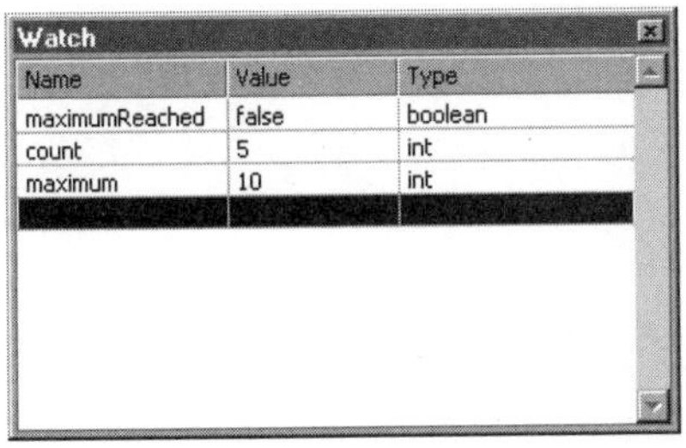

Figure 2-15. *The Watch window with a few variables.*

If you right-click the variable listing in the Watch window, you will see that you have a few options there as well, including removing the watch for that particular variable. Another option is to continue, which we will explore in a moment.

The Immediate Window

Often, in debugging, you need to be able to determine what the value of a variable is as you are stepping through the program. We have seen how to do this with the Watch window. Other debug windows give similar information with their own twist. All of the debug windows are available from both the Debug toolbar and the View menu.

The Immediate window is the only one of these windows that allows us to modify the value of variables by depositing values into the variable at run time. The Immediate window not only allows us to see the value of a variable while the application is running, but also lets us change that value. If you type the name of a variable in the Immediate window and press the Enter key, you will see the value of the variable. To deposit values in a variable, type an assignment expression in the Immediate window.

Using our three variables, *count*, *maximum*, and *maximumReached*, Figure 2-16 shows how they might be manipulated. The user types *count* and presses the Enter key, which causes "5" to appear. This action is repeated for the *maximum* and *maximumReached* variables. The next line (count < maximum) yields *true*. Finally, the user deposits *true* into *maximumReached*, and the assigned value is echoed back.

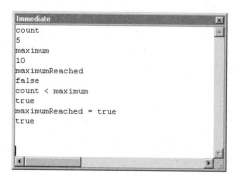

Figure 2-16.   *Changing values of variables using the Immediate window.*

The Output Window

When Java is run from a command-line interface operating system (such as MS-DOS or UNIX), output can be written to the console. Output that goes to the console is character-based (that is, non-Windows-based). We can write output to the console in Visual J++ even though we don't have a command-line interface. We show console output in a window called the Output window. To illustrate this, consider an alternate form of the Hello program:

```
public class Hello
{
    public static void main (String[] args)
    {
        System.out.println("Hello World");
        // writes to the Output window
    }
}
```

This program prints "Hello World" to the screen in command-line operating systems. In Visual J++, "Hello World" appears in the Output window. We can make use of this when debugging our code by placing lines such as

```
System.out.println("Now executing the XYZ method");
```

anywhere in the program where it helps us trace the execution of the code. The string would then be written to the Output window when the line of code is reached, without disturbing the rest of our application.

To bring up the Output window, go to the View menu, and from the Other Windows submenu, select Output. If your output is not appearing in the Output window, make sure that Debug (rather than Solution Builder) appears in the drop-down box at the top of the Output window. When Solution Builder is selected, the Output window shows only output from building your project (compilation errors and the like). We are not building the project now; we are running it. That's why you need to make sure that Debug is selected.

 OTE To use this Hello program, you would want to use a project that doesn't have a form. We haven't done that yet. We'll create projects that don't use forms when we discuss console applications in Chapter 11.

Of course, you want to be sure to remove any calls to *System.out.println* after you are finished debugging.

Getting Going Again

Once you have examined the code you are interested in, and are ready to continue the execution of your program until the next breakpoint, click the Start button again (the ToolTip for the Start button is Continue).

If you want to continue execution until a particular point, but you don't want to set a breakpoint at that location, try using the Run To Cursor button. Clicking this button causes the debugger to execute all the code between the line of code currently executing (possibly the first line of the program if you haven't started the program yet) and the line currently selected. However, if any breakpoints are enabled between the current line and the line selected, the debugger will stop there first. If you want a breakpoint to be ignored, but you don't want to remove it, it must be disabled.

Your other option for resuming execution is to restart the application from the beginning. For this, use the Restart button.

When you are ready to stop the application, you can click the Close button or choose the Stop button on the Debug menu.

Classes and Forms

You've now had a quick tour of the Visual J++ development environment, and you created some simple applications and interacted with the user. Now it's time to delve into the Java programming language itself.

Creating and manipulating classes is the main task of the Java programmer. You can't program in Java without a firm understanding of classes. The Java language supplies us with a large number of powerful, flexible, robust classes that we can use to build our programs, and also allows us to create our own classes to build custom solutions to custom problems.

Along with general Java classes, this chapter also discusses the Visual J++ *Form* class. The forms we introduced in Chapter 2 are members of the *Form* class.

In this chapter, you'll learn about:

■ Classes and objects

■ References

■ The *new* keyword

■ Constructors

■ Special Visual J++ dialog classes

You will get practice using:

- The *MessageBox* class
- The *ColorDialog* class
- The *FontDialog* class

Classes and Objects

Two of the most important organizational tools in Java programming are classes and objects. In order to build Java programs, you must have a handle on both of these concepts. Once introduced, you will see how the Visual J++ development system uses classes and objects to help you create Java programs quickly and easily.

Classes

All programming languages have built-in data types used for creating variables. Built-in types are provided to programmers automatically by the compiler. In programming languages such as FORTAN and C, programmers use built-in types like *int*, *float*, *REAL*, and *INTEGER* to create almost all of their variables. Java has a set of built-in, or *primitive*, types too, which is based on the built-in types of C++. (For more information on Java's primitive types, see Chapter 4.) Like C++, Java also has classes. But Java takes classes one step further than C++ by requiring that *all* code and data belong to some class.

In contrast to a primitive type, a *class* is a user-defined type. Primitive types are fine for many applications, but as software increases in complexity, using built-in types exclusively becomes more difficult. The trouble with primitive types is that they more or less reflect the internals of computer hardware: integers, bytes, floating-point numbers, and so forth. User-defined types (that is, classes) allow us, as programmers, to create variables that are more descriptive of the problem at hand. Every program is intended to solve some problem in the real world. It is important that we be able to relate our solution (a computer program) to the problem that we are solving. Among other things, this makes for programs that are easier to understand and easier to modify to meet changing needs.

Classes provide us with a way to represent complex structures as we create our models of the world inside our programs. Any amount of data can be placed inside a class, and specialized operations can be created to manipulate that data. The operations that a class contains come in the form of *methods* in Java. We will discuss Java methods briefly later in this chapter, and in more detail in Chapter 4.

Classes also include a mechanism for easily extending software, called *inheritance*. Inheritance lets us take an existing solution to a problem and build on it to solve a different, possibly more complex, problem without having to rewrite all the original code. We will be exploring Java's inheritance features in Chapter 5.

In the spirit of using classes to represent real-world concepts, we will use Java to write a Windows-based application that allows the user to submit a bid on a house. Once the bid is submitted, the program will calculate the difference between the asking price and the bid price. Let us say we need this program because we own the "City View House Company" and we build houses with nice views that we want to sell to qualified buyers. To write our program for comparing asking prices to bid prices, we need to be able to represent a house in our code. For this, we use a general-purpose class called *CityViewHouse*. In Java, such a class looks like this:

```
public class CityViewHouse
{
// methods and member variables for the class CityViewHouse
}
```

Except for the comment (which starts with the "//"), the class is left empty for the moment. Typically, a class has methods and member variables, as we will see shortly.

Objects

An *object* is simply a variable of a class type. Usually when programmers use the term "variable" they are referring to a primitive variable. As we discussed, a class is a special kind of type, and so to differentiate variables of a class from variables of a built-in type, the term "object" is used. Whereas a primitive variable is usually pretty simple, an object as the product of a class can be much more complex as well as more versatile. Essentially, to *instantiate* a class is to make an instance of the class, and an *instance* of a class is an object.

An object of class *CityViewHouse* could be created using the following code:

```
public class BidMaker extends Form
{
    private CityViewHouse myHouse = new CityViewHouse();
    // other declarations and code
}
```

In order to understand this code, we must discuss references, member variables, the *new* keyword, and constructors, all of which appear in the following sections.

Creating a New Class

We will now create a new project in Visual J++ and add a general-purpose class to it. Up until this time, our projects have included only forms. Forms are a special kind of class that can contain WFC (Windows Foundation Classes for Java) controls. A Visual J++ class template will help us add our own classes to our projects the way a Form template helped us create forms in Chapter 2. From now on, we also won't be using project wizards to build our project, but will start by creating an empty project and build from there. This allows us to have more control over our project, such as being able to name our forms as we create them rather than using Visual J++ defaults.

Let's begin. Start Visual J++. If you are already in Visual J++, save any work that you might want to keep, and then select Close All from the File menu. Then select New Project from the File menu. (This dialog box comes up automatically when you start Visual J++.) In the New Project dialog box, click the New tab, and from Visual J++ Projects, select Empty Project. Type *BidMaker* in the text box at the bottom of the dialog box, and then click the Open button. See Figure 3-1 for a picture of the New Project dialog box with the Empty Project folder selected.

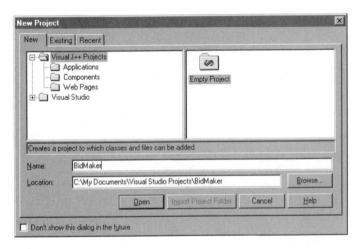

Figure 3-1.   *Starting an empty project.*

When the Project Explorer window appears, right-click the BidMaker project icon, point to Add on the pop-up menu, and then select Add Form. The Add Item dialog box has Form preselected in the left pane. Select Form in the right pane, and name the form file BidMaker.java. Click the Open button, and the form is added to our project. As before, this form will host our WFC controls and act as the interface to our new application.

Now that we have a form in our project, we are ready to add a new general-purpose class. To do this, right-click the BidMaker project icon again, point to Add on the pop-up menu, and then select Add Class. This time, when the Add Item dialog box comes up, it has Class preselected in the left pane.

See Figure 3-2 for a picture of the Add Item dialog box.

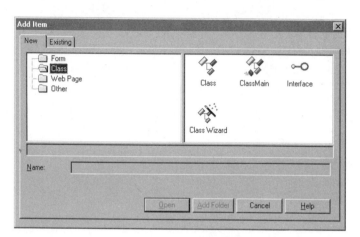

Figure 3-2.   *The Add Item dialog box with Class selected.*

Click Class in the right pane, name the class file CityViewHouse.java, and click the Open button. A code window appears that looks like Figure 3-3.

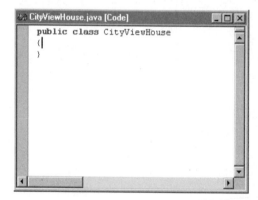

Figure 3-3.   *A newly created class using the class template.*

> **IMPORTANT**   The Java source code for a class must be in a file with the same name as the class. In our example, the file is named CityViewHouse.java and the class is *CityViewHouse*.

Notice the Project Explorer window: your new class appears as a member of the BidMaker project (see Figure 3-4).

Figure 3-4. *The Project Explorer window with your newly created class,* CityViewHouse.

Creating Objects

Now we have a basic understanding of the concepts *object* and *class*, and the relationship between the two. Figure 3-5 illustrates this relationship. Now we will see how the Java language implements class instantiation; that is, we will see how to create objects in Java.

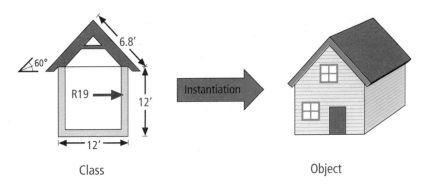

Class   Object

Figure 3-5. *Instantiation is the act of building an object from a class blueprint.*

The phrases "creating an object," "making an instance of a class," and "instantiating a class" all convey the idea that an object is a representation of a class blueprint. In order to create an object in Java, we next need to understand references and the keyword *new*.

References to Objects

References make it possible to access our objects in Java code because Java objects don't have names. Objects can be accessed only indirectly, through *references* that identify an object we want to use. This may seem a little odd, but it works out well, as we will see as we work with Java's references and objects throughout the book. See Figure 3-6 for a representation of a reference. Notice the arrow over the class name *CityViewHouse*. This represents the idea that a reference is not an object of that class, but simply points the way to such an object.

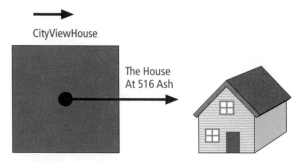

Figure 3-6.　*Picture of a reference and an associated object.*

In order to manipulate an object we need a reference, and in order to obtain a reference we need to declare one. That's what we will do next.

Adding Member Variables to Classes

Member variables are variables that are declared within a class, but not within a method. (We'll see methods after we talk about the *new* keyword.) Member variables are accessible when an object of their class is created, and they live as long as the object of which they are a part lives.

Visual J++ provides a tool for adding member variables to classes. From the Class Outline window, right-click CityHouseView, and then select Add Member Variable. This brings up the Add Member Variable dialog box. Figure 3-7 shows this dialog box.

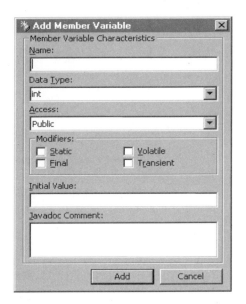

Figure 3-7. *The Add Member Variable dialog box for adding member variables to classes.*

Fill in the text boxes of the Add Member Variable dialog box as follows:

Name	*myHouse*
Data Type	*CityViewHouse*
Access	*Private*

You can leave the rest blank for this member variable. Click the Add button, and *myHouse*, your *CityViewHouse* reference member variable, is added to the code for *BidMaker*.

We will discuss more options for member variables as we go along. For the time being, member variables should have access marked as *private*, and you can leave all the check boxes in the Modifiers section clear. Initial Value is optional, as is a JavaDoc comment. If you do decide to enter a JavaDoc comment (see Chapter 2 for more information on JavaDoc comments), don't include the delimiters (/** and */). Visual J++ adds them for you automatically, and if you add them, the compiler produces a syntax error.

You can dismiss the Add Member Variable dialog box by clicking the Close button in the upper right corner. Examine the code window for the class *BidMaker* and you will see the following line:

```
private CityViewHouse myHouse;
```

Since we left the Initial Value text box blank, the reference *myHouse* begins life without referring to any objects (see Figure 3-8).

```
CityViewHouse myHouse;
```

CityViewHouse

Figure 3-8.   *When a reference variable is first declared, it doesn't refer to anything.*

The black dot in the middle of the box *myHouse* represents the *null* value. As in other programming languages, the *null* value means that the reference *myHouse* doesn't point to anything. Note that we do not yet have a *CityViewHouse* object. We have only a label for the reference to an object we'll be creating at some point. To actually create a *CityViewHouse* object, we need the *new* keyword.

The *new* Keyword

The *new* keyword is what actually allows us to build an object from the blueprint provided by a class definition. When you use the *new* keyword, it instantiates, or creates an instance of, an object of that class. In computer terminology, it allocates computer memory, which is the space that an object needs in order to exist. After it creates that object, it returns a reference value to your Java program. This reference value can then be stored in a reference variable that has already been declared:

```
CityViewHouse myHouse;
myHouse = new CityViewHouse;
```

So, creating an object is a two-step process:

1. Declare the object's reference variable.

2. Call the *new* keyword and store the returned value in the object variable.

We already declared the *myHouse* variable. Step 2 takes place inside the method called *BidMaker*. Notice that the name of the method is the same as the name of the class. We will see why this is significant when we discuss constructors. The *BidMaker* method starts out looking like this:

```
public BidMaker()
{
    // Required for Visual J++ Forms Designer support initForm();

    // TODO: Add any constructor code after initForm call
}
```

Add a new line in the *BidMaker* method that uses the *new* keyword to create a new *CityViewHouse* object, and assign its reference to our object variable *myHouse*. The *BidMaker* method should now look like this:

```
public BidMaker()
{
    // Required for Visual J++ Forms Designer support
    initForm();

    // TODO: Add any constructor code after initForm call
    myHouse = new CityViewHouse();
}
```

We now have a *CityViewHouse* object that our object variable, *myHouse*, points to.

 OTE While it is more descriptive to say that a reference *value* is stored in a reference *variable*, in practice, programmers often simply use the term *reference* to mean either a value (such as one returned by the *new* keyword) or a variable that holds a value. Usually, the intended meaning can be understood from the context.

Methods

Methods describe actions in Java. Java uses methods the way other languages use functions, procedures, and subroutines. However, the methods in Java differ from functions in other languages, in that methods are always members of a class. You can't have a method without having a class to put it in.

We have already seen a few examples of methods in Java. The WFC *Label* class has a *setText* method and a *getText* method, as does the WFC *Edit* class. All event handlers are methods as well (for example, *button1_click*).

Methods also have access modifiers (such as *public* or *private*), return types (for example, *Label.getText* returns a *String* value), names, a parameter list, and a body.

Because methods exist within the context of some class, methods (like properties and other member variables) can be inherited through a class hierarchy. These inherited methods and properties are available for use in other classes. We'll discuss Java's inheritance mechanisms in greater detail in Chapter 5.

 IP For a preview of just how much inheritance affects the building of Java programs, bring up the Class Outline window (from the View menu, select Other Windows, and then select Document Outline). We'll be using the Class Outline window to override methods in Chapter 5.

Let's add a couple of methods to the *CityViewHouse* class (*setAskingPrice* and *getAskingPrice*), as well as a member variable (*askingPrice*). First, from the Class Outline window use the Add Member Variable dialog box to add a *private* member variable called *askingPrice* to the class *CityViewHouse* (following the same procedure that we used to add the *myHouse* object to the class *BidMaker*).

To add a method to the class *CityViewHouse*, right-click *CityViewHouse* in the Class Outline window, and then select Add. This is the Add Method dialog box (see Figure 3-9).

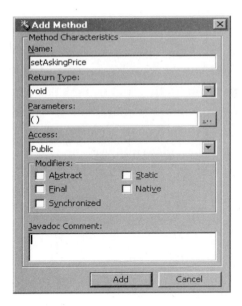

Figure 3-9.   *The Add Method dialog box.*

Name the method *setAskingPrice* and set the return type to *void*. Click the button to the right of the Parameters button.

To add parameters to your method, double-click the Parameters box. This brings up the Edit Parameter List dialog box (see Figure 3-10).

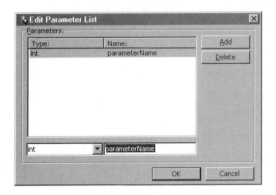

Figure 3-10.   *The Edit Parameter List dialog box.*

In the Edit Parameter List dialog box, click the Add button. In the drop-down list box at the lower left, select the return type *int*. In the text box to the right of that drop-down list box, type *amount* and click the OK button. This brings you back to the Add Method dialog box. Set access to *public*. Repeat the same procedure to create a second method called *getAskingPrice*, which has a return type of *int* and takes no parameters. When you are all finished, your code window for the class *CityViewHouse* should look like this:

```
public class CityViewHouse
{
    private int askingPrice;
    public int getAskingPrice()
    {
        // TODO: Add your own implementation.
        int returnValue;
        returnValue = 0;
        return returnValue;
    }

    public void setAskingPrice(int amount)

    {
        // TODO: Add your own implementation.
    }
}
```

In this example, for the method *CityViewHouse.setAskingPrice*, the access modifier is *public* (meaning, available throughout the project; for more on *public* see Chapter 4); the return type is *void* (meaning, don't return anything); the name is *setAskingPrice*; the parameter list is composed of a single integer value called *amount*; and the body starts and ends with braces ({ }) as all method bodies do. Notice that the simple definition (returnValue = 0) was added to the method *getAskingPrice* so that it is syntactically legal. Select Build from the Build menu, and you will see that the file compiles cleanly.

In order to call either the *getAskingPrice* or the *setAskingPrice* method, we need two things: the code for the bodies of the methods and an object of class *CityViewHouse*. We will complete the code for the methods in the lab for this section, and we will create an object of class *CityViewHouse* later in this chapter.

Identifiers and Naming Conventions

Now that we have a few classes, objects, member variables, and methods of our own, we should consider how best to name them. In this section, we have rules for identifiers and suggestions for naming conventions.

Identifiers

Like every programming language, Java has certain built-in programming elements, or *keywords*, that name characteristics of the language. These are supplied by Java and can't be defined or altered by the programmer. Keywords include words like *class*, *new*, *public*, *static*, *this*, and *null*. The Appendixes include a complete list of Java keywords.

Other programming elements, or *identifiers*, are defined by the programmer and include names of member variables, classes, methods, and objects. Here are some characteristics of legal Java identifiers for the things that you can name:

- They aren't keywords or reserved words.

- They are made up of Unicode characters.

- They start with a Unicode letter.

- They are case-sensitive. (*Bob* and *bob* are distinct identifiers.)

- They cannot include blanks or other white space. (*Hot Dog* is not a legal identifier.)

- They have practically no length limit.

 N OTE "Made up of Unicode characters" means that Java identifiers can contain characters from alphabets other than English, such as Cyrillic. Unicode letters also include the underscore (_) and the dollar sign ($), among others. In this book, when we use the term *character*, we refer to the ASCII character set. Basically, this means *A* through *Z*, *a* through *z*, *0* through *9*, and punctuation.

Naming Conventions

Identifiers follow a naming convention that helps programmers avoid syntax errors and aims toward a consistent style so that anyone who knows the convention can tell at a glance in what general category an item belongs. Here is one naming convention for you to consider as you create your code, and it is what we will use in the examples for this book:

- Start class names with capital letters, and capitalize words within the name (for example, *CityViewHouse*).

- Start member variables and local variable names with lowercase letters, and capitalize words within the name (for example, *bidAmount*).

- Use nouns as member variables and local variables (for example, *bidAmount*).

- Use verbs to start method names, and use the same letter cases as member variables and local variable names (for example, *getAskingPrice*).

- Avoid the use of underscores in general, and in method names in particular, because event handlers use underscores to separate the control name from the event name (for example, *button1_click*).

Using a naming convention takes a little getting used to, but once you do, it is well worth the effort.

Constructors

Each time an object is created (or instantiated), a special kind of method is invoked. This special method is known as a *constructor*, and every class has at least one. Constructor methods allow us to ensure that objects of a specific class are always created correctly. Constructors also initialize objects.

We implicitly call a constructor when we use the *new* keyword. You have already seen the parentheses after the name of the class when using the *new* keyword. Now we will see the code behind the call.

The Default Constructor

Let's look at the use of the *new* keyword in our example with the *CityViewHouse* class. The line that creates an object of type *CityViewHouse* is in the class *BidMaker*. Here it is:

```
myHouse = new CityViewHouse();    // creates a CityViewHouse object
```

Notice that after the *new* keyword is the name of the class followed by a set of parentheses. The parentheses after the class name indicate that a class method exists that has the same name as the class. This method is a constructor for the class, and it ensures that objects of its class follow the class blueprint. If you go back to the definition of the class *CityViewHouse*, you won't see a method there called *CityViewHouse*. This is because if we do not include a constructor method in a class, the Java language provides one for us automatically. This is known as a d*efault constructor*. So, *CityViewHouse* has a default constructor because we didn't explicitly provide a constructor of our own.

A default constructor is really there as a placeholder: it guarantees that every class has at least one constructor method (for following that blueprint). If we could see a default constructor for *CityViewHouse*, it would look like this:

```
CityViewHouse()
{
}
```

Like all constructors, this method has a number of distinguishing characteristics. For one thing, it has no return type. This is not the same as having a return type of *void*. All constructor methods literally have no return type. Also, the name of the constructor method must be the same as the name of the class. That is how we can pick them out in the definition of a class.

Since our example uses a default constructor, there is no code in this method. Of course, constructor methods that we write ourselves have code in them (as you are about to see).

The reason that default constructors exist at all is so that Java's inheritance mechanisms can function correctly. We will see more about inheritance in Chapter 5.

For now, let's add more interesting constructors to our class.

Adding Constructors

Now we can take a more active hand in the creation of our *CityViewHouse* objects. Let's say that we would like the value of *askingPrice* of any given instance of *CityViewHouse* to start at $100,000. What would that code look like? Add the following constructor method inside your *CityViewHouse* class:

```
public CityViewHouse ()   // constructor for class CityViewHouse
{
    askingPrice = 100000;
}
```

Now our class includes the definition of a method that sets the initial asking price of every *CityViewHouse* object to 100000. Whenever a *CityViewHouse* object is created, the constructor method that we provided will be called. Since we are using the naming conventions of capitalizing our class name and beginning method names with a lowercase letter, the constructor is always the only method name in the class that starts with a capital letter.

Whenever we create a new *CityViewHouse* object, we will have a preset asking price of $100,000. This is better than allowing it to default to $0, but wouldn't it be better to state the asking price of each object as it is created? You guessed it. That's the next topic.

Constructors with Parameters

Constructors with parameters allow the code that creates the class to specify values to be passed along to the constructor method as it creates the new object. Let's modify our class *CityViewHouse* to include a parameter with our constructor. Your constructor should now look like the following:

```
public class CityViewHouse
{    // other member variables as before …
    public CityViewHouse (int amount)
    {
        askingPrice = amount;
    }
}
```

Our modified constructor now requires a parameter, so it is no longer legal to create a *CityViewHouse* object without specifying how much the initial asking price should be. The value for the parameter of our constructor must be specified when the object is created. Select Build from the Build menu and you will see the error caused by our change. If the Task List window is not visible, make it visible by selecting Other Windows from the View menu and then selecting Task List. This message appears:

```
Undefined name 'myHouse' (J0049)
```

Double-click this message in the Task List window, and it will take you to this line:

```
    myHouse = new CityViewHouse();
```

The syntax for creating a *CityViewHouse* object with the new constructor is just as it was before, except that a value is placed in the parentheses after the name of the class. Change the line with the error to include the initial asking price (as an *int* value) in the parentheses:

```
    myHouse = new CityViewHouse(250000);
```

With the addition of a parameter to our constructor, we can create multiple *CityViewHouse* objects, each with its own initial asking price as specified when the object is created.

Now that we have our *CityViewHouse* object created correctly, we can use the object to call its methods. The general form of a method call in Java is:

```
object.methodname()
```

In our example for the *setAskingPrice* method, this would be:

```
myHouse.setAskingPrice(260000);    // an increase in asking price
```

And, since *getAskingPrice* returns a value, a call to it would look like this:

```
price = myHouse.getAskingPrice();  // what is current asking price?
```

Lab 3-1: Modifying the BidMaker Project

Lab overview

In this lab, you will practice:

■ Modifying methods of general-purpose classes.

■ Calling methods of general-purpose classes.

You will take an extension of the example code that you just developed and provide some methods with code definitions. You will also call an object method of your class.

Lab setup

1. Start Visual J++.
2. Open the BidMaker starter project (Chapter03\Lab3-1\ BidMaker.sln).

Lab instructions

1. In the Project Explorer window, expand the BidMaker project. The project includes a BidMaker.java file and a CityViewHouse.java file.

2. Right-click BidMaker.java in the Project Explorer window, and select View Code. In the Task List window, a TODO item appears to guide you with the necessary modifications to the BidMaker.java file. Double-click the task item to go to the appropriate section of code where you can make your changes.

3. Repeat step 2 with the CityViewHouse.java file.

4. When you have made the additions, run the project.

5. When the BidMaker form appears, type an integer number (without a dollar sign) in the text box, and click the Accept Bid button.

6. You can check your work against the solution in Chapter03\Sol3-1\BidMaker.sln.

Next steps

Now that we have seen the steps necessary for adding our own classes to our projects, we turn our attention to using some of the predefined classes in Visual J++. In the next section, we learn how to use these classes to create standard Windows dialog boxes in our application. We also see how to add additional forms to our application.

Adding Dialog Boxes and Additional Forms

Visual J++ provides us with a number of predefined classes that make creating powerful Windows-based applications easier. We start with a very handy class that allows us to display alert dialog boxes to the user: the *MessageBox* class.

The *MessageBox* Class

The *MessageBox* class puts messages on the screen. This is just about the easiest way to communicate something to the user that can't be communicated elegantly using the window the user has active at a given moment. The *MessageBox.show* method has three formats that we can use for displaying these alerts.

Start Visual J++ and open the project Chapter03\MessageBox\MessageBoxExamples.sln. Run the project and click each of the buttons on the form. Each button has an associated event handler that brings up one of the forms of a Message Box dialog box. When you are finished, click the Close button in the upper right corner. We'll take a look at the event handlers for each of the buttons and see how each version of *MessageBox.show* is called.

OTE The *MessageBox* class is defined in com.ms.wfc.ui. You will notice that there is an *import* statement at the top of the form code that Visual J++ creates for you that reads:

```
import com.ms.wfc.ui.*;
```

If this line weren't in a Java source code file, the *MessageBox.show* method would have to be called like this:

```
com.ms.wfc.ui.MessageBox.show("Hi User!"); // long name!
```

If you use the *MessageBox* class in one of your own Java files, you need to include this *import* statement or use the long method name.

The source code demonstrates the three formats we can use to call *MessageBox.show*. These formats are summarized in Table 3-1.

MessageBox Format	Description
MessageBox.show(String text)	Message box with message
MessageBox.show(String text, String caption)	Message box with message and window title
MessageBox.show(String text, String caption, int style)	Customized message box

Table 3-1. *The* show *method of the* MessageBox *class.*

Version 1 of *MessageBox.show* looks like this in code:

```
private void simpleBtn_click(Object source, Event e)
{
    MessageBox.show("Simple MessageBox");
}
```

From our earlier exploration, you recognize that *simpleBtn_click* is an event handler. It handles what happens when the button named *simpleBtn* is clicked. The window that this event handler produces is shown in Figure 3-11.

Figure 3-11. *A simple message box.*

Did you notice that this window doesn't have any title? The second version of *MessageBox.show* will change that. Let's change the code just a little to add a title to the window.

```
private void withTitleBtn_click(Object source, Event e)
{
    MessageBox.show("MessageBox with Title","MessageBox Title");
}
```

See Figure 3-12 for the updated message box.

Figure 3-12. *A message box with window title.*

The third version for calling *MessageBox.show* provides us with a way to create all sorts of appearances and behaviors for our message boxes. Let's say that you want a message box with an OK button and a Cancel button, and you want one of those balloon question-mark Windows icons along with your message. To top it off, you want to make sure that your message box has a default response of OK. (The default response button is highlighted and is the one activated when you press the Enter key rather than click the button.) In short, you want a message box that looks like

Figure 3-13. The *withIconsBtn_click* event handler in the example MessageBoxExample project shows what this call to *MessageBox.show* would look like.

Figure 3-13. *Spiffing up your message box.*

Another Java code example for such a message box would be as you see here:

```
private void button1_click(Object source, Event e)
{
    MessageBox.show("Are you sure you're done?", "Tread Lightly",
                MessageBox.YESNO +
                MessageBox.ICONQUESTION +
                MessageBox.DEFBUTTON1);
}
```

The first two parameters are just like the other calls to the method. It's that last one that is a little tricky. Let's take a closer look at it.

The *MessageBox.show* styles

The last parameter to the *show* method is a style value, also called a *flag*. Using that style value, you can specify three things about the message box:

■ The names and number of buttons in the box

■ The special icon that appears next to the message

■ The default button for the box

You could use the numbers that represent these flags; however, the *MessageBox* class provides us with names for these flags. Table 3-2 lists all the style values for the kinds of button sets a message box can have. You can pick any one value from this list for a given call to

MessageBox.show. Some of these flags will not work together; for example, you can't use both MessageBox.OK and MessageBox.YESNO in the same call to *MessageBox.show.*

Button Arrangement	Button
OK button only	MessageBox.OK
OK and Cancel buttons	MessageBox.OKCANCEL
Abort, Retry, and Ignore buttons	MessageBox.ABORTRETRYIGNORE
Yes, No, and Cancel buttons	MessageBox.YESNOCANCEL
Yes and No buttons	MessageBox.YESNO
Retry and Cancel buttons	MessageBox.RETRYCANCEL

Table 3-2. *Button arrangements and corresponding button flags in the* MessageBox *class.*

Going back to that earlier call to *MessageBox.show*, it may be easier to see how the style values work by rebuilding them one by one. Starting with just the button arrangement, we have the following:

```
MessageBox.show("Are you sure you're done?",
    "Tread Lightly",MessageBox.YESNO);
```

Notice that this call works quite well with only the button arrangement flag specified. We don't have to pick an icon value, and the program will pick one of the buttons to be the default if we don't. If we do choose to go on, our next step might be to indicate which icon we want displayed. In order to do this, we determine which flag corresponds to the icon we want to see, and we add that style value to the one we already have in the call. We want the question-mark icon, so now the code looks like this:

```
MessageBox.show("Are you sure you're done?", "Tread Lightly",
    MessageBox.YESNO + MessageBox.ICONQUESTION);
```

It is important to understand that the two flags are added together (using the plus sign) and not separated by commas. Table 3-3 lists all the icon codes for a message box. You can pick any one value from this list to put in a call to *MessageBox.show.*

Icon Code	Icon Description
MessageBox.ICONASTERISK	"i" in word balloon
MessageBox.ICONERROR	Red circle with white "X"
MessageBox.ICONEXCLAMATION	Exclamation point
MessageBox.ICONHAND	Red circle with white "X"
MessageBox.ICONINFORMATION	"i" in word balloon
MessageBox.ICONQUESTION	Question mark
MessageBox.ICONSTOP	Red circle with white "X"
MessageBox.ICONWARNING	Exclamation point

Table 3-3. *Icon codes in the* MessageBox *class, and corresponding descriptions.*

The last style value is the indication of the default button when a message box first appears. The default button is not coded by name, but by placement on the message box. This means that you don't have a flag for indicating that the Yes button in MessageBox.YESNO is the default button. What you do have is a flag for indicating that the first button of the message box is the default. Table 3-4 lists the flags that let you pick which button shows up as the default for the message box. Notice also that the user can still change the default button by pressing the Tab key while the message box is on the screen. Nevertheless, the next time that message box appears, the button that you choose will be the first default.

Default Button	Button Flag
Button 1	MessageBox.DEFBUTTON1
Button 2	MessageBox.DEFBUTTON2
Button 3	MessageBox.DEFBUTTON3

Table 3-4. *Default buttons and corresponding codes in the* MessageBox *class.*

Let's indicate that the first button of the message box should be the default (in this case, the Yes button). We put the last code into the call to *MessageBox.show*, and it looks like this:

```
MessageBox.show("Are you sure you're done?", "Tread Lightly",
                MessageBox.YESNO +
                MessageBox.ICONQUESTION +
                MessageBox.DEFBUTTON1);
```

The *MessageBox.show* return value

We have seen how to customize our message box with different button arrangements and icons, and we have seen how to pick a default button for the box. Now we turn our attention to what happens after the user has responded to the message box. We determine this by the value returned from *MessageBox.show*. This value, along with the corresponding name as shown in Table 3-5, allows us to know exactly what button the user has clicked.

Button Pressed	Value Returned
OK	DialogResult.OK
Cancel	DialogResult.CANCEL
Abort	DialogResult.ABORT
Retry	DialogResult.RETRY
Ignore	DialogResult.IGNORE
Yes	DialogResult.YES
No	DialogResult.NO

Table 3-5.   *Return values and corresponding codes in the* MessageBox *class.*

Using the return code in our event handler, we have the following:

```
private void button1_click(Object source, Event e)

{
    int result;
    result = MessageBox.show("Are you sure you're done?",
                "Tread Lightly",
                MessageBox.YESNO +
                MessageBox.ICONQUESTION +
                MessageBox.DEFBUTTON1);

    if (result == DialogResult.YES)
        {
        Application.exit();
        }
    else if (result == DialogResult.NO)
        {
            // nevermind
        }
}
```

What you see after the call to the *MessageBox.show* method is a test on the value returned. If the user clicks the Yes button, then the result will be equal to DialogResult.NO, and the method *Application.exit* will be called. This method causes the application to terminate. This is a lot like clicking the Close box in the upper right corner of a window. If the user clicks the No button, then the application doesn't do anything. (Of course, the message box itself is already off the screen, so things proceed normally on the *MessageBox.show* form.) It is worth noting that even though no code is executed as a result of the user clicking the No button, the code does include the test. This makes things easier to read for the next programmer (who might be you), and easier to modify when the time comes.

That's the *MessageBox.show* method. It has three formats (simple, with title, and using flags). The *MessageBox* class provides us with names for all the flags and for all the return values. The value returned by *MessageBox.show* corresponds to the button clicked by the user.

Soon we will add a *MessageBox.show* call to a project.

The *ColorDialog* Class

The *ColorDialog* class allows you to provide the user with a way to pick a color for an element of the screen display. You can see the *ColorDialog* class in action by using the Display dialog box. To see the Display dialog box, click the Start button on the Windows taskbar, point to Settings, and then select Control Panel. Double-click the Display icon. Once in the Display dialog box, click the Appearance tab, select the down arrow next to the box labeled Color, and then click the Other button. The Color dialog box shown in Figure 3-14 appears.

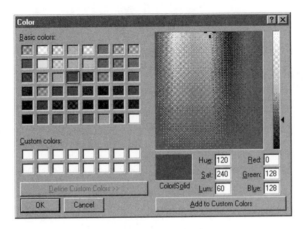

Figure 3-14. *The Color dialog box.*

This is the box that appears when we use a *ColorDialog* object in a Java program. Go ahead and close the Color dialog box. The real fun is bringing up the box from within a Java program. Let's say that you want to allow the user to pick a color for the background of the form in your application. As before, we'll base this action on a button click. To do the job we will need:

■ A *ColorDialog* object

■ Two *Color* objects

■ An integer variable

To do the work, we will need to use the following methods:

- *ColorDialog.setColor* (sets the initial color selected in a ColorDialog object)

- *ColorDialog.showDialog* (activates a *ColorDialog* object)

- *ColorDialog.getColor* (retrieves the color selected in a ColorDialog object)

- *getBackColor* (retrieves the background color of the current form)

Note that the method *getBackColor* is a method of the *Form* class and not of the *ColorDialog* class. Many other classes also include a *getBackColor* method.

A *ColorDialog* object

We start by creating an object of class *ColorDialog*. First we declare a reference to the object, and then we create an object of class *ColorDialog* (using the *new* keyword):

```
ColorDialog myColorDialog;  // a reference to a ColorDialog object
myColorDialog = new ColorDialog(); // creates the ColorDialog object
```

When it is time to actually display the Color dialog box, we will do so by calling the *showDialog* method of this new object.

Two *Color* objects

In order to store the color that the user picks when using the Color dialog box, we must have an object of the proper class, namely an object of the class *Color*. We are not going to look too hard at the class *Color* right now; all we really need is a reference to a *Color* object:

```
Color currentBackgroundColor;  // a reference to a Color object
Color newBackgroundColor;  // ditto
```

A Boolean variable

The user dismisses the Color dialog box in one of two ways: by clicking the OK button or by clicking the Cancel button. An integer value is returned by the *ColorDialog.showDialog* method, which we will see in a moment:

```
int result;
```

getBackColor

Now that we have established our variable storage, we can accomplish our task. First, set up the Color dialog box with the current color of the form background selected. The *getBackColor* method will assign a background color for the form to our *Color* object:

```
currentBackgroundColor = getBackColor();
```

Now our program knows the current background color of the form.

ColorDialog.setColor

Next, we tell our *ColorDialog* object what the background color of the form is. This is done with the *setColor* method of the *ColorDialog* class:

```
myColorDialog.setColor(currentBackgroundColor);  // initial color set
```

ColorDialog.showDialog

Everything is set up to allow the user to pick a color for the form. In order to activate the Color dialog box, we invoke the *showDialog* method. Since we want to know which button the user clicks when finished with the Color dialog box, we will capture the return value of the *showDialog* method by assigning it to the *result* variable. If *result* equals *DialogResult.OK*, we change the background color of the form. If not, the user clicked the Cancel button, and we won't change any colors:

```
if (result == DialogResult.OK)
```

ColorDialog.getColor

Once the user has picked a color and dismissed the Color dialog box, we check to see if the OK button was clicked. If it was, we see what color was chosen by using the *ColorDialog.getColor* method. We store a reference to the new *Color* object in our *Color* object *newBackgroundColor*:

```
if (result == DialogResult.OK)
{
    newBackgroundColor = myColorDialog.getColor();
    setBackColor(newBackgroundColor);
}
```

Putting it together

Taking all these fragments and assembling them in a Click event handler, we have the code that allows the user to change the background color of a form. The complete code is shown in Listing 3-1.

```
private void button1_click(Object source, Event e)
{
    ColorDialog myColorDialog;
    // a reference to a ColorDialog object
    myColorDialog = new ColorDialog();
    // creates the ColorDialog object


    Color currentBackgroundColor;
    // a reference to a Color object
    Color newBackgroundColor; // ditto
    int result;


    currentBackgroundColor = getBackColor();
    myColorDialog.setColor(currentBackgroundColor);
    // initial color set
    result = myColorDialog.showDialog();
    if (result == DialogResult.OK)
    {
        newBackgroundColor = myColorDialog.getColor();
        setBackColor(newBackgroundColor);
    }
}
```

Listing 3-1.   *Event handler for displaying the Color dialog box.*

Start Visual J++ and create a new project with whatever name you like. Add a form to the project, and place a button on the new form. If you leave the button name as *button1*, you can type the above event handler into the code window for your form. Run the project, and use it to change the background color of the form.

The *FontDialog* Class

We can use the same structure that we used with the *ColorDialog* class to manipulate fonts using the *FontDialog* class. Like the *ColorDialog* class, the *FontDialog* class uses the *showDialog* method to activate the dialog box, and returns an integer value that tells us whether or not the user clicked the OK button to close the dialog box.

The *FontDialog* class depends on the *Font* and *Color* classes to store the correct font and color to use when displaying text. We can then use a *FontDialog* object to manipulate the font and color of any particular text. Following the conventions of Visual J++, the *FontDialog* methods that allow us to access these properties are *getColor*, *setColor*, *getFont*, and *setFont*. We will now build an example that allows the user to pick a new font and a new color for the text property of a label. Once again, we base the code on the click of a button on a form. Here we go.

We start with three references (one for the color of the text, one for the font of the text, and one for the *FontDialog* object) and an integer variable. The integer variable allows us to store the result of the *FontDialog.showDialog* method. If the *showDialog* method returns *DialogResult.OK*, then the user clicked the OK button to dismiss the Font dialog box; otherwise, the user clicked something else (such as the Cancel button):

```
private void button1_click(Object source, Event e)
{
    Color fontColor;
    Font font;
    FontDialog fontDialog;
    int result;
```

We use the *getFont* method of the *Label* object to see what the font of the label is before we activate the dialog box, and we do the same for the font color:

```
    font = label1.getFont();
    fontColor = label1.getForeColor();
```

Next, we create a *FontDialog* object. Once the *FontDialog* object is created, we can activate the dialog box with a *showDialog* method. We'll store the result of the *showDialog* method in the integer variable *result*:

```
fontDialog = new FontDialog();
result = fontDialog.showDialog();
```

Once we have checked to see if the user clicked OK (the value of *result* is *DialogResult.OK*), we get the font setting and the color setting from the *FontDialog* object:

```
if (result == DialogResult.OK)
    {
        font = fontDialog.getFont();
        fontColor = fontDialog.getColor();
```

Then we take the new font and color values and use them to change the *Label* object:

```
        label1.setFont(font);
        label1.setForeColor(fontColor);
    }
}
```

That's all there is to it!

If you want to see the *FontDialog* class in action, start Visual J++ and create a new project. As with the *ColorDialog* test that we did earlier, add a form to the project. The form will need a Button control (named *button1*) and a Label control (*label1*). Add the code for *button1_click* to your form. Run the project and use it to change the font and color of the label.

Adding Another Form

It's a pretty rare application that requires only one window. Adding a new form to your project is simple. Start by selecting Add Form from the Project menu and create a new form. (Later, if you have a form in mind for your project that you or anyone else created previously, you can click the Existing tab and add that form.)

Because we got to the Add Item dialog box through the Add Form menu item, the Form folder is already selected. Select the icon labeled Form to create a new form for your project. You can do the same thing by right-clicking the project icon in the Project Explorer window or clicking the Add Item button on the toolbar (it's usually second from the left on the toolbar).

Showing Another Form

Activating a *Form* object is a matter of creating an object of your *Form* class and calling the *show* method of that form. Say we have a project with two forms. On the first form we place a button that accesses the other form. The code would look like this:

```
public class Form1 extends Form
{
    private void button1_click(Object source, Event e)
    {
        Form2 secondFrm;    // a reference to a Form2 form object
        secondFrm = new Form2();    // create the new Form2 form object
        secondFrm.show();    // display the new Form2 form object
    }
// class Form1 continues. . .
```

What this event handler does is to declare a reference to the new form, then create the *Form* object (with the *new* keyword), and then call the *show* method of the new form.

Once the new form displays itself, the input focus is transferred to the new form, and the user can interact with it. When the user is finished with the form, the form can be dismissed with the normal window controls at the right end of the title bar.

Another way to dismiss the form is to call the *dispose* method or the *hide* method of the form. After you've added a button and the appropriate code to your first form, add another form. Then put a button on the second form and call either method as shown in the following code:

```
public class Form2 extends Form
{
    private void button1_click(Object source, Event e)
    {
        hide();   // or dispose();
    }
// class Form2 continues . . .
```

The difference between the *dispose* method and the *hide* method is that the *hide* method only makes the window invisible without removing it from memory, whereas the *dispose* method recycles the memory as well. If you intend to use the same form again shortly, then the *hide* method is a better choice.

 NOTE   Viewing the properties of a second form is a little tricky. If the first form is selected, you can't go to the Properties window and see the properties of the second form. To see the properties of the second form, you must first select the second form in the Project Explorer, click the View Designer button, and then go to the Properties window to view the properties of the form.

Notice that each form can have its own button called *button1*. Note that the Text property of each form serves as the title of the form window so that you can tell them apart at run time.

Run the project, and click the buttons to make the *Form2* object appear and disappear. Close the running application by clicking the Close button at the top of the *Form1* window.

Lab 3-2: House For Sale

We've explored predefined dialog box classes and multiple form applications in Visual J++. Let's apply that knowledge to create a Java application.

Lab overview

In this lab, you will practice:

- Creating objects.
- Using *FontDialog*.
- Using *ColorDialog*.
- Using *MessageBox*.
- Creating and displaying forms.

This lab project consists of two forms. The first form will present three buttons: one for changing the font and font color, one for changing the background color, and one for viewing those changes on a second form. The second form contains a mock-up of a house ad. The second form will present a button to allow the user to make a bid on the house in the ad. As a result of pressing this button, a message box will appear with information about the house.

Lab setup

1. Start Visual J++.
2. Open the HouseForSale starter project (Chapter03\Lab3-2\ HouseForSale.sln).
3. Look in the Project Explorer window. If necessary, expand the list to display the files associated with this project.
4. Select CustomizeAd.java, and at the top of the Project Explorer window, click the View Code button.

Lab instructions

1. The comments of the code contain a number of TODO tokens. Each of these TODO comments describes what the code there should look like when you are finished.

   Write code that:

   - Creates, modifies, and displays a form
   - Adds a member variable to the class
   - Displays a Color dialog box and makes appropriate changes if the user clicks OK

2. Scout around the code to see if you can pick up any other hints about your new code. (In particular, check out the *pickFontBtn_click* method). It may also help to look at the HouseAd.java code to see what the methods look like there.

3. When you are done with CustomizeAd.java, modify HouseAd.java to display the Message Box dialog box as indicated in the comments of the source code for HouseAd.java.

4. When you have made your modifications, click the Start Without Debugging button. When you click the Fonts button, the Font dialog box should appear, and when you click Background, the Color dialog box should appear. Clicking the View Ad button should display the form of class *HouseAd* with your customization.

5. You can compare your work to the solution files in Chapter03\ Sol3-2\HouseForSale.sln.

Next steps

You have seen how to create a decent Windows-based application with forms, controls, standard methods, and standard dialog boxes. As we move on, we will take a closer look at the Java language and expand our knowledge of WFC controls.

Menus, Types, and Methods

In the last chapter, you learned about Java classes and objects. Classes provide a Java program with its fundamental structure. Into this structure are placed methods and member variables. In this chapter, we explore the methods and member variables that populate classes. In addition, to help you improve the usability of your Windows-based applications, we will work with the Visual J++ Menu Designer.

In this chapter, you'll learn about:

- Java's built-in data types and predefined classes
- Boolean logic
- The Menu Designer and putting menus on forms
- Methods

You will get practice using:

- Java's built-in types
- The Visual J++ Menu Designer
- The Class Builder

Built-In Types

The Java language has a number of primitive types, in addition to classes, for characterizing variables. These built-in types are simpler than classes and more efficient for many simple jobs.

NOTE   Programmers generally use the term *type* to mean either a primitive type (for example, *int, float, byte*) or a *class*. For example, "A parameter can be of any type" means that a parameter can be of any type or of any class. To avoid confusion as you start out, we will use the terms as follows: *types* (the set of all built-in types and all classes), *built-in types* (predefined types), and *classes* (whether provided by Java, Visual J++, or a programmer).

Table 4-1 provides a list of all the primitive types and some of their characteristics.

Type	Values	Initial Value
boolean	true and false	false
byte	8-bit integer values between −128 and 127	0
char	16-bit Unicode characters between \u0000 and \uFFFF	\u0000
double	64-bit floating-point numbers	+0.0
float	32-bit floating-point numbers	+0.0
int	32-bit integer	0
long	64-bit integer	0
short	16-bit integer	0

Table 4-1.   *Java's primitive types.*

Most of these types are part of Java's legacy from its predecessors C and C++, but Java has its own twist on them. In this section we will talk briefly about each of Java's built-in types.

The Boolean Type

Boolean is a system of logic. Using the keyword *boolean*, you can define your own Boolean values. As with any type, it has values, and it has operations on those values. Let's start with values.

Boolean values

In a Boolean system, the two possible values are *true* and *false*. In Java, when we create a variable of type *boolean*, we are indicating that this variable can only be evaluated as *true* or *false*.

 OTE C/C++ programmers take heed: Boolean values are not 0s and 1s, and cannot be treated as such.

The declaration of a Boolean variable looks like this:

```
boolean tooLarge;
```

A value could be assigned to this variable using any operator whose result is either *true* or *false*. The equality operator (==) is just such an operator. Notice that the equality operator is a double equal sign; remember not to confuse equality with assignment (=). Let's say we create a couple of variables to hold integer values. The code is as follows:

```
int upperLimit = 100;
int count;
```

As the program executes, the variable *count* will increment periodically. If we want to find out whether *count* is at the maximum allowed value of *upperLimit*, we could compare the values of *count* and *upperLimit* this way:

```
count == upperLimit
```

Since *count* is either equal to *upperLimit* or not, we see only two possible values for this expression: *true* or *false*. If we want to assign the value of this expression to our Boolean variable, it looks like this:

```
tooLarge = count == upperLimit;
```

If all those equal signs look strange to you, consider doing it this way:

```
tooLarge = (count == upperLimit);
```

Don't hesitate to use parentheses if you feel that it makes the code easier to read and understand.

Having said all this about Boolean variables, it is also worth mentioning that they are rarely assigned in practice. More often than not, programmers simply use a Boolean expression such as

```
count == upperLimit
```

directly in code, and omit the assignment to the Boolean variable. Still, it is important for you to understand what Boolean expressions are and how they fit into your code.

Boolean expressions are used in *if* statements, *while* loops, and *do while* loops. Here are a couple of examples:

```
// if statement
if (count == 100)
{
    // code executes only if count is 100
}
// while loop
while (size == 0)
{
    // code executes repeatedly as long
    // as size is zero
}
```

Notice that Boolean expressions are always enclosed within parentheses. See the appendixes for a summary of some of Java's syntax.

Boolean operations

In addition to equality, Boolean expressions also support operators such as less-than (<), greater-than (>), less-than-or-equal-to (<=), and greater-than-or-equal-to (>=) as well as logical AND (&&), OR (| |), and NOT (!). To illustrate logical AND, here is an *if* statement that tests to see if the value of the variable *score* is between 80 and 90:

```
if ( (score >= 80) && (score <= 90) )
{
    // code executes only if score is 80 or greater
    // and also 90 or less
}
```

The Boolean NOT operator is the exclamation point (!). It reverses whatever value a *Boolean* expression has. That is, if the value of the expression is *true*, then the NOT operator results in *false*, and vice versa. Here's a *while* loop that uses the NOT operator:

```
while (!done)  // read this as "while not done"
{
    // code executes repeatedly until done is true
}
```

The NOT operator can also be used with equality to change the meaning to NOT equal:

```
if (score != 100)  // read this as "if score is not 100"
{
    // code executes if score is anything other than 100
}
```

Numeric Types

The numeric types are for holding the values of numbers. In computer programs, numbers come in two flavors: integer values and floating-point values. Integer values are the whole numbers, and floating-point numbers can include fractional values after the decimal point. So, 432 is an integer value and 432.2 is a floating-point value.

To represent integer values, Java includes *int*, *byte*, *long*, and *short*. To represent floating-point values, Java has *float* and *double*.

Alphabetic Types

The Java language uses the Unicode character set. Unlike the ASCII character set (which uses 7-bit characters) or even ISO Latin-1 (which uses 8-bit characters), Unicode uses 16-bit characters. This gives us over 65,000 possible characters. Java programmers can use characters from various languages, such as Greek, Arabic, hiragana, or even Devanagari. To store theses characters in our programs, we use variables of two types: *char* and *java.lang.String*.

Single-character values: *char*

For single Unicode characters, we use the built-in type *char*.

 OTE   Unicode characters include many special characters used in written languages around the world. In this book, when we use the term *character*, we refer to the ASCII character set. Basically, this means *A* through *Z*, *a* through *z*, *0* through *9*, and punctuation.

Since variables of type *char* are somewhat limited in applicability, the predefined class *String* is preferred for most character manipulation.

Series of characters: The *java.lang.String* class

For holding values of more than one Unicode character at a time, we use the predefined class *java.lang.String*. Since all the classes in the java.lang package need java.lang in front of them in order to be used in code, most people refer to this class simply as *String*.

Here's an example of declaring a *String* variable:

```
String name;
name = "Bob White";
```

The type of the text property (a property of many WFC controls) is *String*. Therefore, the type of the value returned by the *getText* method is *String*. Here's an example:

```
// event procedure for an EditBox object
private void edit1_textChanged(Object source, Event e)
{
    String name;
    name = edit1.getText();
}
```

The method above creates a variable called *name*, and assigns to it the text property of the EditBox control *edit1* every time the *edit1* control receives a Change event.

Similarly, the *setText* method takes a *String* value as a parameter. If we expand the above example to also set the text property of a Label control called *label1*, it looks like this:

```
private void edit1_textChanged(Object source, Event e)

{
    String name;
    name = edit1.getText();
    label1.setText(name);
}
```

In fact, we can even do away with the intermediate *String* variable by
having the value returned from the *getText* method sent directly to the
setText method. The following code example does this:

```
private void edit1_textChanged(Object source, Event e)
{
    label1.setText(edit1.getText());
}
```

Which version you use depends on personal preference and your
particular situation and needs. Use the one that makes the most sense
to you.

Be careful when making *String* comparisons! There is a subtle, but critical,
difference between comparing *String* values (that is, the contents of a
String variable) and *String* references. For instance, study the following:

```
String firstName = "Bob";
edit1.setText("Bob");
firstName == edit1.getText()            // is false!
firstName.equals(edit1.getText())       // is true
edit1.getText().equals(firstName)       // is also true
```

Look at the last line of code. We have an object (*edit1*), followed by a
method (*getText*), followed by another method (*equals*). What we are
seeing here is that a method can be called using a value returned by the
first method. The type of the value returned by *getText* is *String*, and
String values can be used to call the *equals* method. Whew!

Be sure to use the *equals* method when comparing *String* values. Don't
use the equality operator. For more information on values vs. references,
refer back to Chapter 3.

To see representative variables of all of Java's primitive types, open the
Visual J++ project called BuiltIn, located in Chapter04\BuiltIn\
BuiltIn.sln. Run the project, and then check out the Java code.

Member Variable Modifiers

The Java language provides us with a rich set of member variable modifiers that allows us to establish the scope and visibility of variables. In this section, we will discuss the options you have as you populate your classes with member variables.

Access Modifiers

The first option is the access modifier of the member variable. The access modifier controls which methods can examine and modify a given member variable. The four access modifiers are Default (package), *public*, *protected*, and *private*. Table 4-2 contains a short description of each of these options.

Modifier	Description
Default (package)	Member variables of Default access can be accessed by any member function in the same package.
public	Member variables of *public* access can be accessed by any method in the Visual J++ project; access is unrestricted. To avoid unwanted modifications to your class, we recommend that you don't use the *public* access modifier with member variables.
protected	Member variables of *protected* access can be accessed by any method in the same class hierarchy.
private	Member variables of *private* access can be accessed only by methods in the same class as the member variable. The *private* access modifier is often your safest choice for member variables.

Table 4-2.   *Java's access modifiers.*

Notice that *public*, *protected*, and *private* are keywords, while the "Default (package)" option simply means no access modifier is present.

Chapter 5 says more about the *protected* keyword in the discussion of Java inheritance, and the default package is explained in Chapter 10 in the discussion of Java packages. For now, we'll sum up access modifiers on member variables by saying that almost all member variables should be private.

Static Member Variables

Up to this point in our discussion, member variables have been non-static. This means that every time you created an object of a class, that object was itself a copy (new instance) of the class with its own set of member variables for the class. Now, we'll contrast that with the behavior of static member variables.

In Visual J++, open the project Gizmo located in Chapter04\Gizmo\Gizmo.sln. Run the Gizmo project, and create a few gizmos by clicking the Make A Gizmo button. Gizmos appear at the bottom of the form. The text at the top of the form changes to reflect the fact that a gizmo is now in service. However, make another gizmo in the same way, and you will see that while a new gizmo appears at the bottom of the form, the text at the top of the form still says that only one gizmo is in service. To see why this is, take a look at the code for the *Gizmo* class. Here's a portion of Gizmo.java:

```
public class Gizmo
{
    private String manufacturer = "Gizmo Products, Inc.";
    private int gizmosInService = 0;
    private int length;
    private int width;
    private int depth;
    public Gizmo (int len, int wid, int dep)
    {
        gizmosInService = gizmosInService + 1;
        // more code …
    }
    // more methods …
}
```

At the top of the class are five member variables. Each instantiated object of class *Gizmo* gets its own copy of each of these variables. Each time a gizmo is created, the member variable *gizmosInService* is created and initialized to 0. The *Gizmo* constructor method is also called, and it adds 1 to *gizmosInService* for the object being created. This means *gizmosInService* is always 1. These member variables are also called *instance variables* because a copy of them exists for each instance (that is, each object) that is created. In this case, however, what we really want is a class variable. A *class variable* is a member variable that has a modifier of *static*, and it does not belong to any particular object of a class but to the class as a whole. Only one copy exists of any static member variable. So let's change *gizmosInService* to be a static member variable by placing the keyword *static* in its definition, like this:

```
private static int gizmosInService = 0;
```

Now run the program again, and notice that the correct number of gizmos appears at the top of the form as gizmos are created. See Figure 4-1 for a diagram of the static member variable *gizmosInService* for the class *Gizmo*.

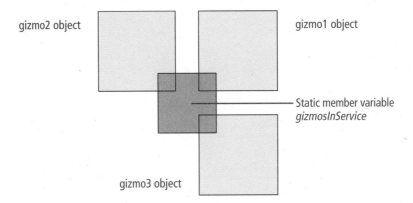

gizmo2 object

gizmo1 object

Static member variable
gizmosInService

gizmo3 object

Figure 4-1. *Static member variables are shared by all the objects of a given class.*

You don't want to set the value of a static member variable in a constructor, because if you do, every time an object of the class is created, the static member resets to the same value. You can modify static member variables in constructors, however, as we did by adding 1 to *gizmosInService* above.

Our *Gizmo* class also includes information about the name of the manufacturer of a gizmo: the class that does not change, regardless of the number of objects. Consider making that member variable both static and final. See the next section for information about the *final* keyword.

Final Member Variables

Final member variables are "final" in the sense that whatever value they have when you create them is the only one that they are ever going to have. Other languages would call a final member variable a constant. Going back to the *GizmoFactory* example, consider this code:

```
public class Gizmo
{
    private String manufacturer = "Gizmo Products, Inc.";
    private static int gizmosInService = 0;     // class variable
    private int length;
    private int width;
    private int depth;

    // code omitted for brevity

    public String getManufacturer ()
    {
        return manufacturer;
    }
}
```

We see that the member variable *manufacturer* is effectively a read-only member variable. We don't want this variable's value changed, and we can be assured of this by declaring the member variable *final*. Usually, final variables are also made static because there is no sense in making copies of constant values. Making it static would change our variable declaration of *manufacturer* to look like this:

```
private static final String manufacturer = "Gizmo Products, Inc.";
```

Any attempts to change the value of a final variable are met by a compilation error message, as you would expect.

Rather than using a literal value, we can also use static final member variables to give meaningful names to numbers. We saw this in Chapter 2 when we changed the background color of the form:

```
setBackColor(Color.BLUE);     // sets the form background color to blue
```

The value *BLUE* is actually a member variable declared *public static final int* in the class *Color*. This is one of the few times that it makes sense to make a member variable public, rather than private. For our gizmo example, add the following lines of code to the class *Gizmo*:

```
public static final int awake = 0;
public static final int asleep = 1;
private int status = asleep;
public void setStatus (int stat)
{
    status = stat;
}
public int getStatus ()
{
    return status;
}
```

Our gizmos now have a status. They can be either "awake" or "asleep." They are born asleep, but their status can be changed with the *setStatus* method. The *getStatus* method tells us what the current status of a gizmo is. Notice that the member variables we declared *static final int* are also public so that they can be used outside the class.

Working with Menus

Designing your menus and determining exactly how they should behave can be a major part of building a user interface. This is why you are going to like the Visual J++ Menu Designer. Visual J++ makes the menu building process straightforward with a WYSIWYG (What-You-See-Is-What-You-Get, pronounced "wizzywig") tool called the Menu Designer.

Using the Menu Designer

Putting a menu on a form is as simple as adding any other control—simpler, in fact, because it doesn't much matter where you place the control on the form, but the menu titles and items always appear at the top of the form. Using the Menu Designer is so easy, you will wonder how you got along without it.

Start Visual J++ if it is not running. As before, you should save any work in progress, select New Project from the File menu, and then create an empty project. Name the project MenuTest or some other name that makes sense to you. Once the project is created, go the Project menu and select Add Form. Just to keep things simple, give your form file the same name as your project (for example, "MenuTest.java").

You will use the Toolbox window to add a menu to your form. If the Toolbox is not visible, click Toolbox on the View menu. In the Toolbox, click the WFC Controls button. Select the MainMenu control and drag it onto the form. A visual marker, "Type Here," appears at the top of the form. If you don't like the drag-and-drop approach to placing WFC controls on your forms, you can double-click the control in the Toolbox, and Visual J++ will place the control on the form for you. Letting Visual J++ place the control on the form for you is fine for a Menu control, since it doesn't matter where it is positioned on the form. From this point on, it's pretty much a matter of typing what you need for menu titles and items.

Two visual markers appear directly to the right and below to signify the next available editing location. Type the name of your first menu title in the default location text box. (For example, type *File* to add the File menu.)

The menu title is added to your menu, and the default location text box moves to the next menu title location. Continue typing your menu titles until all your titles are complete. See Figure 4-2 for a view of the Menu Designer in action.

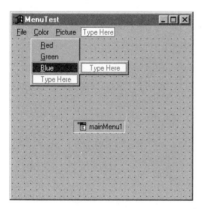

Figure 4-2.   *Using the Menu Designer: the MainMenu control on a form.*

As with the other WFC controls we have seen, menu items have properties. Forms can have several menu items, such as File/Save and File/SaveAs, that change depending on the state of the application. Using properties for each menu item, menu items can be enabled or disabled, checked or unchecked, made visible or hidden. You can also change a menu item's text property in the Properties window, but usually it's easier to use the Menu Designer. One special feature of the text property in menus is the ability to establish an *access key*. An access key is the key in the Alt+key sequence that allows you to access a menu item without using the mouse. If you put an ampersand (&) in front of a letter in the text property of a menu item, then instead of the ampersand showing up in the menu, the letter immediately following the ampersand will be underlined. For example, if the text property for a menu item is *&File*, the menu item appears like this:

File

This means that the user can activate that menu without a mouse by pressing the Alt key followed by the letter F.

For this example, we want our menus to have the menu settings shown in Figure 4-3. Note that menu titles are the names on the menu bar itself, while menu items are the names of the options that appear in the menus underneath the menu titles.

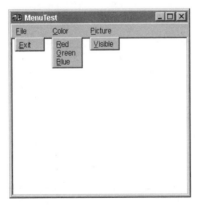

Figure 4-3.   *Menu titles and items for our Menu Designer project example.*

IMPORTANT   Don't double-click any of the menu elements in the View Designer just yet. It is especially important that we modify the name property of the menu item before trying to write any event handlers for it. An application tends to have several menu items, and using the default names of *menuItem1*, *menuItem2*, and so forth, can be quite awkward.

Menu Item Names

For every menu title and every menu item, a new control is created for your form. Each of these controls defaults to the name *menuItem* plus a number that represents the order in which the item was created for the form (for instance, the first control is called *menuItem1*). It is up to us to give the controls more meaningful names by changing their name properties.

So, before we jump in and start coding event handlers, we'll rename the menu items. For most programmers, *menuItem1* through *menuItem100* are not the best names: "Let's see, was *menuItem57* Delete or Rename?" One hundred menu items may sound like a lot, but it doesn't take long to put together an application with 10 menu titles and 10 menu items in each title.

Set the name property of each menu item as shown in Table 4-3.

Menu Text Property Value	Menu Name Property Value
&File	*fileMnu*
E&xit	*fileExitMnu*
&Color	*colorMnu*
&Red	*colorRedMnu*
&Green	*colorGreenMnu*
&Blue	*colorBlueMnu*
&Picture	*pictureMnu*
&Visible	*pictureVisibleMnu*

Table 4-3.　*Text property values and corresponding name property values for our menu titles and items.*

In this example, we apply a naming convention that uses the menu title for the menu item, followed by the suffix *Mnu*.

While you are in the Properties window modifying the name property called *pictureVisibleMnu*, change the checked property to *true*. This causes a check mark to appear next to the menu item in the Menu Designer. As we have seen with many properties of WFC controls, the value of this property can be changed during design or in code (with the method *setChecked*, in this case); we will, in fact, do this in the lab exercise that follows.

Another thing the Menu Designer can do for you is to help you create *hierarchical menus*. That is, you can build submenus off any menu item. To see this happen with the Menu Designer, simply type a name in one of the menu item fields and notice that another "Type Here" box appears to the right of it. This represents the first item in the submenu. If you don't want a submenu, just don't type anything here. What could be easier? We won't be using hierarchical menus in this example, but the approach is the same.

Menu Events and Event Handlers

Menus are activated by a click of the mouse (or an access key sequence), and Click is the name of the event for which we will write event procedures. The menu item receives a Click event whenever the user selects it by, well, clicking on it.

When you have completed your menu layout (using the Menu Designer) and given your menu items meaningful names, it is time to attach event handlers to each menu item. Double-clicking the menu item in the View Designer creates the shell of an event handler in the code window. It is then up to us to fill in the body of the event handler.

In the View Designer, start by selecting the File menu. This opens the File menu. From here you can add event handlers to items on this menu. Double-click the menu item Exit.

When you double-click a menu item, a code window opens for the form that contains the control for that menu item. A skeleton for the event handler appears in the code window. Here is the event handler for the *fileExitMnu* control:

```
private void fileExitMnu_click(Object source, Event e)
{
    Application.exit();  // ends the application
}
```

The *exit* method stops the running application in a graceful way. Run the project, and a form window appears. Test the menu bar. Of course, since we haven't added any event handlers to the other menu items, they won't do anything when selected.

Menu shortcuts can also be added to controls, using the Shortcut property. A menu *shortcut* is the control-key or function-key equivalent of selecting the menu item with a mouse. To associate a shortcut with a menu item, just click the shortcut property of the menu item in the Properties window, and then click the down arrow that appears next to the shortcut property menu. You can accomplish the same thing using the Menu Designer. If you click to the right of the menu item, a pop-up menu of all the possible menu shortcuts appears, with the current shortcut selected. For our example, let's modify the *menuItem* objects to have the shortcuts shown in Table 4-4.

Menu Item	Shortcut
colorRedMnu	Ctrl+R
colorGreenMnu	Ctrl+G
colorBlueMnu	Ctrl+B

Table 4-4. *Our menu items and corresponding shortcuts.*

When you have added these shortcuts, go back to the Menu Designer, and you will see that each menu item with an associated shortcut has the corresponding shortcut displayed next to it on the menu.

Lab 4-1: Building a Hello Application with Menus

We now have menus to work with as we build our applications. This lab gives you a chance to practice the skills you acquired earlier as we build a form that has a menu.

Lab overview

In this lab you will practice using:

- The Menu Designer.
- Menu event handlers.

The goal of this exercise is to build an application (much like the Hello application we created in Chapter 2) that includes menus.

If you have been following the example, you can skip to the lab instructions.

Lab setup

1. Start Visual J++.

2. Open the MnuHello starter project (Chapter04\Lab4-1\ MnuHello.sln).

Lab instructions

1. Using the Menu Designer, double-click each of the menu items in the Color menu (not the Color menu title itself) in turn, and add an appropriate event handler. The event handler associated with Red looks like this:

```
private void colorRedMnu_click(Object source, Event e)
{
    setBackColor(Color.RED);
}
```

The event procedures for Green and Blue behave similarly for their colors.

2. The event handler for the Visible menu item in the Picture menu should include code for toggling the check mark on and off. To turn the check mark on and off, modify the checked property. We started by setting checked to *true* in the Properties window for *pictureVisibleMnu*. In the event handler, reverse the value of the property, using the method *setChecked*. The method *getChecked* returns the current value of the checked property, and the logical NOT operator (!) can be used to reverse that value (yielding *true* if *getChecked* returns *false*, and vice versa). If Visible is selected, the picture *forestPic* should be visible on the form. Selecting the menu item Visible when it is already checked should remove the check mark and make the picture invisible. This is reversible by selecting (toggling) Visible again.

3. Once you have gotten the check mark to appear and disappear in the menu correctly, use the *setVisible* method of the picture *forestPic* to make the picture visible or invisible as appropriate.

4. Type the event handler for the OK button:

```
private void OkBtn_click(Object source, Event e)
{
    if (nameEdt.getText().length() != 0)
        {
        nameLbl.setText("Hello" + nameEdt.getText());
        }
}
```

5. Run the project and test the menus. The solution files for this project are in Chapter04\Sol4-1\MenuHello.sln.

Next steps

We have seen examples of Java methods in our previous work. In the next section, we take a closer look at methods. This allows us to make the most of powerful Java mechanisms such as overloading and inheritance.

Methods

Methods (called functions, subprograms, procedures, or subroutines in other programming languages) are the services that a class, or an object of a class, provides to the programmer. Many methods are available to the Java programmer right from the start, and you can add to that list by writing your own methods.

Method names often include a verb (such as "get" or "set") to indicate that some action is taking place. While naming your methods using verb forms is not required, verb forms are going to make the most sense to other people reading your code. You'll probably find this style to be the most natural, because methods really are the verbs of the Java language.

One interesting thing about a Java method, as opposed to similar features in almost every other programming language, is that it must be a member of a class. In almost every other language, subroutines are not closely associated with any particular object (if that language even has objects), but instead are in what is often referred to as the "global" scope. Java enforces organization of programs by insisting that every method— every piece of code—be in the context, or scope, of some class.

Consider the following code from the previous Gizmo example. (For simplicity, the class for this method is not shown here.)

```
public int getInServiceCount()
{
    return gizmosInService;
}
```

Picking out the name of the method with all those other keywords in front of it can be a little confusing. Fortunately, when we see this code inside Visual J++, the keywords (in this case, *public* and *int*) stand out from the method name by their color. Either way, the name of the method is the identifier immediately in front of the set of parentheses: *getInServiceCount*.

 OTE   Visual J++ methods provided by Microsoft use the naming convention of adding a "get" or "set" in front of a property name. For example, the *Label* class has a text property, and therefore, also has a *getText* method and a *setText* method.

Parameters

In order for a method to do work for you, many times the method needs some information first. Methods get their information "passed in" to them by means of parameters. The syntax for telling the compiler that a method has parameters is to indicate the type name, followed by the name of the parameter. If you want a method to take more than one parameter, simply follow the first parameter with a comma (,) and supply the type and name of the next parameter. In this way, your methods can have as many parameters as you like.

In the *Gizmo* class, the constructor method takes three parameters, all of type *int*:

```
public Gizmo (int len, int wid, int dep)
{
    gizmosInService = gizmosInService + 1;
    length = len;
    width = wid;
    depth = dep;
}
```

The names of the parameters for the constructor *Gizmo* are *len*, *wid*, and *dep*. Of course, your parameters can have any type and any name that you choose. However, it is a good idea to give your parameters names that indicate why that parameter is being passed to the method. In this case, the names are short for length, width, and depth, respectively. Why don't we just use the natural names (*length*, *width*, and *depth*)? We can't use the natural names because those names would interfere with the names of the member variables. For more on this subject, and to see how Java deals with the problem, see "The *this* Keyword" later in this chapter.

If your method requires no additional information to be passed to it, leaving the parentheses empty is just fine:

```
public int getInServiceCount()
{
    return gizmosInService;
}
```

 NOTE Because of the way Java supplies parameters with values, parameters of predefined types (such as *int*) cannot change values outside the method. Inside a method, change the value of an *int* parameter all you want; it has no effect on the outside. This is different from many other computer languages (the Basic language, for example).

Return Types

Methods can also sometimes require information to be passed in using parameters, and sometimes they can hand information back to the code that called them. The Java mechanism for doing this is the *return* keyword. We saw this in the *getInServiceCount* method:

```
public int getInServiceCount()
{
    return gizmosInService;
}
```

The value being returned is the current value of *gizmosInService*. Notice
that every value in Java has a type, whether primitive or class, associated
with it. In this case, the type is *int*. The method says that it is going to
return an *int*, and the member variable *gizmosInService* is an *int*, so the
code is consistent. The type returned by a particular method is indicated
by the keyword immediately before the name of the method.

Some methods don't return values. For these methods, use the return type
void to signify that the method does not return a value. We don't have any
void methods in the *Gizmo* class, but we might add one that would allow
us to set the gizmo's depth. It wouldn't need to return a value, so it would
look like this:

```
public void setDepth (int dep)
{
    depth = dep;
}
```

The *this* Keyword

In Java, all of the action, that is, the executable code, takes place within
methods. Methods, in turn, are always contained inside a class. This
is different from most other programming languages, where code can
execute without a context. Code that executes without a context is often
referred to as *global*. There are no global methods in Java.

 OTE   This discussion of the *this* keyword excludes static methods.
Technically, only nonstatic methods have current objects and *this* references.
We'll explore static methods in the next section.

In order to invoke a method, you need an object. The object that is used
to call a method is known as the *current* object. The *this* keyword allows
the programmer to refer to the current object. Because of the *this* keyword,
a method always knows which object was used to call it. (The value of the
this keyword is a reference value, so sometimes people call it the *this*
reference.) Using the *this* keyword is especially helpful when a member

variable has the same name as a parameter. Any discussion of the *this* keyword can get very confusing, but once you get the hang of using *this* in your code you'll wonder how you got along without it.

The constructor method of the *Gizmo* class is an example of how using *this* can work. Previously, the names of the parameters were slightly modified to keep from clashing with their corresponding member variables (for example, parameter *len* corresponds to member variable *length*). Rather than compromise the names of either parameters or member variables, we now modify the code to use more natural parameter names and the *this* reference:

```
public Gizmo (int length, int width, int depth)
{
    gizmosInService = gizmosInService + 1;
    this.length = length;
    this.width = width;
    this.depth = depth;
}
```

In the code above, the member variables have the same identifiers as the parameters, but the use of *this* eliminates ambiguity. Just what would happen if the lines had been coded without *this*? Consider replacing the last three assignments in the method with these three lines:

```
length = length;
width = width;
depth = depth;
```

Not only is this confusing, it doesn't work. The most that these lines would ever do would be to assign the parameter value back to the parameter variable, leaving the member variables of the object untouched. In cases where *this* is not needed (for example, cases where the parameter names are distinct from the member variable names), the keyword can be omitted, and often is. Of course, any time you feel that placing *this* before a method or data member adds clarity to the code, by all means use it.

Try changing all of the parameters in the *Gizmo* class so that they match the member variables. Use the *this* keyword where appropriate to ensure that the right variable is being modified.

In Visual J++, using the *this* keyword can be a handy way to remind yourself which methods apply to the class for which you are writing a member function. Let's say you want to get the background color of a form, but you can't remember exactly which method is required. If you type the keyword *this* followed by a period (.), a pop-up menu appears listing all of the possible methods that can be applied to a current object of this class. Figure 4-4 shows an example of using the *this* keyword in this way.

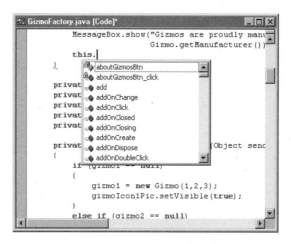

Figure 4-4. *Using the* this *keyword to display a list of available methods.*

Static Methods

When we discussed static member variables earlier, we saw that they don't belong to any individual object in the class, but to the class as a whole. Nonstatic member variables are known as instance variables, and static member variables are known as class variables. The same logic applies to methods.

Static methods are *class* methods, and are the only kind of method that can be invoked without instantiating an object. Because class methods can be invoked without an object, they aren't allowed to access any of the instance member variables of their class. For the same reason, class methods can't use the *this* reference. On the other hand, class methods can use class member variables, since neither requires the existence of a class.

We already made use of class methods when we called the *show* method of *MessageBox* in Chapter 3. *MessageBox* is a class, not an object, so the *show* method must be static.

Returning to the *Gizmo* class example, consider the two methods we have that return a class member variable value: *getInServiceCount* and *getManufacturer*. Since these methods could reasonably be called, even when no objects of the class exist, we should consider making them static.

We can easily modify the code for the *getInServiceCount* and *getManufacturer* methods. Repeat this procedure for the *getManufacturer* method. When you are done, your code should look like this:

```
public class Gizmo
{
    private static final String manufacturer = "Gizmo Products, Inc.";
    private static int gizmosInService = 0;

    // code omitted for brevity

    public static int getInServiceCount ()
    {
        return gizmosInService;
    }
    public static String getManufacturer ()
    {
        return manufacturer;
    }
}
```

Now that we have changed the *getManufacturer* method to be static, we can remove a bug from the code. Run the GizmoFactory project. If you click the About Gizmos button before you create any gizmos, an error occurs. This happens because the reference *gizmo1* has a value of *null*, which means that it does not yet point to an object. In the file GizmoFactory.java, find the call to *getManufacturer*, and change it so that it doesn't use an object, but instead uses the class *Gizmo*:

```
private void aboutGizmosBtn_click(Object source, Event e)
{
    MessageBox.show("Gizmos are proudly manufactured by " +
                    Gizmo.getManufacturer());
}
```

This change removes the bug from the code. While we are at it, we should also change the call to *getInServiceCount* to use the class *Gizmo*, as well:

```
gizmoInfoLbl.setText("There are currently " +
                        Gizmo.getInServiceCount() +
                        " gizmos in service");
```

Run the project, and verify that the error has been fixed.

Because class methods are available even without having to instantiate an object of their class, they are an ideal place for code that may need to be invoked irrespective of an object. A lot of system code is written this way. Look at the *main* method in *GizmoFactory* (or in any class, for that matter):

```
public static void main(String args[])
```

The *main* method is a class method. It has to be: *main* is the very first method executed by Visual J++ when it runs your project, and there are no objects before the project is started.

Overloading Methods

Often when we create a method for a class, we need to use that method in more than one way. As we saw in Chapter 3 when we looked at constructors, we may want to have a constructor without parameters, as well as a version with parameters. Any time you have two methods in the same class with the same name, this is called *overloading*. All methods are candidates for overloading. Consider this class fragment:

```
public class Television
{
    public void setAspectRatio (int width, int height)
    {
        //TODO: complete setAspectRatio
    }
    // other members as necessary …
}
```

The method *setAspectRatio* allows the user to modify the image on the television screen. A regular TV image's aspect ratio is 4:3. This means that for every four units of width, there are three units of height. For example, a 20-inch TV screen is 16 inches wide and 12 inches high, because the 20 inches are measured diagonally. In the near future, digital TV signals will become the standard. With the new signal standard, the aspect ratio will change to something closer to that of a cinema movie screen (something like 7:3).

So, having your TV change its aspect ratio will be a handy function: you can watch reruns of *My Mother the Car* at 4:3, and watch new movies at 7:3. Our *setAspectRatio* method takes two *int* parameters for the width and height of the screen. This method is absolute because it sets the width and height to specific values, without regard to the current width and height of the screen.

Since we also might want to specify the aspect ratio in a relative way using a double floating-point value, a different method would preserve the previous screen size while adjusting the ratio between width and height. Let's add a second method to the class that takes a floating-point value:

```
public class Television
{
    public void setAspectRatio (int width, int height)
    {
        // code omitted
    }
    public void setAspectRatio (double ratio)
    {
        // code omitted
    }
    // other members as necessary …
}
```

Now we have a class that has two methods with the same name.

Overload Resolution

How can the Java compiler tell apart two methods with the same name? Pretty much the same way we, as humans, do. We notice the parts that are different when we call the method. Each method has a parameter list, and by the types in that list (including the order in which they appear), we can uniquely identify any method. Using the example above with the TV aspect ratio, we see that the two overloaded methods have distinct parameter lists.

The parameter list of the first method consists of two *int* parameters. The parameter list of the second method consists of one *double* parameter. So, in calling the methods, there is no confusion about which is which:

```
public class AspectViewer extends Form
{
    private Television tv;
    public AspectViewer()
    {
        // Required for Visual J++ Forms Designer Support
        initForm();

        // TODO: Add any constructor code after initForm call
        tv = new Television(viewScreenPic);
    }
    private void tvBtn_click (Object source, Event e)
    {
        tv.setAspectRatio(100,75);
    }
    private void movieBtn_click (Object source, Event e)
    {
        tv.setAspectRatio(7.0/3.0);
    }
    // AspectViewer class continues …
}
```

You can have as many methods with the same name in a class as you like, as long as they have unique parameter lists.

Method overloading can also be used to provide us with default versions of methods. In the following *Television* class, we can set the aspect ratio as a width and height (the *int* version), as a ratio (the *double* version), or just use the default (the parameterless version):

```
public class Television
{
    public void setAspectRatio (int width, int height)
    {
        // code omitted
    }
    public void setAspectRatio (double ratio)
    {
        // code omitted
    }
    public void setAspectRatio () //is called with no parameters

    {
        setAspectRatio(100,75);  // standard, default TV aspect ratio
    }
    // other members as necessary …
}
```

Lab 4-2: Setting the Aspect Ratio

In this lab, you use method overloading to create three different versions of a method; that is, one method name shared by three methods, all in the same class, each with distinct parameter lists.

Lab overview

In this lab, you will practice:

■ Creating overloaded methods.

■ Calling overloaded methods.

■ Resizing *PictureBox* objects.

The supplied code for this lab contains a form with a picture box and four buttons. Your task is to add the event handler code for three of the buttons. Each of these buttons sets the aspect ratio of the picture box.

Lab setup

1. Start Visual J++.

2. Open the View Aspect Ratio starter project (Chapter04\Lab4-2\ AspectViewer.sln).

Lab instructions

1. In the Code View window, modify the class *Television*. Write three versions of the *setAspectRatio* method. The return type of each of these methods is *void*. The access modifier is *public*. So, each method starts like this:

```
public void setAspectRatio (parameter_list) …
```

Remember, the parameter list can be empty (that is, the method takes no parameters). These methods are to behave as follows:

- The method with two *int* parameters should call the *viewScreen.setSize* method and pass the two parameter values to that method. The object of class *PictureBox* is *viewScreen*, and the *setSize* method allows the picture box to be resized.

- The method with no parameters should call the values *viewScreen.setSize* method with the parameters *100* and *100*.

- The body of the method with a *double* parameter should look like this, where *ratio* is the name of the *double* parameter of the double floating-point version of *setAspectRatio*:

```
{
    int baseHeight = viewScreen.getSize().y;
    viewScreen.setSize((int)baseHeight*ratio),baseHeight);
}
```

2. In any order, modify the buttons so that:

- The button labeled Movie causes the double floating-point version of the *setAspectRatio* method to be called with the value *7.0/3.0*.

- The button labeled Square calls the version of the *setAspectRatio* method with no parameters.

- The button labeled TV causes the two *int* versions of the *setAspectRatio* method to be called with the values *100* and *75*.

The easiest way to modify each button is to double-click the button on the form in design mode. This takes you to the Java code window and the event handler of the correct name. When you have added the code for that event, go back to the form, and double-click the next button.

3. Run the completed project and click each button to see its aspect ratio.

4. Compare your work to the solution files in Chapter04\Sol4-2\ AspectViewer.sln.

Next steps

We've come to the end of another chapter. Take a look at all the material we have covered so far: forms, projects, WFC controls, events and event handlers, classes, objects, member variables, methods, constructors, standard dialog boxes, built-in types, menus, and finally, overloaded methods. Wow! You have accomplished quite a bit and can now write a pretty fair Windows-based application, using only what we have seen so far.

In the next chapter, we are going to take our knowledge and multiply it, by bringing in the concept of inheritance. We'll be able to leverage a vast amount of existing Java code without having to rewrite it. Instead, we'll use that existing code as a basis for greater things.

Inheritance

In the Java programming language, *inheritance* allows you to take an existing class and extend its capabilities. This existing class can be one that is provided by the language itself, one that some other programmer has written, or one that you yourself wrote earlier. Inheritance is everywhere in Java, and we have been using it implicitly from the beginning of this book. Now we'll see how that implicit use takes place.

In this chapter, you'll learn about Java inheritance mechanisms and concepts, including:

■ The *extends* keyword

■ The *super* keyword

■ Method overriding

■ Inheritance modifiers

You will get practice using:

■ The Visual J++ Class Outline

Superclasses and Subclasses

The terms *superclass* and *subclass* describe a relationship one class has with another. As you might expect, a superclass is a kind of parent to its subclass. A superclass is a class that has one or more *extensions*, or classes that use the superclass as a starting point and build from there.

The neat thing about subclasses is that they have all the functionality of their superclasses. This is analogous to the way consumer products are marketed in the real world. You can get a basic TV or you can get the super-deluxe model. The basic TV is an instance of a superclass, say the *Television* class. You can turn it on and off, adjust the volume, change the channel, and that's about it. If you wanted to describe the super-deluxe version of *Television* (sometimes called a *specialization*), you might start by saying, "It's everything a basic TV is, with some additional features."

A subclass of *Television* might be called *WideScreenTv*, and it would include all the bells and whistles that we have come to expect in a high-end electronic home-entertainment center. Rewriting all the code that went into the original *Television* is pointless, so why not just copy it when defining *WideScreenTv*?

It turns out that every class in Java, except one, is a subclass. All classes in Java are descended from the class *java.lang.Object*. The *Object* class is Java's ultimate superclass. To see this for ourselves, all we have to do is create a simple class and examine it in Visual J++, using the Class Outline window. See Figure 5-1 for a diagram of the relationship of classes *Object*, *Television*, and *WideScreenTv*.

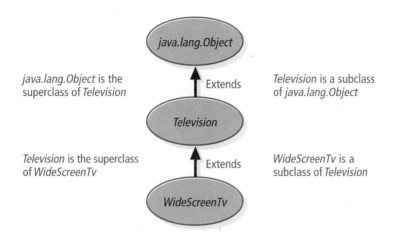

java.lang.Object is the superclass of *Television*

Extends

Television is a subclass of *java.lang.Object*

Television is the superclass of *WideScreenTv*

Extends

WideScreenTv is a subclass of *Television*

Figure 5-1.   *Superclass and subclass relationships.*

Working with the Class Outline Window

To help us work more effectively with classes, the Visual J++ development environment provides us with the Class Outline window. With it, we can easily see where our class fits in the class hierarchy. A *class hierarchy* describes the relationship of subclasses to their superclass and to each other. Technically, all classes in Java are related to one another because all classes are extensions of *java.lang.Object*; however, we can speak about a class hierarchy starting at any class we choose, and in general, we take superclass to mean a base or simple class like *Television*.

We'll use the Class Outline window to view a simple class called *Box*.

In Visual J++, open the BoxStarter project, located in Chapter05\BoxStarter\Box.sln, and bring up the Class Outline window. To make the Class Outline window visible, point to Other Windows from the View menu, and then choose Document Outline. The Class Outline window will contain the following message:

```
There are no items to show for the selected document.
```

To bring up something more interesting in the Class Outline window, go to the Project Explorer window, and expand the list for the BoxStarter project. Then select Box.java, and click the View Code button (or double-click Box.java). Expand Box in the Class Outline window. The Class Outline window then resembles Figure 5-2.

Figure 5-2.   *The Class Outline window, examining the* Box *class.*

Glancing at the Class Outline window, we see that *Box* has member variables *open* and *content*, and methods *Box*, *setOpen*, *getOpen*, *getContent*, and *setContent*. If you open the Superclasses folder, you will see that *Box* is a subclass of *java.lang.Object*. Open the Inherited members folder, and you will see several methods. Where do these methods come from? From the class *java.lang.Object*, because that is the superclass of *Box*. So, an instance of *Box* can do all these things, and we hardly had to lift a finger.

Here's the definition of the *Box* class, and we see that the description of the class matches what the Class Outline window told us about it:

```
public class Box
{
    private boolean open;
    private String content;

    public Box (String content)
    {
```

```
        open = true;
        this.content = content;
    }

    public void setOpen (boolean open)
    {
        this.open = open;
    }

    public boolean getOpen ()
    {
        return open;
    }

    public String getContent ()
    {
        return content;
    }

    public void setContent (String newContent)
    {
        this.content = newContent;
    }
}
```

The class *Box* doesn't have a lot of personality. You can create a box, put stuff inside it, close the box, open the box, and take stuff out. However, it is a good place to start a class hierarchy. In this example, we say that *Box* is the superclass of the hierarchy we are interested in.

The *extends* Keyword

We used the *Box* class to start our hierarchy; now let's expand it with a specialization of the *Box* class. Our specialization will include the ability to lock boxes. We can create a class *LockableBox* using the *extends* keyword in the class definition to indicate that *LockableBox* is a subclass of *Box*.

LockableBox does everything *Box* does, and more. Add this class to the BoxStarter project:

```
import com.ms.wfc.ui.*;
public class LockableBox extends Box
{
    private String password;
    private boolean locked;
}
```

Just like *Box*, an instance of *LockableBox* can be opened, closed, and so forth. A *LockableBox* object has this functionality because the methods of *Box* have been copied into *LockableBox*. This saves us from having to copy the code ourselves. What we still need to do is to override any methods copied from *Box* that are inappropriate for *LockableBox*, and write the code for any new functionality that we want *LockableBox* to have.

With *LockableBox* visible in your code window, go to the Class Outline window and examine the class *LockableBox*. What is its superclass? What are its inherited methods? Where do they come from? Notice that *LockableBox* has two classes in its Superclasses folder. The *Box* class is its direct superclass.

The Inherited Members list of *LockableBox* includes the members of *Object* as well as the members of *Box*.

If you would like to switch back and forth between viewing class *Box* and class *LockableBox* in the Class Outline window, open the Default package icon at the top of the Class Outline window, and you will see all the classes in your project. Double-click any one of these to examine it in the Class Outline window.

The *super* Keyword

With our hierarchy in place, our next step is to differentiate *LockableBox* from its superclass. Let's add a constructor to *LockableBox*. Add this code to your *LockableBox* class:

```
public LockableBox (String password)
{
    super("");
    this.password = password;
    super.setOpen(true);
}
```

This constructor uses two keywords (*super* and *this*). We have seen the use of the *this* reference before (in Chapter 4), but the *super* keyword is new. The *super* keyword allows us to take advantage of one of the greatest strengths of object-oriented programming: you never have to write code when you can use code that is already written. Here, the *super* keyword allows us to do just that.

When invoked from within a constructor method, the *super* keyword calls the constructor of the direct superclass (in this case, the *Box* constructor method). Used this way, the subclass constructor makes sure that the *Box* part of a *LockableBox* object is initialized correctly. In order for this method to work, the *super* call must be the first thing in the code of the subclass constructor, even before any local variables are defined. In this example, the call to the superclass constructor requires a *String* parameter.

The other use of *super* in this method is to call the *setOpen* method of the superclass *Box*. So, *super* can also be used to call any method of the superclass. We didn't really have to call the *setOpen* method of *Box* here, because the *Box* object is set to *open* by the *Box* constructor method. If the constructor method for *Box* did not require any parameters, we wouldn't have to call the constructor for *Box* explicitly; it would be called automatically. What this means is that whether you include it in your code or not, the superclass constructor is called. The reason we don't see the call to the constructor method for the *Object* class in the constructors of direct subclasses of *Object* (such as *Box*) is that the constructor for *Object* doesn't take any parameters. This explains why classes must have a default constructor if you don't supply one. Refer to Chapter 2 for information on default constructors.

Naturally, in order for the *super* keyword to work, we must have access to its method. Back in Chapter 4, we saw that member variables have four levels of visibility: Default (package), *public*, *protected*, and *private*. These same levels apply to methods. For our example, we'll be using only *public* methods and *private* member variables.

Use of the *super* keyword is not limited to methods. The same syntax can be used to refer to member variables of the superclass as well. The *super* keyword is not used this way as often for two reasons: member variables are *private* more often than not (which means they are not visible in subclasses, no matter what syntax you use); and unless you have a member variable in the superclass with the same name as a member variable in the subclass, you don't need to specify *super* in front of the member variable.

Overriding Methods

Sometimes when inheritance is used to create a new subclass, the inherited definition of a method is not sufficient for the subclass. With our *Box* example, the *setOpen* method is not sufficient; we must first determine whether or not the box is locked. The Java mechanism for this is called *overriding*. Overriding occurs when we create a new method in the subclass with the same name and parameter list as a method in the superclass.

We will override the *setOpen* method of *LockableBox* using the Class Outline. Bring up *LockableBox* in the Class Outline window, open the folder called Inherited Members, and find the *setOpen* method. When you right-click the method, a pop-up menu appears. Select Override Method from this menu. Visual J++ knows the access modifier, the return type, the name, and the parameter list of the method being overridden, and will copy them into your class. This is a handy way to override methods of classes, especially when you can't remember exactly how a method should appear in code. As we progress through the book, we will override many unfamiliar methods. Let Visual J++ handle the details for you by using the Class Outline.

When you select Override Method, the following line appears in the code for *LockableBox*:

```
public void setOpen(boolean open)
{
    super.setOpen(open);
}
```

We see that the automatically supplied method simply calls the superclass version of *setOpen*. While this is not required (you could delete the line `super.setOpen(open);`), it is a good practice to explicitly handle initializing the superclass and then do the specialized work for the subclass. In our case, however, we don't want to open the *Box* object if it is locked.

Modify the overridden *setOpen* method to look like this:

```
public void setOpen (boolean open)
{
    if (this.locked && open == true)
        {
        MessageBox.show("Sorry, box is locked. Unlock the box first",
            "Box is locked", MessageBox.ICONEXCLAMATION);
        }
    else
        {
        super.setOpen(open);
        }
}
```

In the code above, if the box is locked (this.locked), and an attempt is made to open it (open == true), then a message appears on the screen saying that this is not allowed. Otherwise, the superclass version of *setOpen* is called.

The Class Outline can also be used to quickly find method definitions. Bring the *Box* class into the Class Outline window, and when you find the *getOpen* method, double-click it. The *getOpen* method appears in the middle of the code window. Right-click any item in the Class Outline window to see a context menu with additional options.

While we have *getOpen* available, take a look at its definition. Notice that not all inherited methods need to be overridden. This is a method that can be inherited into *LockableBox* as is.

Lab 5-1: Building on *LockableBox*

We will now use the Visual J++ Class Outline to override some of the methods of *Box* inherited into *LockableBox*.

Lab overview

In this lab, you will practice:

- Overriding methods.

- Using the Class Outline.

Starting with *Box*, a fragment of *LockableBox*, and a form that displays the current state of a *LockableBox* object, you will fill in the details of *LockableBox* by overriding the inherited versions of the *getContent* and *setContent* methods.

Lab setup

1. Start Visual J++ and open the Box project (Chapter05\Lab5-1\ Box.sln). This code is an extension of the code that you have been building as you followed along with this chapter. (You have been following along, right? If not, no problem; that's what the Box project is for.)

2. Run the project code.

3. Create a box by clicking the Create Chest button.

4. Type a content string for the box and a password. Notice how the password characters show up as asterisks (*). This was predefined by setting the passwordChar property of the edit box to *.

5. Use the radio buttons to close and lock the box.

6. Click the Examine Contents button. A message box appears with the contents of the box (the string you typed earlier). Our job is to fix the code so that contents of the box cannot be examined when the box is locked.

Lab instructions

1. Use the Class Outline to override the method *getContent*. Double-click LockableBox in the Project Explorer. (Double-clicking a Java file in the list brings up the View Designer if the file is attached to a form; otherwise, View Code is activated.) In the Class Outline window, locate LockableBox (you may have to open the Default package icon and double-click LockableBox). Underneath LockableBox, open the Inherited Members folder and find getContent. Right-click getContent and select Override Method from the pop-up menu that appears. The default version of the overridden *getContent* method looks like this:

```
public String getContent ()
{
    return super.getContent();
}
```

2. Modify *getContent* so that it checks to see if the box is locked. Use the value of the Boolean member variable *locked*. If the box is locked, use *MessageBox.show* to put out a message stating that the box is locked and to return a *null* value. If the box is not locked, return the value of *super.getContent*.

3. Use the Class Outline to override the method *setContent* in the same way that you overrode the *getContent* method. The default version of the override of *setContent* looks like this:

```
public void setContent (String newContent)
{
    super.setContent(newContent);
}
```

4. Modify the new *setContent* method so that it checks to see if the box is locked. If the box is locked, use *MessageBox.show* to tell the user that the box must be unlocked before the content can be changed. If the box is not locked, call the superclass version of *setContent* and pass it *newContent*.

5. Run the project code to verify that the contents of the box cannot be examined when the box is locked. To keep things simple, the contents of the box can be examined even if the box is closed. Only when the box is closed and locked are the contents not available. You can compare your work to the solution located in Chapter05\Sol5-1\Box.sln.

Next steps

We have seen the basics of inheritance with the use of *extends*, *super*, and overriding methods. We now move on to some inheritance modifiers for classes and methods: *abstract* and *final*.

Abstract Classes and Methods

When we used the Add Method dialog box (in Chapter 3), we skipped a couple of modifiers: *abstract* and *final*. Both of these modifiers relate to inheritance.

When we create a class, we must include the code for all its methods. While this may seem blindingly obvious, there are times we need only a placeholder for a method, without any method code. That's when we use the keyword *abstract*.

To understand the use of an abstract class, remember that when we use Java's inheritance, we are building a class hierarchy of increasing specialization. We used a general class, *Box*, to build a specialized class, *LockableBox*, earlier. As we extend one class into another, each new subclass is more specialized than its superclass. An abstract class, on the other hand, is a class in a class hierarchy that is so general that no objects can be created using it. An abstract class exists only to be extended.

You can't make an object of an abstract class, because an abstract class need not contain code for all of its methods. Abstract classes are useful only when a subclass extends them. See "The *extends* Keyword" earlier in this chapter for details.

An abstract class is allowed to have definitions (code) for some, all, or none of its methods. The *abstract* keyword gives us the option of leaving out the method definitions, and it guarantees that no objects are created using it. You can extend from an abstract class and create objects of the subclass. To create an object of the subclass, all abstract methods of the abstract class must be literally defined in the subclass.

Start Visual J++ and create a new project called Shapes. Add a class to this project, and call it *Shape*. Let's now add an abstract method called *area* to our abstract class. The method returns a *double*, takes no parameters, and has public access. Your code for the *Shape* class should now look like this:

```
public abstract class Shape
{
    public abstract double area();
}
```

Abstract methods serve as placeholders in an abstract class definition. They exist only to force subsequent subclasses to implement them.

Note again that since *area* is abstract, *Shape* must also be abstract. If any of the methods in a class are abstract, the entire class must be designated as abstract. You can, however, have an abstract class that contains no abstract methods. You might do this to prevent anyone from instantiating that class.

Turning our attention to the method *area*, we see that it looks a little different from other methods we have seen in Java. First, of course, it includes the keyword *abstract*, and second, the parentheses are followed by a semicolon (;). This leaves the method without any code. This is all right, because the class *Shape* is so general that the definition for area is difficult to write. Exactly what kind of shape is it? What are its dimensions? We can't create an object of class *Shape*; we have to extend from it, and we must be more specific.

So, the *area* method is a placeholder that requires one of two things of the classes that extend from it: that they be abstract themselves, or that they define exactly what the *area* method does. Eventually, of course, you must define what the *area* method does, or you can't create any objects.

Using the Project Explorer window, add a new class called *Rectangle* to the project. Your new class should look like this:

```
public class Rectangle extends Shape
{
}
```

Modify the *Rectangle* class so that it has two *double* member variables (length and width). Also include a constructor that assigns values to length and width. Finally, override the method *area* using the Class Outline window and the Inherited Members folder as we did with the *getContent* and *setContent* methods of *LockableBox*. When you are finished, your class should look like this:

```
public class Rectangle extends Shape
{
    private double length;
    private double width;
    public Rectangle (double length, double width)
    {
        this.length = length;
        this.width = width;
    }
    public double area()
    {
        return length * width;
    }
}
```

A rectangle is a more specific thing than a shape, so now we can define what the *area* method does.

Final Classes

The use of the *extends* keyword has no limit. You can keep applying the *extends* keyword to class after class after class. Most of the time, this is fine. At times, however, you want to prevent a class from being extended. The class *java.lang.System* is an example of a final class. It's final because you can't subclass the class *System*. The *final* modifier is generally used for security purposes: since you can't extend a final class, you can't override any of its methods. This guarantees that the methods in the class will not be overridden in a way other than what the class author intended. For example, you might have a class that includes a method that can determine whether the user is from the local intranet or the global Internet. If you were to allow this class to be extended, the overridden version of the security method might be modified to always indicate that the user came from the local intranet. In practice, however, unless you are writing classes for a sensitive system, it is almost always better to leave the class extendable (that is, non-*final*), and mark individual methods as final. We'll discuss final methods in the next section.

Consider the example of the class *Rectangle*. We could create squares using the class *Rectangle* in two ways. We could simply instantiate the class with the same value for length and width:

```
Rectangle square = new Rectangle(5,5);   // a 5X5 square
```

Or, we could extend the class *Rectangle* into the class *Square*:

```
public class Square extends Rectangle
{
    public Square (double length)
    {
        super(length,length);
    }
}
```

In the above code, the call to the superclass constructor (the constructor for *Rectangle*) creates a rectangle where all four sides are of equal length. We could then create a square like this:

```
Square square = new Square(5);   // a 5X5 square
```

Each approach has its advantages and disadvantages, depending on your situation. If you want to prevent the definition of class *Square* as seen above, you can modify *Rectangle* to be a final class:

```
public final class Rectangle extends Shape
{   // ...code continues
```

Given this version of *Rectangle,* the only way to create square objects would be:

```
Rectangle square = new Rectangle(5,5);   // a 5X5 square
```

Final Methods

When you use the keyword *final* in a method definition, it means that no further overriding is possible for that method. The earlier section on overriding tells us that each subclass in a hierarchy can have its own definition for a method that it inherits. However, you can defeat the ability to override a method by using *final*.

The main reason to use *final* is to guarantee that a particular method has only one definition from that point on in the class hierarchy. As we discussed in the section on final classes, this can be necessary in an environment where security is an issue. Knowing that a method won't be overridden in later classes, you can allow for some optimization of the Java code as well.

The usual inheritance mechanism of Java is to inherit the non-private methods of a class, and to allow the overriding of code for those methods. The *final* keyword allows the programmer to force the inheritance of the method without the option to override the code.

If we change our *area* method of the *Rectangle* class to be final, we prevent a subclass such as *Square* from overriding it:

```
public class Rectangle extends Shape
{
    private double length;
    private double width;
    public Rectangle (double length, double width)
    {
        this.length = length;
        this.width = width;
    }
    public final double area()
    {
        return length * width;
    }
}

public class Square extends Rectangle
{
    public Square (double length)
    {
        super(length,length);
    }
    public double area ()   // illegal, method is final in superclass!
    {
        // …
    }
}
```

Because *area* is a final method in *Rectangle*, it can't be overridden in *Square*. This makes sense because further subclasses of *Rectangle* should use the same method to determine their areas.

Lab 5-2: Drawing with Windows Foundation Classes

Here we build on the *Shape* hierarchy discussed in the previous sections. The new class will represent ellipses.

Lab overview

In this lab, you will practice:

- Overriding abstract methods.

- Using the *final* modifier.

The starter project includes a form that allows users to see rectangles of various sizes; the program includes the area of each rectangle. The exercise is to add a class that calculates the area in an ellipse.
The starter code includes the code necessary to draw the ellipses.

Lab setup

1. Start Visual J++.

2. Open the project DrawingWithWFC (Chapter05\Lab5-2\ DrawingWithWFC.sln). The project includes a form that uses scroll bars to resize two kinds of shapes: rectangles and ellipses. As each shape is drawn, the area covered by that shape is displayed at the bottom of the form.

3. Run the project to see how rectangles are drawn and how their areas are given.

Lab instructions

1. Add a new class, called *Ellipse*, to the project. The class *Ellipse* should look like the following:

```
public class Ellipse extends Shape
{
    private double majorAxis;
    private double minorAxis;
    public Ellipse (double majorAxis, double minorAxis)
    {
        this.majorAxis = majorAxis;
        this.minorAxis = minorAxis;
    }
    public final double area()
    {
        return Math.PI * majorAxis / 2.0 * minorAxis / 2.0;
    }
}
```

IP   Look at the use of the *Math* class in the preceding definition of *Ellipse.area*. The value *java.lang.Math.PI* is a member variable declared *public static final double* that represents the mathematical value *pi*. If you are searching for a math function, the place to look is in the Java class *Math*.

2. Two areas in the form file RectAndEllipse.java are marked with TODO tokens stating that they should be removed when the class *Ellipse* is completed. Remove the comment lines that have TODO tokens, and uncomment the code that uses the class *Ellipse*.

3. Run the project again. This time, you are able to draw some ellipses.

4. You can check your work against the solution in Chapter05\Sol5-2\ DrawingWithWFC.sln.

Next steps

Now that we have tackled the basics of inheritance, we'll build on our hard-won knowledge by examining what first made Java famous: the applet.

6

Creating an Applet

Until now, we've been working with applications. However, where the Java language has made a name for itself is with Java applets created to run on Web pages. While applications are stand-alone programs, applets require Web browsers or some other appletviewer in which to execute. The neat thing about Java applets is that they can run on anyone's computer as long as it has the Virtual Machine for Java, which includes just about every computer that surfs the Internet.

In this chapter, you will learn about:

- Java applets
- Associating applets with Web pages
- HTML (Hypertext Markup Language)

You will get a chance to:

- Build a Java applet using the Visual J++ applet template.
- Embed your applet in a Web page.
- Use the Java drawing package java.awt.
- Respond to events using the Java 1.02 event model.

Applets

In our quest to learn Java and Visual J++, we have seen forms, classes, objects, controls, events, properties, event procedures, and more. All of this will help us in our exploration of applets, HTML, and Web pages.

As we have seen, a class is a blueprint for an object. Once you create an object of a class, you can call the methods of that object as defined by the class.

A form is simply a class we can place controls on. Controls, such as Button, Label, and ListBox, are classes provided to you by the Visual J++ environment, specifically the WFC library. When you drag a control onto a form in the Forms Designer, you are creating a member variable of that class in your *Form* class. Remember, a form that you create (by default called *Form1*) is a subclass of the Visual J++ class called *Form*.

A Java applet is very similar. Every applet is a subclass of a class called *Applet*. So in the same way that *Form* is the superclass of all form classes, *Applet* is the superclass of all applets.

Running an applet requires the support of an *appletviewer*. The most commonly used appletviewers are Web browsers, such as Microsoft Internet Explorer. For a Web browser to function as an appletviewer, it must be *Java enabled*, as most Web browsers are these days. Less complex appletviewers are also available that simply provide us with a quick way to view an applet without having to bring up a Web browser. As we will see shortly, Visual J++ provides this kind of simple appletviewer.

The java.applet Package

The *Applet* class is defined in the java.applet package. In fact, the only class inside java.applet is the *Applet* class. The rest of the definitions are *interfaces*. We'll be covering interfaces in Chapter 8.

Specifically, the interfaces defined in java.applet are:

- *AppletContext* (used to help applets communicate with any other applets running at the same time)

- *AppletStub* (used for writing appletviewers; this interface is rarely used by applet programmers)

- *AudioClip* (used when you need your applet to play a sound file)

We will be using *AppletContext* and *AudioClip* in Chapter 7. In this chapter, we focus on the class *java.applet.Applet*.

Web Pages

A Web page acts as the host of a Java applet. Made up of HTML commands, a Web page is meant to be displayed using an Internet browser. The beauty of Web pages is that they allow everyone access to information in a similar format, without regard to the particular computer hardware or software.

We won't go into all the intricacies of HTML in this book, but we will see enough HTML to help you support your applets nicely.

Portability

An applet can run on any computer in the world, provided that the computer has the Virtual Machine for Java and some sort of appletviewer. As we develop our applets, we will see what a running applet looks like in Visual J++ Quick View and in Microsoft Internet Explorer.

For painting graphics on almost any screen display connected to the Virtual Machine, Java provides the Abstract Window Toolkit (AWT) package called java.awt. We will be using the AWT package to draw some simple graphics on a Web page.

Security

With the potential to run on almost any computer on the planet, Java applets had to be designed with an eye toward security. When you run a Java applet from a Web browser, the applet cannot:

- Access your local hard drive.

- Use any server except the one from which it was launched.

The only pieces of your hardware that the applet has access to are your screen display, mouse, and keyboard.

This does not mean that a Java applet cannot be useful or interesting. Java applets can gather input, provide demonstrations, calculate values, display animations, enhance Web site navigation, or simply add a little flash to a Web page. The security restrictions keep applets under control, and they make the Web a safe place to surf.

Creating Your Applet

We will now create our own applet using an applet template in Visual J++. This is similar to the Form template that we used to create an application in Chapter 2. Using this tool, we can have a new Java applet up and running in no time. Later, we will see how to build an applet from scratch.

Using the Applet Template

Start Visual J++, and select New Project from the File menu if it does not come up automatically. In the left pane under the folder Visual J++ Projects, select the folder called Web Pages. In the right pane, we see the Web page templates that Visual J++ provides for our use. We'll be building a regular applet, so select Applet On HTML. This choice provides us with a Visual J++ applet template. Type *MyFirstApplet* for the project name. This name will be applied to both the folder created in the specified directory and the solution file in that folder. See Figure 6-1 for an example of using the applet template.

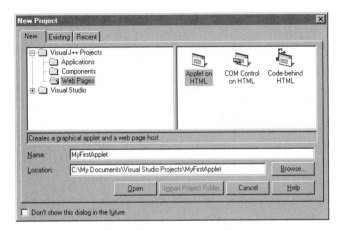

Figure 6-1. *The New Project dialog box using the applet template.*

Click the Open button, and the system goes to work creating the files needed to support your applet. In the Project Explorer window, you see the solution icon and underneath it the project icon. Expand the project, and you will see the two source code files supporting your applet: Applet1.java and Page1.htm. The Java file is where the code for the applet itself resides, and the HTML file is a basic Web page for hosting your applet (see Figure 6-2).

Figure 6-2. *The Project Explorer window after using the Visual J++ applet template.*

The applet template provides a complete applet ready to be run from within the context of a Web page. It doesn't do much, but everything that you need for a basic applet is there. From the Debug menu, select the menu item Start Without Debugging. Internet Explorer starts, and the HTML Web page that was automatically created is loaded into the browser. Hosted on this page are your applet and a short message (see Figure 6-3). Now close Internet Explorer to return to the Visual J++ environment.

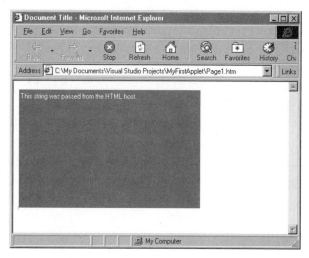

Figure 6-3.   *Viewing the applet with Internet Explorer.*

Using the applet template feature of Visual J++, we have just created an applet and an HTML Web page, embedded the applet on the Web page, and displayed the results in Internet Explorer. That's quite a bit. However, when it comes to extending the *Applet* class, using a template to generate an applet is probably not the best solution. We can actually build a pretty good applet without having to use all the features of an applet template. Keep in mind, though, that an applet template is a good reference tool to use after you have mastered a few more concepts.

For now, let's look at some of *MyFirstApplet* so we can see what to look for when we build an applet from scratch. We will start a selective tour by looking at the Java applet code created by the template.

In the Project Explorer window, right-click the Java file Applet1.java, and select View Code. (You may notice that the View Designer button is dimmed; this is normal. Unlike Visual J++ forms, the View Designer does not allow you to design your Java applet visually.) The file starts like this:

```
import java.awt.*;
import java.applet.*;
```

The two *import* statements indicate the Java packages that provide support for this applet. The first line imports Java's AWT. This is where you will find all of Java's built-in graphics capabilities. Using the AWT, we can draw text, lines, arcs, rectangles, polygons, and other shapes inside an applet window. We will use this package later to draw in our applet.

The second line imports the package where the *Applet* class itself is defined. All Java applets are subclasses of the class *java.applet.Applet*. Since we have imported the java.applet package, we can refer to the *java.applet.Applet* class simply as *Applet*.

The code continues with a JavaDoc comment and then the first line of our applet class:

```
/**
 * This class reads PARAM tags from its HTML host page and sets
 * the color and label properties of the applet. Program execution
 * begins with the init() method.
 */
public class Applet1 extends Applet
{
```

This line indicates that our applet class (*Applet1* in this case) is descended from *Applet*.

Before we build our own Java applets, let's turn our attention to the HTML document that supports the applet code.

A First Look at HTML

To see the HTML code Visual J++ generated to host our applet, go to the Project Explorer window and double-click the Page1.htm icon. Notice the three tabs at the bottom of the HTML code window. If the Design tab is not selected, click it now. What you see in the code window looks similar to Figure 6-4.

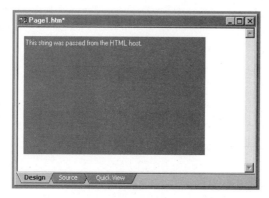

Figure 6-4.   *The HTML code window with the Design tab selected.*

The view of the project from the Design tab is analogous to the view in the View Designer (which we used to develop our Java application). It shows the HTML page with all of its components. The HTML page doesn't have any components other than the Java applet, so that is all we see. If you go to the Toolbox window and click the HTML button, you will see that the controls are enabled (that is, not dimmed as they have been previously). If you drag an HTML Intrinsic control onto the form, it appears on the form just as controls did for Java applications. We'll look at HTML controls in Chapter 7.

What Does HTML Look Like?

Click the Source tab to the right of the Design tab to view the HTML code for the project. We see an HTML file with code for the applet embedded in it (see Figure 6-5).

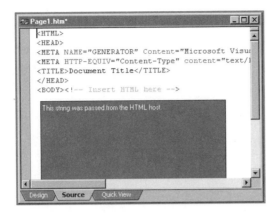

Figure 6-5. *The HTML code window with the Source tab selected.*

In order to see the HTML code that embeds the Java applet in the Web page, right-click the picture of the applet, and select Always View As Text from the pop-up menu that appears. What you see is a collection of HTML tags. An HTML tag is an instruction to the Web page about how to display the current page. HTML tags are easy to pick out because they start and end with angle brackets (< >). Some tags also include HTML attributes inside the angle brackets. These attributes allow us to specify certain values to be associated with the HTML tags. Looking at the HTML code for Page1.htm, we see a handful of tags, attributes, and values that are going to support our applet.

Here is the HTML code, line by line:

```
<HTML>
```

This tag identifies the code that follows it as HTML information that should be interpreted for display by a Web browser. At the end of the file is </HTML>, which specifies the end of the HTML code. A number of tags start and end using this same convention; that is, a closing tag indicates the end of a particular HTML tag's instruction.

```
<HEAD>
```

Continuing down the page, everything between <HEAD> and </HEAD> provides information about the document.

```
<META NAME="GENERATOR" Content="Microsoft Visual Studio 98">
```

The <META> tag is used for such things as identifying what program created the HTML document, who the author of the document is, and which Web site the document came from.

```
</HEAD>
```

This tag ends the <HEAD> section.

```
<BODY>
```

The <BODY> tag is placed just before the actual contents of the document. It creates a home for all of the HTML components on the page. The <BODY> tag often contains attributes indicating the background color for the page. The <BODY> tag also contains the <APPLET> tag, which is where applet code is placed.

```
<P> </P>
```

This code is the HTML way of placing a blank paragraph above the applet display area. That way, there will be a bit of blank space surrounding it.

```
<!-- Insert HTML here -->
```

The text <!--Insert HTML here--> comments and marks the place for you to add your HTML tags and text. As you become more adept at using HTML code, you may want to place additional tags in the body section of the HTML document. This is also where the Forms Designer places the HTML tags necessary to create the HTML Intrinsics controls (buttons, labels, and so forth). Right now, the only tags in the <BODY> area are <APPLET> and the supporting <PARAM> tags. This is where our applet comes into the picture.

```
<APPLET
code=Applet1.class
name=Applet1
width=320
height=200 VIEWASTEXT>
```

The <APPLET> tag has three required attributes: CODE, HEIGHT, and WIDTH. The NAME attribute is optional.

The CODE attribute's value is the name of the class file associated with the applet. The class file is not the Java source code file, but the *compiled* Java code for the *Applet1* class (the filename has a .class extension).

The NAME attribute is only necessary if you want to make an applet communicate with another applet on the same page running at the same time (which we will do in Chapter 7).

The HEIGHT and WIDTH attributes tell the browser how much space to set aside for the applet when it draws that page. The VIEWASTEXT option tells the HTML code window to display the applet code instead of the applet design.

```
<PARAM NAME="label" VALUE="This string was passed from the HTML
    host.">
<PARAM NAME="background" VALUE="008080">
<PARAM NAME="foreground" VALUE="FFFFFF">
```

Next are the <PARAM> tags. <PARAM> tags must appear within the <APPLET> tags and are generally the place where "command line" parameters are located for an applet. The reason for this is that applets have no command line, so you can't append parameters that modify the applet when it starts up. The tags here are setting the foreground and background colors and passing a string that will print in the applet when it is run. We will discuss how to use <PARAM> tags from within an applet in Chapter 7.

```
</APPLET>
```

This ends the <APPLET> tag.

```
</BODY>
```

This ends the body of the HTML document.

```
</HTML>
```

And this ends the HTML document.

The <APPLET> Tag

We saw the <APPLET> tag in action in Page1.htm. This is the applet programmer's most important HTML tag because it allows applets to run inside Web pages. Table 6-1 shows a summary of <APPLET> tag attributes. Note that HTML tags are not case-sensitive. They are capitalized here by convention.

Attribute	Use	Value	Required?
CODEBASE	Alternative location for files	URL	No
CODE	Name of Java class file	Java class filename	Yes
NAME	Names running applet	String	No
ALT	String to be displayed if Java is disabled on Web browser	String	No
ALIGN	Applet placement on page	*Left*, *Right*, *Top*, *Middle*, or *Bottom*	No
HEIGHT	Vertical size of applet's display area	Number	Yes
WIDTH	Horizontal size of applet's display area	Number	Yes
HSPACE	Amount of horizontal space around applet	Number	No
VSPACE	Amount of vertical space around applet	Number	No

Table 6-1.   *Summary of the HTML <APPLET> tag attributes.*

Some Other Interesting Tags

HTML 3.2 contains about 70 tags used to display HTML documents as Web pages. We won't be using them all in this book. Table 6-2 summarizes a handful of tags that will be useful to us right away.

Tag	Attributes	Use
<BODY>	BACKGROUND, BGCOLOR, TEXT, LINK, VLINK, ALINK	Contains the HTML code for displaying the page; can be used to specify background characteristics
 	CLEAR	Forces a line break
<HEAD>	—	Contains the HTML code describing the document itself, as opposed to its display
<P>	ALIGN	Indicates a paragraph on the page
<HR>	ALIGN, NOSHADE, SIZE, WIDTH	Draws a horizontal line across page; useful for visual separation
<HTML>	VERSION	Contains all the HTML code for the entire document
<TITLE>	—	Title of document displayed as title of window

Table 6-2.   *Summary of HTML tags commonly used by applet programmers.*

Here is an example HTML document that uses each of the tags described above:

```
<HTML>
<HEAD>
<TITLE>Demonstration of HTML tags</TITLE>
</HEAD>
<BODY>
<P>This is a paragraph on the page.</P>
<P>This is a second paragraph with
two forced <BR>line breaks<BR> in it.</P>
<HR>
<P>This paragraph is surrounded
 by horizontal lines.</P>
<HR>
</BODY>
</HTML>
```

If you open this file from within a Web browser, the title bar of the browser window contains "Demonstration of HTML tags" with the paragraph text (<P>...</P>) displayed in the window itself. Notice that the second paragraph does not contain a line break after the word "with," but breaks only where specifically instructed to by the <BR> tag. If you change the width of the browser window so that it is not wide enough to display a paragraph on one line, it wraps to a second line.

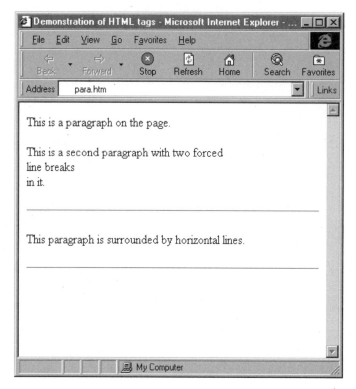

Figure 6-6.   *The HTML page with paragraphs and line breaks.*

Creating an Applet from Scratch

We have used a Visual J++ applet template to build an applet. We have looked at the Java file containing the applet code and the HTML document. We have run the applet in the context of a Web page by selecting Start from the Visual J++ environment. Now it is time to build our own applet from scratch. We will create a new, empty project and populate it with Java and HTML code files.

Select New Project from the File menu. If you are prompted to save any open work, go ahead and do so. Be sure the check box labeled Close Current Solution is selected. In the left pane of the New Project dialog box, select the folder Visual J++ Projects. (Don't select Web Pages!) In the right pane, select the Empty Project folder. Type *ScratchApplet*, and click the Open button.

In the Project Explorer window, right-click the ScratchApplet project icon and, from the pop-up menu, point to Add, and then select Add Class. This causes the Add Item dialog box to appear with Class preselected in the left pane. Select Class in the right pane, and enter *ScratchApplet.java* as the name for the class. Click the Open button.

We are now presented with a code window with an empty class in it. Our first modification will be to add a couple of handy *import* statements. We saw these earlier in MyFirstApplet.java. Again, they are:

```
import java.awt.*;
import java.applet.*;
```

Now we are ready to connect our class to the *java.applet.Applet* class. Simply type *extends Applet* after the name of your class:

```
public class ScratchApplet extends Applet
{
}
```

We now have the stub of an applet class. Our next step is to add a Web page to our project.

In the Project Explorer window, right-click the project icon and, from the pop-up menu, point to Add, and then select Add Web Page. The Add Item dialog box appears with Web Page preselected in the left pane. Select Page in the right pane, and type *ScratchApplet.htm* for the name.

When the code window for the HTML document appears, click the Source tab. You will see that an HTML skeleton has been created for you. Change the text between <TITLE> and </TITLE> to Scratch Applet. After the <P> and </P> line of code, add an <APPLET> tag, as in the following HTML code:

```
<HTML>
<HEAD>
<META NAME="GENERATOR" Content="Microsoft Visual Studio 98">
<TITLE>Scratch Applet</TITLE>
```

```
</HEAD>
<BODY>
<P> </P>
<APPLET CODE=ScratchApplet.class HEIGHT=200 WIDTH=200>
Hello World! Your Browser does not support Java.
</APPLET>
</BODY>
</HTML>
```

Note that the text between the beginning and ending <APPLET> tags is displayed only if your browser does not support Java or has support for Java disabled. If your browser does support Java, then the applet is displayed. At this point, the applet shows only a background, which is pretty dull. Now that we have the basis for our applet in place, we can move to the next section where we draw a few things in the applet using the Abstract Window Toolkit package.

The java.awt Package

With Java's Abstract Window Toolkit, you can draw graphics such as circles, ovals, rectangles, and polygons. You can add controls to the applet just as you did with the WFC controls in Chapters 2, 3, and 4, and you can create layouts for the elements placed on an applet display area using layout managers (introduced in the "Panels and Layouts" section later in this chapter).

In this first look at the AWT package, we will be drawing graphics. Note that with the AWT, displaying text is considered to be a graphics and not a text operation. So, we'll start out using graphics methods to "draw" text in the applet display area.

Inheritance and Applet Classes

Applet classes work because the Web browsers that invoke them already know which methods to call. This is because a Java-enabled Web browser knows which methods the *java.applet.Applet* class contains. If we create a method in our applet that does not exist in some form in the *Applet* superclass, the Web browser does not know that the new method exists. The contents of the *Applet* superclass define a protocol for applets. In order to write code for our applet class, we must stay within this protocol. This doesn't mean that we can't create new methods for our applets; it just means that the Web browser cannot call those methods directly. Just as we have done with other Java classes, we can add methods that provide our applet with special functionality, or we can add methods simply to break up the work our applet does into smaller chunks. The difference is that a Web browser can only use one of the new methods if a call to the new method is included in an overridden definition of one of the inherited methods.

The protocol between an applet class and a Web browser is established using the class hierarchy of *Applet*. In order to determine all of the methods available to an applet, go to each superclass in turn (that is, follow the hierarchy) and look for its methods. In some cases, the inherited method may only be an empty method with no code, but the method is there nonetheless.

Figure 6-7 shows the class hierarchy of the class *Applet*.

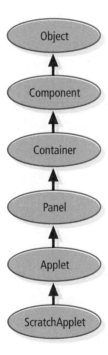

Figure 6-7.   *The* ScratchApplet *family tree.*

In order to use a method from a superclass in our applet, we apply the overriding technique that we discussed in Chapter 5. Visual J++ has a tool that makes this easy, and we will use it in a moment. In this chapter and in Chapter 7, we also cover the most commonly overridden applet methods.

Adding Drawing Text

The initial code for our applet class will print out a message. For this bit of graphics we use the *paint* method. The *paint* method is one of those methods that is available to all applet classes through inheritance (*paint* is specifically inherited from *java.awt.Container*). To create a different definition for the *paint* method in our applet class, we override its superclass definition.

As before, in order to override a method in a class, you can type the new method or use the Class Outline window to assist you. To use the Class Outline to override a method in your applet, bring up the code window for ScratchApplet.java. Then go to the Class Outline window and open the icon for the applet class. Open the Inherited Members folder, and scroll down to the *paint* method. As you can see, we have a lot of methods here to choose from. Fortunately, they are listed alphabetically, and typing the first letter of the method name you are interested in (*paint*) moves you down to methods that start with the letter *p*. The *paint* method happens to be the first one. Right-click the *paint* method and select Override Method from the pop-up menu.

This code appears in your applet:

```
public void paint(Graphics p1)
{
    //TODO: Add your own implementation.
    super.paint(p1);
}
```

As always, it is a good practice to call the superclass method that you are overriding, and this line is provided automatically if we override methods using the Class Outline window.

Add the following line after the call to *super.paint*:

```
g.drawString("Hello",50,50);
```

It's a good idea to change the name of the *Graphics* parameter to something more meaningful than *p1*. The conventional name for this parameter is *g*, as we have used here. (The type *Graphics* is defined in java.awt.) Don't forget to change this name in the call to the superclass method of *paint* as well. The completed version of your Java file now looks like this:

```
import java.awt.*;
import java.applet.*;

public class ScratchApplet extends Applet
{
    public void paint(Graphics g)
    {
        super.paint(g);
        g.drawString("Hello",50,50);
    }
}
```

When you start your applet after adding this method, Internet Explorer loads the applet, and your window will look something like Figure 6-8.

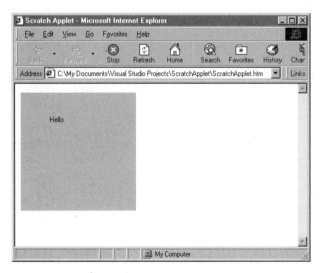

Figure 6-8. *Your applet with a new* paint *method.*

The Web browser creates and maintains the *Graphics* object that is passed to the *paint* method, so we, as applet programmers, don't have to. This is another example of how applets and Web browsers work together.

Next we will look at how the AWT package deals with events.

Responding to Applet Events

We have already seen how Visual J++ deals with events and event handlers. In Chapters 2, 3, and 4, we used event handlers to interact with the user. Those events and procedures are part of WFC, but not part of Java. Java has its own way of dealing with events within the AWT package. In this section, we will write code to handle events in applets.

Event-Handling Models in Java

The AWT package has two distinct event models. The first was part of Java version 1.02, and the second is part of Java 1.1. The version 1.02 model is smaller and simpler than the version 1.1 model, but it is also less functional and not as adept at dealing with large applications. Each model has its own benefits. We use the 1.02 model in this book because the applets we build will be small.

Just like applet classes, the Java 1.02 event handler makes use of the inheritance model and overriding methods. In short, if you want to handle events, just override the proper method. The method names indicate which event they handle. We will look at handling mouse events first.

 OTE Because there are two event models in Java, the older one has been *deprecated*. This means the 1.02 model has been superseded by the new one in Java 1.1, and support for it will eventually be removed from the language. The Task List window indicates this for each event handler that you override in your applet class. These messages can be ignored for now because the old model will be around for a while yet. However, if you plan on writing a lot of event-handling code in your applets, you should consider learning the new model and be aware that code you write for the old model will eventually become obsolete.

Adding Event-Handling Code to Our Applet

Returning to our ScratchApplet example, we decide that we want to intercept a mouse click. In order to find the correct event handler to override, it is helpful to know that all the events associated with the mouse start with the word "mouse," and in Java's 1.02 event model there is no "click" event, per se. What happens instead of "click" is the combination of a mouse-down event followed by a mouse-up event. The event we will handle here is the mouse-up event. The method to override for a mouse-up event is called *mouseUp*. Here's a *mouseUp* method that changes the background color of the applet window:

```
public boolean mouseUp(Event e, int x, int y)
{
    setBackground(Color.red);
    repaint();
    return true;
}
```

Add this new method to your applet and run it. When you click the applet display area in the Web browser, the call to *setBackground* changes the background color to red. The parameter value is a constant called *red*, which comes from the *Color* class of the AWT package. Note that this is not the same constant *RED* that comes from the *Color* class we used in Chapter 4 (although the effect is the same). The call to the *repaint* method causes the change to be seen in the display area. Changes to the values of properties (such as the color of the background of an applet) aren't seen until an update to the screen display is needed. Calling *repaint* forces an intrinsic call to *paint*, and so the appearance of the applet changes. Notice that we can't call *paint* directly, because it requires a parameter value of type *Graphics* that our event doesn't contain.

Finally, we return the Boolean value *true*. Returning the value *true* from an AWT event handler means we have handled the event and it need not be passed along to any other event handlers.

The next method override will be a little more dynamic. If we add a label, a layout manager in which to place the label, and a *mouseMove* event handler, we can track the cursor as it moves inside our applet. The code for this is:

```
private Label mousePositionLbl = new Label();
public boolean mouseMove(Event e, int x, int y)
{
    mousePositionLbl.setText("Cursor is at "+x+","+y);
    repaint();
    return true;
}
```

The first line creates an AWT Label component. The *mouseMove* method changes the text of that label to be the current position of the mouse. It does this every time the mouse moves. Don't forget to call *repaint* to actually effect a change to the display area. However, if you run the project after adding this method, you will see that the applet still appears to be unchanged. In order for the label to appear in the applet display area, it must be explicitly added to the applet.

Adding Components to Applets

Arranging components for applet user interfaces is not as simple as placing WFC controls on forms. Applet components are placed in containers by one of five layout managers: *FlowLayout*, *GridLayout*, *BorderLayout*, *CardLayout*, and *GridBagLayout*. We will discuss these in more detail later in this chapter. For this first example, we will use a *BorderLayout* manager and add our component to it.

After we have created a layout manager, we can add the component to the layout rather than directly to the applet. When we built Windows-based applications using Visual J++, we used the Visual J++ Forms Designer to place WFC controls onto forms. When we drop a WFC control on a form using the Forms Designer, a lot of Java code is generated for us by Visual J++. This automatically supplied code ensures that the WFC control appears exactly as we have specified. However, to place AWT controls in the applet display area, we must supply the Java code ourselves. Additionally, we must be sure to place the code in the right methods so that the AWT controls appear when we want them to.

In this example, we want our AWT controls to appear immediately—that is, as soon as the Web page that contains our applet is downloaded by a Web browser. In order for the AWT controls to appear immediately, we override the *init* method of the class *Applet*. The Web browser executes the *init* method of our applet right after it creates the applet instance. The *init* method for our example applet class is shown in the following code:

```
public void init()
{
    super.init();
    setLayout(new BorderLayout());
    add("North",mousePositionLbl);
}
```

Let's examine the three lines of code above. The call to *super.init* is, of course, the call to the superclass method of *init*. The *setLayout* method is called with a newly created *BorderLayout* object. *BorderLayout* objects allow us to specify whether components are placed at the top (*"North"*), bottom (*"South"*), left (*"West"*), or right (*"East"*) part of the applet display area. To get the label to appear at the top of the display area, we call the *add* method with the parameter *"North"* and the name of the component. Again, this is just a first example to get things rolling; we will look at the details of layouts later in this chapter.

Once you have added this code to the applet, run it and move the cursor around the applet display area to see what happens. Figure 6-9 shows an example of the applet running.

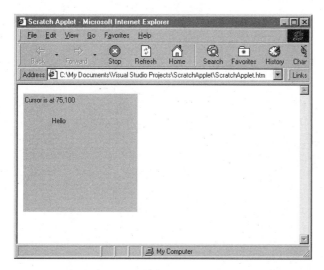

Figure 6-9.   *The* ScratchApplet *applet reporting the mouse cursor position using an AWT Label component.*

Drawing Using an AWT *Graphics* Object

As we saw before, the three required attributes for <APPLET> are CODE, HEIGHT, and WIDTH. The Web browser uses the values that we choose for HEIGHT and WIDTH to specify an applet display area for the Web page we can draw in using a *Graphics* object. To draw in the applet display area we use the *paint* method. The drawing display is mapped out using *x* and *y* coordinates, with 0,0 in the upper left corner of the display (see Figure 6-10).

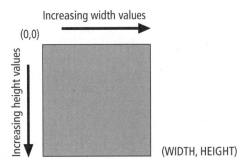

Figure 6-10. *The display coordinate system of an applet.*

For example, say you had an applet class called *MyApplet*. You might put that applet in the Web page using this tag definition:

```
<APPLET CODE=MyApplet.class WIDTH=50 HEIGHT=100></APPLET>
```

The browser then sets aside a display area for your applet of 50 pixels wide by 100 pixels high. The following override of the *paint* method in your applet class draws a line from the upper left corner to the lower right corner (see Figure 6-11):

```
public void paint(Graphics g)
{
    g.drawLine(0,0,50,100);
}
```

Figure 6-11. *The* drawLine *method in action.*

If you attempt to draw beyond the space set aside by the browser, the graphics will not appear on the Web page; but of course, the applet doesn't know this.

The parameter of the *paint* method is of type *java.awt.Graphics*. This type of object allows us to draw text and graphics in the display area of our applet. We have already used the *drawString* method to display text, and we just saw the *drawLine* method drawing a diagonal line. We can also use this object to draw rectangles, ovals, and polygons, among other things.

When we draw shapes with *Graphics* objects, we have the choice of filling in the shape or just drawing the outline of the shape. The *drawRect* method draws only the outline of a rectangle, and the *fillRect* method draws the shape and fills in the rectangle. The following code uses *fillRect* and *drawRect* to draw two squares:

```
public void paint(Graphics g)
{
    g.fillRect(10,10,80,80);   // draws a solid square
    g.drawRect(100,10,80,80);  // draws a square outline
}
```

The first two parameters of both the *fillRect* and *drawRect* methods represent the *x* and *y* coordinates of the upper left corner of the rectangle. The third parameter is the width of the rectangle, and the fourth is its height (see Figure 6-12).

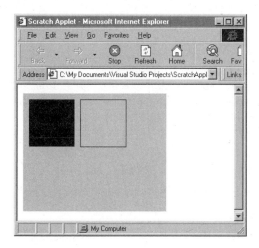

Figure 6-12. *A solid square and a square outline drawn using* fillRect *and* drawRect, *respectively.*

Here is a sample call for another *Graphics* method, *drawOval*:

```
g.drawOval(10,10,80,80);
```

This call draws a circle within the display area with an upper left corner of 10,10 and a lower right corner of 80,80. That is, the first two parameters are the *x* and *y* coordinates of the upper left corner of the square, and the second two parameters are the height and width of the oval (see Figure 6-13).

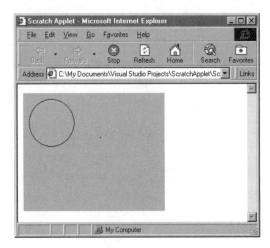

Figure 6-13. *A circle drawn with the call* drawOval(10,10,80,80).

The *fillOval* method behaves the same way, but fills in the oval.

 OTE Since squares and circles are, respectively, simply rectangles and ovals of equal proportion, the *Graphics* methods for handling instances of these object pairs is the same. Specifically, *drawRect* and *fillRect* are used to draw and fill both squares and rectangles, and *drawOval* and *fillOval* are used to draw and fill both circles and ovals (ellipses). In the case of squares and circles, the third and fourth parameters of these method calls are equal.

The arc drawing routines (*drawArc* and *fillArc*) work just like the oval-drawing routines but require two additional parameters representing the starting angle to begin drawing the arc, and the angle of the sweep of the arc.

The following call to *fillArc* draws a solid arc in the display area with an upper left corner of 10,10 and a lower right corner of 80,80:

```
g.fillArc(10,10,80,80,10,90);
```

Drawing begins at 10 degrees above the *x*-axis and continues for 90 degrees in a counter-clockwise direction (until the 100-degree mark is reached). See Figure 6-14 for a picture of the arc.

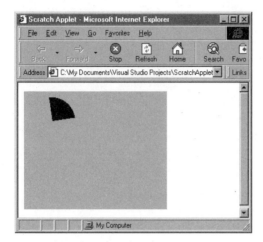

Figure 6-14. *An arc drawn with the call* fillArc(10,10,80,80,10,90).

Lab 6-1: Building a Quadrant Applet

In this lab, we build an applet that draws shapes in a quadrant of the applet, based on mouse position.

Lab overview

You will practice:

- Using Visual J++ to create an applet from scratch.

- Adding data variables to an applet.

- Writing an AWT *mouseMove* event handler.

- Using AWT drawing methods.

As with the *ScratchApplet* applet we just created, our applet in this lab will watch the mouse as it moves through our applet. This time, however, we'll only be interested in which quadrant of the applet display area the mouse is in. We will use AWT routines to draw a shape in that quadrant.

Lab setup

1. Start Visual J++.

2. In the New Project dialog box, create an empty project called Quadrant.

3. Add a Java class to the project called *Quadrant* (filename Quadrant.java).

4. Add a Web page to the project (filename Quadrant.htm) and an <APPLET> tag.

Lab instructions

1. Add data variables to the *Quadrant* class.

   ■ Add the data variables *clear*, *circle*, *square*, and *arc* of type *int* to the class. Each of these variables should have the modifiers *public*, *static*, and *final*. For example, here is the definition of *clear*:

   ```
   public static final int clear = 0;
   ```

   It doesn't matter what values you give the other static final data members, as long as each one has a unique value.

   ■ Add the data variable *drawnShape*, and initialize it to the value of *clear*.

2. Override the method *init*. Remember to call *repaint*.

3. Override the method *paint*.

   This method should first clear the display area with a call to the method *clearRect*:

   ```
   g.clearRect(0,0,200,200);
   ```

4. Divide the applet display area into quadrants.

   ■ Call the *Graphics* method *drawLine* twice: first to draw a horizontal line midway between the top and bottom of the display area, and then to draw a vertical line midway between the left and right boundaries of the display area.

▪ Number quadrants as follows: upper left is one, upper right is two, lower left is three, and lower right is four.

5. Use an *if* statement to compare the value of *drawnShape* with *circle*, *square*, and *arc*. Depending on the value of *drawnShape*, draw either a circle outline in quadrant one, a solid square in quadrant two, or a solid arc in quadrant three. You can pick any starting angle and sweep angle that you like for the arc.

6. Override the method *mouseMove*.

   Use an *if* statement to determine which quadrant the mouse is currently in. Test the values of the second parameter (the *x*-value parameter) and the third parameter (the *y*-value parameter) to make this determination. If the mouse is in quadrant one, set the data variable *drawnShape* to be a circle. If the mouse is in quadrant two, set *drawnShape* to be a square. If in the third quadrant, set it to be an arc. And if the mouse is in the fourth quadrant, set *drawnShape* to clear.

7. After setting the value of *drawnShape*, call the *repaint* method to display the results. Return the value *true*, indicating that you have handled the mouseMove event and no other methods need to see it.

8. Use the <APPLET> tag to embed your applet inside the HTML Web page file Quadrant.htm.

9. Run your applet and see what happens when you move the cursor around inside the display area of the applet. You can compare your work to the solution located in Chapter06\Sol6-1\Quadrant.sln.

Next steps

We can now build basic applets and handle some events. Let's explore AWT components further. We will see how to create them, place them in our applet display area, and handle their events.

Components in the AWT

The java.awt package includes components for building a user interface similar to what we saw previously with forms and WFC controls. These components include support for buttons, labels, check boxes, radio buttons, text entry, and more. In this section, we will populate our applet display area with some of the more commonly used AWT components and write the event-handling code for these components.

Labels

Label components in the AWT are just like the Label controls of WFC. They allow us to place text in the display area that the user cannot modify directly.

Most of the time, you create a label and assign a string to it with a statement such as the following:

```
Label myLabel = new Label("This is my label");
```

You can find out what the text of a label is with the *getText* method:

```
String myLabelText = myLabel.getText();
```

And you can change the text of a label with the *setText* method:

```
myLabel.setText("New Label Text");
```

To place a label in the applet display area, we use the *add* method of the *Applet* class.

Buttons

Button components are basically labels that the user can click to communicate with the program. Also, like labels, buttons have a *getText/ setText* pair of methods for manipulating what text appears on the button.

Where buttons (and other components, as we shall see) differ from labels is in their use of a method called *action*. Here's an example of creating a button inside an *Applet* class:

```
class AppletWithButton extends Applet
{
    private Button button1 = new Button("Click Here");
}
```

Of course, creating a button in and of itself is not of much use. We must make the button appear in the applet display area and attach an event handler to it to make it do something if it's clicked. The event-handling part of the puzzle is in the next section.

Responding to AWT Component Events

We handle events by overriding inherited event-handling methods. In the Java 1.02 event-handling model, only four event-handling methods are associated with components, and three of these are often ignored. That makes it pretty easy, doesn't it? The four event-handling methods are *action*, *gotFocus*, *lostFocus*, and *handleEvent*.

The *action* event handler is by far the most-often used of these methods. When the user triggers a component, the *action* method is called. It is then up to us to put the proper code in the *action* method so that we can determine exactly what happens. We will see an example of this shortly.

The methods *gotFocus* and *lostFocus* are activated when a component gains or loses focus as a user tabs through an interface. For example, when a button gains focus, the default is for the button text to receive a black outline; when focus is lost, the black outline disappears.

Any other events are handled by *handleEvent*. We will use an override of this method to do text entry in an applet display area.

Let's create and add an override of the *action* method to the class
AppletWithButton:

```
class AppletWithButton extends Applet
{
    private Button button1 = new Button("Click Here");
    public boolean action(Event e, Object helper)
    {
        if (e.target == button1)
        {
            setBackground(Color.green);
        }
        repaint();
        return true;
    }
    public void init ()
    {
        add (button1);
    }
}
```

The override of the *action* method for this *Applet* class checks to see if
button1 was pressed; if it was, the background color of the applet display
area becomes green. Starting at the top of the method, we see that *action*
takes two parameters. The first is the *Event* object that knows everything
about what event just took place, and the other is a sort of helper object.
For example, the *Event* object contains a reference to the component that
signaled the event. Since we have only one component, the component
signaling the event must have been *button1*. Because the signaling
component was a *Button* object, the second parameter is actually a *String*
object whose value is the text on the button (in this case, that string would
be "Click Here"). Each component object has its own helper object that
will be passed to the *action* method.

The *if* statement in the code checks to see if the target of the event was
button1. Of course, it has to be, because that is our only component, but
it never hurts to check (and this makes it easier to add another component
later). Once we have determined that it was in fact *button1* that was
pressed, we change the background color of the display area to green.
(Remember, you must repaint the applet if a control is supposed to change
the appearance of your applet.)

Next, if your event-handling method has done everything that needs to be done (that is, "consumed" the event), then you should return the value *true*. If you would like to pass the event along to some other method, return *false*, and then other components can see the event and react appropriately. In our case, nothing more needs doing, so we return *true*.

Finally, in order to make a *Button* object available in the display area, we must call the *add* method. Since we want *button1* to appear right away, we override the *init* method and place the call to *add* there. At this point we don't have much say about where the button appears in the display area. In order to gain more control over where our components appear (and we usually want to), we need to use layouts. We've almost reached that discussion.

Text Fields and Keyboard Events

If we want our applet to react to individual keystrokes, we can override either the *keyDown* or *keyUp* method. Strictly speaking, these events are not component events. The component events are handled by *action*, *gotFocus*, *lostFocus*, and *handleEvent*.

The following override of the *keyDown* method senses characters typed by the user, and changes the color of the display area's background accordingly:

```
public boolean keyDown(Event e, int keyValue)
{
    switch (keyValue)
    {
        case 'r' : setBackground(Color.red);
                    break;
        case 'g' : setBackground(Color.green);
                    break;
        case 'b' : setBackground(Color.blue);
                    break;
    }
    repaint();
    return true;
}
```

The second parameter of the *keyDown* method is the integer value of the key on the keyboard that the user pressed. A *switch* statement then allows us to select which key it is and take the appropriate action. See Chapter 11 for more information on the *switch* statement.

Note once again that changing the background color value does not change the display area itself, and so we call *repaint* to update the display. Last, we return the value *true*, because no other methods need to deal with this event.

If you want to deal with nonprintable keys (like the function keys F1 through F12), the *Event* class has defined names to help you. If we change the *switch* statement above to the following, then pressing F1, F2, and F3 changes the background color to red, green, and blue, respectively:

```
switch (keyValue)
{
    case e.F1 : setBackground(Color.red);
              break;
    case e.F2 : setBackground(Color.green);
              break;
    case e.F3 : setBackground(Color.blue);
              break;
}
```

Not all keys have names in *Event*, so we must use their numerical values from the Unicode character set. If you have used the ASCII character set before, it's handy to know that the first 128 values in the Unicode character set are the same as the ASCII character set. Also, the numeric value of the Unicode character for Ctrl-A is 1, Ctrl-B is 2, Ctrl-C is 3, and so on. Let's modify the *keydown* method so that instead of function keys, the program accepts control keys. That is, this time the user must hold down the control key (Ctrl) together with a letter key to get the colors to change:

```
public boolean keyDown(Event e, int keyValue)
{
    switch (keyValue)
    {
        case 18 : setBackground(Color.red); // control r
                break;
        case 7 : setBackground(Color.green); // control g
                break;
```

```
        case 2 : setBackground(Color.blue); // control b
                break;
    }
    repaint();
    return true;
}
```

If you want to know whether a modifier key was held down, without regard to which key it was, use the methods *shiftDown*, *controlDown*, and *metaDown* inside the *Event* class. Here's an example of sensing a right click:

```
public boolean mouseDown(Event e, int x, int y)
{
    if (e.metaDown())
    {
        // right click detected
    }
}
```

Once you have identified the events you want to handle, two components in the AWT assist you in dealing with text. These are the classes *TextField* and *TextArea*. *TextField* allows for only one line of input, while *TextArea* supports multiline input. They are both descended from *TextComponent* and so have many methods in common. We will restrict ourselves to *TextField* for this discussion.

When you create a *TextField* object, you can leave its size unspecified:

```
TextField firstNameTxt = new TextField();
```

Or you can specify how many characters wide the field is:

```
TextField lastNameTxt = new TextField(10);
```

Or you can specify what text goes into the field initially:

```
TextField jobDescriptionTxt = new TextField("Computer Bum");
```

Or you can specify both:

```
TextField currentPostTxt = new TextField("Flunky",20);
```

As with the other components and controls, you have at your service a *getText* and *setText* pair. *TextField* also lets us manipulate the selected area of text. *TextField* has a *getSelectedText* method for dealing with user selections of text. Here's an example:

```
public class ShowSelectedText extends Applet
{
    private TextField blankTxt = new TextField(10);
    private Label message1 = new Label("Selected Text is ");
    private Label message2 = new Label("            ");
    public void init()
    {
        add(blankTxt);
        add(message1);
        add(message2);
        super.init();
    }

    public boolean keyDown(Event e, int keyValue)
    {
        message2.setText(blankTxt.getSelectedText());
        return super.keyDown(e, keyValue);
    }
}
```

If you run this applet and select some text in the *TextField* object called
blankTxt, the text will be echoed in the value of the *Label* object
message2. However, you will notice a couple of strange things going on.

First, if you select the text in the text field with the mouse, nothing shows
up in the *message2 Label* object. This is because the only event handler
that we have overridden is *keyDown*, and therefore *keyDown* is the only
method that can modify the text property of *message2*. If we wanted the
program to react to text selection using the mouse, we would have to
override a mouse event handler, such as the *mouseMove* method.

Second, if you use the Shift key and the arrow keys to select text inside the
text field *blankTxt*, you will notice that the value displayed appears to be
one keystroke behind the actual selection. Say, for example, that the text
in the text field is "Java," and the first *a* and the *v* are selected
(highlighted). Only the *a* would appear after "Selected Text is." If you
expanded the selection to the second *a*, then *av* would appear after
"Selected Text is." This occurs because this version of *keyDown* is being
called before the text property of *blankTxt* has been updated to include
the second *a*. Under normal circumstances, this is okay, because
expanding the selection using the arrow keys is not the event that causes
the selection to be examined. Normally, a button, a control sequence (such

as Ctrl+C for copying), or an access key (such as Alt+F for pulling down the File menu) is the event that triggers an examination of the currently selected text.

A "more intelligent" event handler for this example might look like this:

```
public boolean keyDown(Event e, int keyValue)

{
    // if the user pressed control c or control x, update the
        displayed selection
    if (keyValue == 3 || keyValue == 24)
    {
        displaySelection();
    }
    return super.keyDown(e, keyValue); "
```

Panels and Layouts

So far, we haven't had much control over where the components that we place in the applet display area show up. Layouts allow us to specify the general behavior and location of a component—"general" because we can't place a component in the display area to the exact pixel, as we can with WFC. This is because Java applets are explicitly intended to run on any display (regardless of resolution) on the World Wide Web. Using a relative approach to arranging our applet layout, rather than an exact pixel approach, ensures the best possible display of our applet on any screen. To do this, we let AWT layout objects handle the job for us.

The java.awt package provides us with five kinds of layout manager:

- *FlowLayout* is the default layout; it is what we get if we don't specify our own layout manager. *FlowLayout* simply places the next control to the right of the last component added and wraps around to the next line if necessary.

- *GridLayout* allows us to set up a grid for our components. Each component is given one cell in a grid, and all components are the same size (the size of one cell in the grid).

- *BorderLayout* works like a map. When we use a *BorderLayout* layout manager, we specify a compass direction as a string (*"North"*, *"East"*, *"South"*, *"West"*, and *"Center"*), and the control is then placed at the top, right, bottom, left, or center of the display area.

- *CardLayout* is for stacking components, one on top of the other, like a deck of playing cards. This works well if we want only one component in a set to be available at a time.

- *GridBagLayout* is like *GridLayout*, but allows for more complex layouts. With *GridLayout*, each of the components fits into one cell, and all cells are the same size. With *GridBagLayout*, there is no such restriction. However, the flexibility comes at a price: *GridBagLayout* is also the most complicated layout to set up. Because of the complexity of setting up a *GridBagLayout* layout manager, we will not go into detail here about how it is done.

We will now see examples of using *FlowLayout*, *GridLayout*, *BorderLayout*, and *CardLayout* to arrange components in an applet display area.

Remember, at the time the applet is created, we arrange the applet's components by overriding the *init* method. We don't need to look at all the code that might go into an applet class to understand layout managers, so rather than show the entire applet code, we will narrow our view to the supporting data variables and the *init* method. Of course, you are free to create, arrange, and add components to the display area at any time in the applet's life cycle. You'll see more about an applet's life cycle in Chapter 9.

Let's put some components in a display area by using *FlowLayout* (the default layout manager). We'll use buttons here, but any component can be arranged in a display area in this way; buttons are just simpler to work with for these examples.

Our first step is to create the layout manager:

```
FlowLayout flowingButtons = new FlowLayout();
```

This creates a *FlowLayout* object that starts placing components at the left side of the display area until it runs out of room. After that, it wraps down to the next line and begins placing components on the left side of that line. You can also specify an alignment, as the following line of code does:

```
FlowLayout flowingButtons = new FlowLayout(FlowLayout.CENTER);
```

Here the components are placed with an equal amount of blank space to the left and right of the components. The alignment options are LEFT, RIGHT, and CENTER.

If you don't like tightly packed components, you can specify the number of pixels between the components:

```
FlowLayout flowingButtons = new FlowLayout(FlowLayout.CENTER,10,15);
```

This separates the buttons horizontally by 10 pixels and vertically separates the rows by 15 pixels.

As with components, simply creating the layout manager doesn't affect the applet much, so we have to call the applet's *setLayout* method to apply the layout to the applet display area. Here's that code:

```
setLayout(flowingButtons);
```

Once we have applied the layout manager to the applet, we can add the components. Here's an applet fragment that creates a few buttons, sets up a layout manager, and adds the buttons in the *init* method:

```
Button ok = new Button("OK");
Button cancel = new Button("Cancel");
Button apply = new Button("Apply");
Button options = new Button("Options…");
Button properties = new Button("Properties");
public void init ()
{
    FlowLayout flowingButtons = new
FlowLayout(FlowLayout.CENTER,10,15);
    setLayout(flowingButtons);
    add(ok);
    add(cancel);
    add(apply);
    add(options);
    add(properties);
}
```

Figure 6-15 shows this layout manager in action with these buttons.

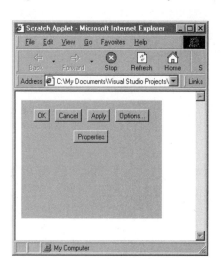

Figure 6-15. *Buttons displayed with the* FlowLayout *layout manager.*

 IP Another way to see buttons "flow" in a display is to bring up the Properties dialog box of your project (under the Project menu), and click the Launch tab. In the drop-down box labeled When Project Loads, Run, select your applet class. Now when you run the project, the applet code runs without Internet Explorer; instead, the applet runs in the Visual J++ appletviewer. The appletviewer window can be easily resized to show you how your applet will appear using different window sizes.

Here's that same set of buttons using *GridLayout*:

```
public void init ()
{
    GridLayout gridButtons = new GridLayout(0,3,10,15);
```

The first two parameters in the construction of a *GridLayout* object are the number of rows and columns in the grid. The number of rows here is zero, because *GridLayout* allows you to specify only the number of rows or the number of columns. In this example, since we are adding five buttons in a grid that always has three columns, the grid automatically has two rows. If you try to specify both rows and columns, the value for columns is ignored. The last two parameters specify the number of pixels between each column and the numbers of pixels between each row, respectively.

```
    setLayout(gridButtons);
```

The preceding line sets the layout for the applet as before. Then, the buttons (or any components) are added as usual:

```
add(ok);
add(cancel);
add(apply);
add(options);
add(properties);
}
```

Figure 6-16 shows a picture of this layout.

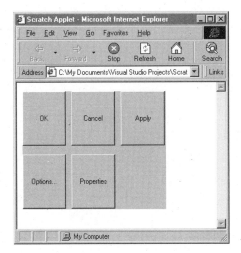

Figure 6-16.   *Using the* GridLayout *layout manager.*

BorderLayout works like a map. In order to create a *BorderLayout* layout manager for an applet, you must add the buttons using an additional parameter value (*"North"* for the top of the display area, *"East"* for the right side, *"West"* for the left, *"South"* for the bottom, and *"Center"* for anything else). Here's an example:

```
public void init ()
{
    BorderLayout borderButtons = new BorderLayout(10,15);
    setLayout(borderButtons);
    add("North",ok);
    add("East",cancel);
    add("West",apply);
    add("South",options);
    add("Center",properties);
}
```

The code above creates the *BorderLayout* object with 10 pixels of empty space between columns on the horizontal and 15 pixels of empty space between rows on the vertical.

The *add* method is what differentiates *BorderLayout* from the two previous layout managers. Specifying the directional parameter tells the layout manager where to place the buttons.

Figure 6-17 shows a picture of this layout.

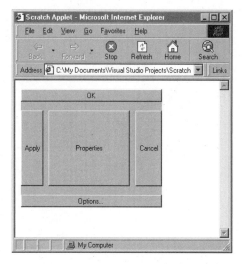

Figure 6-17. *Arranging buttons with a* BorderLayout *layout manager.*

A couple of important notes about *BorderLayout*: If you don't specify a directional parameter, the component won't show up in the display area at all; and if you specify two components using the same direction, then the last one added will completely cover the first one.

Before we discuss the *CardLayout* layout manager, let's talk about panels for a moment. The *Panel* class hosts AWT components much as the *Form* class of WFC hosts WFC controls. In fact, the reason that an applet class can host components is that the *Applet* class is a subclass of *Panel*.

To have more control over the placement of components in our applet display area, we can group components in panels. If we take the last three examples of layout managers and place them all in the display area at the same time, but each on a different panel, the display area looks like Figure 6-18.

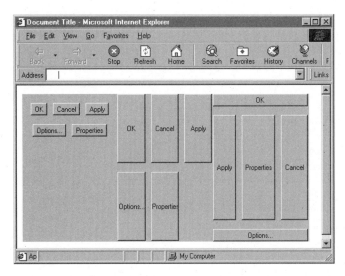

Figure 6-18. *An applet displaying three panels using three different layout managers.*

Admittedly, the design is a bit messy, but this demonstrates how you can arrange components in a display area using more than one layout manager. Keep in mind that we are using buttons in the example, but you can put any sort of component on a panel. You might have a panel full of radio buttons and check boxes as part of an Options dialog box.

This next example shows how you might arrange components in an applet display area using three panels. Note that since you can't add the same component to more than one panel at a time, two additional sets of our five buttons are needed for the second and third panels. For our example, we will assume that we've taken the code we used to define the original set of buttons and made the panel components unique by simply appending a digit to their names (for example, *ok*, *ok2*, and *ok3*).

```
public void init ()
    {
```

First, we create a new *Panel* object:

```
Panel flowPanel = new Panel();
```

And then a new layout manager:

```
FlowLayout flowingButtons = new
FlowLayout(FlowLayout.CENTER,10,15);
```

Next, we apply the layout manager to the panel, rather than to the whole applet as we did before:

```
flowPanel.setLayout(flowingButtons);
```

Finally, we add the components to the *Panel* object, rather than directly to the display area:

```
flowPanel.add(ok);
flowPanel.add(cancel);
flowPanel.add(apply);
flowPanel.add(options);
flowPanel.add(properties);
```

We repeat the process with another panel and another layout manager:

```
Panel gridPanel = new Panel();
GridLayout gridButtons = new GridLayout(0,3,10,15);
gridPanel.setLayout(gridButtons);
gridPanel.add(ok2);
gridPanel.add(cancel2);
gridPanel.add(apply2);
gridPanel.add(options2);
gridPanel.add(properties2);
```

And then another:

```
Panel borderPanel = new Panel();
BorderLayout borderButtons = new BorderLayout(10,15);
borderPanel.setLayout(borderButtons);
borderPanel.add("North",ok3);
borderPanel.add("East",cancel3);
borderPanel.add("West",apply3);
borderPanel.add("South",options3);
borderPanel.add("Center",properties3);
```

Our last step is to create a layout for the applet as a whole and then add the panels to the display area:

```
        GridLayout appletLayout = new GridLayout(0,3);
        setLayout(appletLayout);
        add(flowPanel);
        add(gridPanel);
        add(borderPanel);
    }
```

This brings us back to the last layout manager, *CardLayout*. If you didn't want to see all the panels in your layout at once, you might place your *Panel* objects using *CardLayout* so that only one panel is seen at a time.

If you replace the last five code lines in the previous example with the following code, then each panel will be on a card in a *CardLayout* object:

```
        CardLayout appletLayout = new CardLayout();
        setLayout(appletLayout);
        add(flowPanel);
        add(gridPanel);
        add(borderPanel);
        flowPanel.show(false);
        gridPanel.show(true);
        borderPanel.show(false);
```

This example hides *flowPanel* and *borderPanel* while displaying the *gridPanel* layout. Elsewhere in the applet might be an override of the *action* method that brings the *flowPanel* layout or the *borderPanel* layout to the front while hiding *gridPanel*.

Lab 6-2: Revisiting Hello as an Applet

In this lab, we will create an applet that behaves much the same way as the Hello application that we created in Chapter 2.

Lab overview

You will practice:

- Creating an applet with AWT components.

- Embedding your applet in an HTML document.

As with the application version of this lab, this applet will allow you to type a name into a text field and then click the OK button to see a change in the greeting at the top of the applet display area.

Lab setup

1. Start Visual J++ and create an empty project called HelloApplet.

2. Add a Java class to the project called *HelloApplet* (filename HelloApplet.java).

3. Add a Web page to the project called HelloApplet (filename HelloApplet.htm) and an <APPLET> tag with HEIGHT and WIDTH attributes.

4. Run your project code to make sure that everything is set up correctly. If it is, a gray box 200 pixels wide and 200 pixels high (or whatever height and width you specified) will appear inside an Internet Explorer window. You can close the window and return to the Visual J++ environment to work on your applet.

Lab instructions

1. Add member variables to your applet for a text field, a button, and a label.

2. Override the *init* method in your applet to create objects for these references. Place the components in your applet display area using *FlowLayout*. Call the *repaint* method at the end of the *init* method.

3. Override the *action* method of your applet. If the target of the event that caused the *action* method to be called was the OK button, then set the text of the *Label* object to be *Hello* plus the text of the *TextField* object.

4. Run your project, type your name in the text field, and click the OK button. You can check your work against the solution in Chapter06\Sol6-2\HelloApplet.sln.

Next steps

We can now build basic applets and populate them with AWT components. Next we will add images and sounds to our applets.

Enhancing Your Applet

Now that we can create a basic applet with a few AWT components, our next step is to add the multimedia capabilities for which Java is so famous on the Internet. We'll start with pictures and sound, and then move on to reading parameters into our Java applet from the HTML host file. Finally, we'll see how we can add JScript code to our Web pages to bring them alive.

In this chapter, you will learn about:

- Playing sounds and displaying pictures in applets
- Changing applet characteristics using the HTML <PARAM> tag
- Using JScript to communicate with applets

You will get a chance to:

- Play sound files.
- Display image files.
- Communicate with your applet via a <PARAM> tag in an HTML document.
- Customize the behavior of your applet using JScript.

Using Media Files in Applets

Java applets come equipped to use pictures and sound. All we have to do is fill in the blanks. In this chapter, we will see how to place images and sounds in our applets. Later, we will use this foundation to build applets that provide animation.

Showing an Image in an Applet

To display an image in an applet, we start by creating a member variable of type *Image*. Then, when we need to bring the image into our program, we call the *getImage* method of the *Applet* class. Finally, to display the image, we call the *drawImage* method of the *Graphics* class. Typically, *getImage* is used in our override of the *init* method, and *drawImage* is evoked through our override of the *paint* method. What follows is an example of an applet class that displays an *Image* object.

All the resources that we need are in either the java.applet package or the java.awt package, so we add these two *import* statements:

```
import java.applet.*;
import java.awt.*;

public class DisplayImage extends Applet
{
```

The member variable *balloons* is used to access our *Image* object:

```
    private Image balloons;
    public void init ()
    {
```

As we initialize our applet, we call *getImage* to get a reference to the *Image* object that we will later display on the screen:

```
        balloons = getImage(getCodeBase(),
            "Balloons.jpg");
    }
```

Finally, in order to show the image, we call the *drawImage* method of the *Graphics* class:

```
public void paint (Graphics g)
{
    g.drawImage(balloons,0,0,this);
}
}
```

Taking a closer look at the call to the *getImage* method, we see that it takes two parameters:

```
balloons = getImage(getCodeBase(),
            "Balloons.jpg");
```

The first parameter specifies the location of the image file. To acquire this information, we've used a call to another method of the applet class: *getCodeBase*. The return value of the *getCodeBase* method is the value of the CODEBASE attribute supplied in the HTML file associated with the applet. This value will be the name of the folder where files that support the execution of the applet can be found. If the CODEBASE attribute is not included in the HTML file, then the return value of the *getCodeBase* method will be the directory of the applet bytecode file (with the file extension .class). Consider this example of an <APPLET> tag in an HTML file:

```
<APPLET
CODE=Applet1.class
CODEBASE="file://C:\My Documents\Visual Studio Projects\images"
NAME=Applet1
WIDTH=320
HEIGHT=200>
```

Since the CODEBASE attribute of this <APPLET> tag is "file://C:\My Documents\Visual Studio Projects\images," the *getCodeBase* method returns this pathname.

In our *DisplayImage* example, the class files we're accessing are in the same place as our Java source code and Web files, so we haven't used the CODEBASE attribute in our HTML file. Therefore, the call to *getCodeBase* returns the folder of our applet. The advantage of using *getCodeBase* is that if you move your files into another folder, everything still works as long as they all get moved together and you include or change the value of the <APPLET> CODEBASE attribute. The second parameter of the *getImage* call is the name of the image file to be loaded.

Here we are loading a JPEG image into our program (file extension .jpg), but we could also have loaded a GIF image (file extension .gif).

The Graphics method *drawImage* is then used in the *paint* method to actually render the image:

```
g.drawImage(balloons,0,0,this);
```

The *drawImage* method is overloaded, so there is more than one way to call it. The *drawImage* method we are using here takes the *Image* reference variable, followed by the coordinates of the upper left corner location of the image in the display area, and finally by the host for the image. In this case, we have placed the image directly in the applet display area by specifying the keyword *this*.

Playing Sounds in an Applet

Playing sounds from our applet is a three-step process. First, we create an *AudioClip* reference variable. *AudioClip* is located in the java.applet package. Second, we call the *getAudioClip* method to load the audio file. Third, we call the *play* method of the *AudioClip* object when we're actually ready to play the audio file.

We will use a button in the display area to activate the *AudioClip* object from within the applet. Here's how we will do that:

```
import java.applet.*;
import java.awt.*;

public class PlaySound extends Applet
{
```

Here's the *AudioClip* member variable:

```
    private AudioClip drip;
    private Button playDrip;
    public void init ()
    {
```

This is where we associate our *AudioClip* member variable with the audio file. Notice that the *getAudioClip* method, like the *getImage* method we discussed in the previous section, also has a parameter that serves to tell the method where to look for the audio file. The second parameter is the name of the audio file:

```
        drip = getAudioClip(getCodeBase(),"drip.au");
        playDrip = new Button("Drip");
        add (playDrip);
}
public boolean action (Event e, Object helper)
{
        if (e.target == playDrip)
        {
```

Our *action* method is where we activate the *AudioClip* object using the *play* method:

```
        drip.play();
}
        return super.action (e, helper);
    }
}
```

The audio files that you can play from within your applets are sound clip files (file extension .au).

Sending Parameters to an Applet

Often, the key to a good applet is flexibility, and flexibility is what the <PARAM> tag provides. By allowing those who embed our Java applets in their HTML documents the chance to customize some of the behavior or characteristics of our running applet code, we are making our programs more useful in more situations and for more people on the World Wide Web.

The <PARAM> Tag

The mechanism for pulling external information into our applet comes in two parts: the <PARAM> tag with its associated attributes and the *getParameter* method. The tag shows up in an HTML document, and the *getParameter* method is typically called inside the *init* method of an applet.

Let's construct a variation on the *Hello* applet using <PARAM> and *getParameter*. We start by creating a new empty project in Visual J++. Then we add a Web page, and we replace the line

```
<!-- Insert HTML here -->
```

with the following:

```
<APPLET CODE=HelloName.class WIDTH=200 HEIGHT=200>
<PARAM NAME="who" VALUE="Java Applet Master">
</APPLET>
```

As we learned in Chapter 6, <PARAM> tags are closely associated with the <APPLET> tag. The two attributes of <PARAM> are NAME and VALUE. The name of a parameter (that is, the value of the NAME attribute) must be known by the applet code in order for the applet to use the associated value. While the name of the parameter (for example, *"who"*) is predetermined in the applet code, VALUE can be any string. It is up to you as the applet programmer to provide anyone using your applet with a list of the available parameters.

Reading Parameters into an Applet

Our next step is to write the code in the applet to read the value for the parameter from the HTML file. Here is the applet code for doing that. Things start out the same as in our other applets:

```
//HelloName.java
import java.applet.*;
import java.awt.*;

public class HelloName extends Applet
{
```

We declare a *String* member variable that holds the value read in from the applet <PARAM> tag:

```
    private String who;
```

Then comes the initialization routine, *init*:

```
    public void init ()
    {
```

We call the *getParameter* method with a *String* parameter whose value matches the value of the NAME attribute of a corresponding <PARAM> tag in the HTML file. The method returns the value of the VALUE attribute associated with NAME. In this case, since we pass it the NAME value of *"who"*, it returns the string *"Java Applet Master"* and assigns that value to the *who* member variable:

```
who = getParameter("who");
```

It is good practice to verify that a value was returned and provide for that eventuality:

```
if (who == null)
{
    who = "World";
}
}
```

If the *who* member variable is *null*, then either the <PARAM> tag was not included in the HTML document, or the applet may be executing from within an appletviewer that does not interpret HTML code. In any case, if *who* is *null*, we want to provide a default generic greeting:

```
public void paint(Graphics g)
{
    super.paint(g);
```

All that is left to do is construct the text string to be drawn in the applet display area and use the *drawString* method to display it:

```
g.drawString("Hello " + who + "!",50,50);
}
}
```

If you want to see the effect of not including the <PARAM> tag when running this applet, comment it out by placing

```
<!--
```

in front of the <PARAM> tag, and

```
-->
```

after it. If you have commented it out correctly, the text between these tokens should turn gray. Rerun the applet and see how it behaves.

Here's another example, which sets the background color of the applet display area to the color red. We start again with the required HTML <APPLET> tag with the accompanying <PARAM> tag:

```
<APPLET code=RedApplet.class HEIGHT=200 WIDTH=200 >
<PARAM NAME="background color" VALUE="Red">
</APPLET>
```

The applet code looks like this:

```
import java.applet.*;
import java.awt.*;

public class RedApplet extends Applet
{
    public void init ()
    {
```

Once again, we call the *getParameter* method to get the contents of the VALUE attribute using the value of the NAME attribute:

```
        String backgroundParameter =
            getParameter("background color");
```

Then we can test the return value of *getParameter* and take the appropriate action:

```
        if (backgroundParameter.equals("Red"))
        {
            setBackground(Color.red);
        }
        else if (backgroundParameter.equals("Blue"))
        {
            setBackground(Color.blue);
        }
    }
}
```

Try changing the <PARAM> tag NAME attribute to *"Blue"* (take care to match the case of the letters) in order to change the background color from red to blue.

Lab 7-1: Working with Images, Sounds, and the <PARAM> Tag

We have seen how to render images, play sounds, and customize our applets using the HTML tag <PARAM>. In this lab we bring all of those elements together.

Lab overview

In this lab, you will practice:

■ Loading and displaying *Image* objects.

■ Loading and playing *AudioClip* objects.

■ Embedding <PARAM> tags in HTML files.

■ Reading the value of <PARAM> tags from within Java code.

The applet that you write for this lab will render an *Image* object and play an *AudioClip* object. It will determine which image file to display and which sound clip file to play based on the value of two HTML <PARAM> tags.

Lab setup

1. Copy the *.au and *.jpg files from Chapter07\Lab7-1 to the directory you will use for this project.

2. Start Visual J++, and create an empty project called AudioImage.

3. Create a class file for your Java applet and an HTML file for your Web page.

Lab instructions

1. In your applet code file, create member variables of types *Image*, *AudioClip*, and *Button*.

2. Override the *init* method, and create local variables for storing the *String* values of the image file and sound clip file.

3. Provide the local *String* variables with values by assigning them the return values of two calls (one for the *Image* parameter and one for the *Audio* parameter) to the *getParameter* method.

4. Check each of the local *String* variables to see if they are *null*. If either is *null*, assign it a default filename. Place two image files and two sound clip files in your project directory for testing the return value of *getParameter*.

5. Create a *Button* object and assign its reference to your *Button* member variable.

6. Add that button to your applet display area using the *add* method.

7. Override the *paint* method to use *drawImage* to display the *Image* object.

8. Override the *action* method to play the sound clip file if the button is pressed.

9. Include the following HTML code in your project Web page (this HTML code goes between <BODY> and </BODY>):

```
<APPLET CODE=AudioImage.class WIDTH=200 HEIGHT=200>
<PARAM NAME="Audio" VALUE="drip.au">
<PARAM NAME="Image" VALUE="Balloons.jpg">
</APPLET>
```

10. Run the project. You should see the image in the applet display area. Click the button, and you should hear the sound clip file being played. You can compare your work to the solution located in Chapter07\Sol7-1\AudioImage.sln.

11. Remove the two <PARAM> tags from the HTML file. How does your applet behave differently?

Next steps

We have seen how an applet can be embedded in a Web page, and we have used the <PARAM> tag to communicate with the applet from HTML. This use of an applet in a Web page is mostly passive. Our next step is to write programming code in the Web page itself using JScript.

Applets and the Web Page

The World Wide Web was originally intended to be a mechanism for distributing literature. Web pages were more or less pages of text that could be electronically published quickly and easily for distribution around the world. The leap to electronic publishing was impressive, but people quickly hungered for a more interactive sort of Web page. Interactive pages provide an effective interface through the use of elements such as buttons and check boxes, and they respond dynamically and adapt to users.

HTML does a lot of things, but it is not a programming language and was never intended to be. JavaScript was developed to extend HTML functionality by allowing scripts, or interpreted programming code, to be embedded in HTML code.

The variant of JavaScript that we will be using is called JScript. JScript code can interact with an applet to customize the behavior of the applet. This allows us to reuse the applet code with different Web pages and modifiable JScript to achieve different effects without having to recode and recompile the Java applet.

Although JScript was developed to fill the gap between passive HTML and a full-power Java applet, it is a programming language in its own right. Our discussion of JScript will provide only a glimpse of its capabilities. What we will do here is build a Web page with Visual J++, using an applet and embedded JScript to demonstrate how all of these basic elements work together.

Applet-to-Web Page Communication

Our first step in building an active Web page that interacts with an applet is to create an applet that includes one or more *public* methods and *public* member variables that can be accessed by the JScript functions we include in the HTML document.

 OTE   When writing JScript code, it is important that you directly reference an applet's variables only if they are declared *final*, and use the applet's *public* methods to access any of its non-final variables. This will help you achieve the desired effect from your Web page.

Our exercise at the end of this section is to complete a Web page using HTML, an applet, and JScript code. The Web page displays houses for sale and simple descriptions of them for viewing on the Internet by prospective clients. The applet for this exercise is supplied to you and contains Java code with which you are familiar from previous discussions. Before we start the exercise, let's examine key pieces of this code so that you can see how they will connect with the JScript code that we will write.

If you would like to preview the code as we cover the information, preliminary files can be found in the House project (Chapter07\House\ HouseDisplay.sln). Open the project in Visual J++ and double-click HouseDisplay.java.

```
public class HouseDisplay extends Applet
{
```

To start, we declare three *public* member variables. These constants are used by JScript to tell the Java applet which house's picture we want to display on the Web page. Any element in the applet code marked *public* is available to the JScript code. The remaining declarations create typical member variables for an applet:

```
public static final int house1 = 1;
public static final int house2 = 2;
public static final int house3 = 3;

private boolean showHouse = false;
private Font font = new Font("TimesRoman", Font.BOLD, 14);
private Image house1Img;
private Image house2Img;
private Image house3Img;
private Image currentImg;
private String message;
```

The JScript code we are creating passes values to the *setDisplay* method that tell the applet which of the three possible images should be rendered. Notice the call to *repaint* at the bottom of this method, which causes the newly selected image to be displayed:

```
public void setDisplay(int houseNumber)
{
    if (houseNumber == house1)
    {
        currentImg = house1Img;
        showHouse = true;
    }
    else if (houseNumber == house2)
    {
        currentImg = house2Img;
        showHouse = true;
    }
    else if (houseNumber == house3)
    {
        currentImg = house3Img;
        showHouse = true;
    }
    this.repaint();
}
```

The applet also gives us the option of displaying an image or a text message. Later, we will make use of this option by writing JScript to either display a picture or draw text in the applet display area. Which one we choose depends on what is more appropriate to the situation as our applet executes. Here's the method that our JScript code will use to set the text of the message to be displayed:

```
public void setMessage (String text)
{
    message = text;
    showHouse = false;
    this.repaint();
}
```

The override of the *paint* method for this applet displays either a text message or an image, as determined by calls to *setDisplay* and *setMessage*. Notice the use of the *getSize* method, along with the *width* and *height* member variables, in the following code to determine the size of the applet on the Web page. The value of *getSize().width* allows us to determine the value of the WIDTH attribute associated with the

<APPLET> tag in the HTML file. The call to *g.clearRect* clears a rectangle, starting in the upper left corner of the applet display area, for the width and height of the entire display area. By calling the *Graphics* method *drawImage* with *x* and *y* offsets, we can center the image on the display area:

```
public void paint (Graphics g)
{
    int imageWidth;
    int imageHeight;
    int xOffset;
    int yOffset;

    g.clearRect(0,0,
        this.getSize().width,
        this.getSize().height);
    if (showHouse)
    {
        imageWidth = currentImg.getWidth(this);
        imageHeight = currentImg.getHeight(this);
        xOffset = (this.getSize().width - imageWidth) /2;
        yOffset = (this.getSize().height - imageHeight) /2;
        g.drawImage(currentImg,xOffset,yOffset,this);
    }
    else
    {
        g.setFont(font);
        g.drawString(message,5,50);
    }
}
```

Here's the method that reads the parameter values in the <PARAM> tag on the Web page. If *houseGif* is *null*, then the <PARAM> tag for this value is not included on the Web page; or, if *houseGif* is an empty string (""), then a <PARAM> tag is included, but no image file is specified in the VALUE attribute. We use a default image ("NoPicture.gif") to handle either possibility:

```
private void getParameters()
    {
        String houseGif;
        houseGif = this.getParameter("house1");

        if (houseGif == null || houseGif.equals(""))
        {
            house1Img = getImage(getCodeBase(),"NoPicture.gif");
        }
        else
        {
            house1Img = getImage(getCodeBase(),houseGif);
        }

        houseGif = this.getParameter("house2");
        if (houseGif == null || houseGif.equals(""))
        {
            house2Img = getImage(getCodeBase(),"NoPicture.gif");
        }
        else
        {
            house2Img = getImage(getCodeBase(),houseGif);
        }

        houseGif = this.getParameter("house3");
        if (houseGif == null || houseGif.equals(""))
        {
            house3Img = getImage(getCodeBase(),"NoPicture.gif");
        }
        else
        {
            house3Img = getImage(getCodeBase(),houseGif);
        }
    }
```

The override of the *init* method calls *getParameters*. The *getParameters*
method loads the appropriate image files as specified by the values of the
<PARAM> attributes. The applet is then fully initialized and ready to
interact with the user:

```
public void init()
{
    super.init();
    getParameters();
}
}
```

Our first step is complete: we have an applet with a few *public* methods and variables that JScript can use to customize the run-time behavior of the applet. Next, we build a host HTML Web page for the applet, HTML controls, and JScript code.

Using HTML Controls

We can use Visual J++ to build controls on a Web page in much the same way that we build Windows application interfaces by dropping WFC controls onto forms. Once we have the controls on the Web page, we can add event handlers to particular events just as we did with Windows applications. In our HTML Web pages, these event handlers will be written in JScript.

If you have not already done so, open the preliminary House project (Chapter07\House\HouseDisplay.sln). Add a Web page to the project, and call it HouseOfHouses.htm. This brings up a blank HTML code window with the Design tab selected. Type the following text into the HTML file window:

```
Welcome to The City View House Company's "House of Houses" Homepage!

To read a description of a house for sale, just move the cursor over
one of the buttons. To see a picture of the house, click the button.
```

To see how this text looks in HTML code, click the Source tab. Visual J++ has automatically added all the appropriate HTML code around your text. Click the Design tab again, and we'll add some buttons to the Web page. Bring up the Toolbox window, and select the drop-down box labeled HTML at the top. See Figure 7-1 for a picture of the Toolbox window with the HTML tools displayed.

Figure 7-1. *The Toolbox window's HTML components.*

From the HTML Toolbox, select a Button component and drag it to the HTML page. Put the button beneath the text you typed. To make sure of this alignment, you can add a carriage return after the text, or position your cursor directly before the button, and then double-click the Line Break component. (You can see the difference in the HTML code by clicking the Source tab.) Add a space (use the Spacebar, or double-click Space in the Toolbox), and then add another button to the right of the first. Add a third button to the right of the first two.

If you click a button with the cursor, you will see that you can change the caption of the button. Change the three buttons to use the captions *City View House*, *Cute 1 Bedroom*, and *Lakeside Beauty*, respectively.

Click the Source tab, and add the following HTML <APPLET> tag after the code for the third button and before the end of the HTML body (</BODY):

```
<APPLET code=HouseDisplay.class name=housedisplay
height=300 width=500 >
    <PARAM NAME="house1" VALUE="CityView.gif">
    <PARAM NAME="house2" VALUE="Cute1Bedroom.gif">
    <PARAM NAME="house3" VALUE="LakeSide.gif">
Your Browser must be Java-enabled to see City View's Houses
</APPLET>
```

This <APPLET> tag with its associated <PARAM> tags installs the *HouseDisplay* applet on the Web page and passes it the names of the three GIF files to be displayed as the user requests. These filenames are then *parsed* (read and processed) by the *getParameters* method in *HouseDisplay*.

Click the Quick View tab of the HTML window, and you will see that a 500×300 pixel area has been set aside for the applet display area on your Web page. Figure 7-2 shows an example of how this looks.

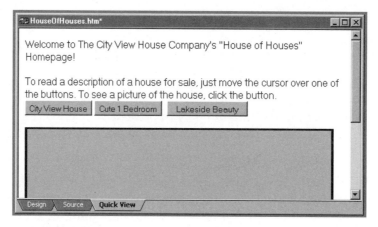

Figure 7-2.   *Your HTML page for HouseOfHouses.*

HTML Outline

Back in Chapter 5, we used the Class Outline window to help us see the overall structure of our application. A similar tool, known as the HTML Outline window, works with HTML files. You get to this window by selecting Other Windows from the View menu, and then selecting Document Outline. When you select Document Outline with an HTML file active, Visual J++ brings up an HTML Outline window, rather than the Class Outline window that we saw in Chapter 5. When the Quick View tab is selected, the HTML Outline window displays the following message:

```
There are no items to show for the selected document.
```

Click the Design or Source tab, and you will see that the HTML Outline window looks like Figure 7-3.

Figure 7-3.   *The HTML Outline window.*

Click any of the elements in the HTML Outline window, and you will see that same element selected in the HTML code window. Select button1 in the HTML Outline window, and then click the Source tab of the HTML code window. Notice that the cursor is focused at the point in the HTML code where *button1* is defined. Click button3 in the HTML Outline window, and the cursor moves to find the definition of *button3*. Click housedisplay in the HTML Outline window to see the <APPLET> tag that you typed earlier. If you right-click the applet placeholder in the code window, you can view the <APPLET> code by selecting the Always View As Text check box. Clearing Always View As Text returns you to the placeholder.

HTML Properties

Just as we set the properties of WFC controls using the Properties window, we can change the properties of our HTML components using the Properties window. In the HTML code window, click the Design tab. In the HTML Outline window, select <BODY>. The top of the Properties window indicates that we are now looking at the properties of DOCUMENT. If the

Properties window is not visible, you can bring it up by selecting Properties Window from the View menu. Figure 7-4 shows the DOCUMENT component in the Properties window.

Figure 7-4.   *The Properties window with DOCUMENT selected.*

In the Properties window, locate the background property and change its setting to *Background.bmp.* Your applet background will now change as this file is loaded. In the HTML Outline window, select *button1*. Scroll in the Properties window to the backgroundColor property, and choose a color for *button1* from the Color dialog box that appears. Repeat the process with the other two buttons. Select DOCUMENT from the drop-down box at the top of the Properties window, and change the setting of the title property to *City View House Company.* If you look at the HTML source code, you will see that the <TITLE> tag reflects this change. It now looks like this:

```
<TITLE>City View House Company</TITLE>
```

To give your applet a nice border, select the applet in the HTML Outline window or the HTML code window, go to the Properties window ("<APPLET>" should appear in the drop-down box at the top), and set borderBottom, borderLeft, borderRight, and borderTop to *solid.*

You can change the identification of any HTML component by changing the (Id) property of that component in the HTML Properties window. Since the (Id) property name includes the parentheses, it appears at the top of the HTML Properties window list. Changes to the (Id) property of a component are reflected in the HTML Outline window. We want to keep things simple for our example, so we leave the (Id) properties of the HTML button components with their default values of *button1*, *button2*, and *button3*.

Script Outline

The Script Outline window is just about your best friend when it comes to keeping track of the JScript code that you are going to write or have already written. We will use this tool to insert JScript code into our HTML page. It will help us keep track of many of the structural details of the JScript code in our HTML page, freeing us to concentrate on writing the actual code.

With the Source tab selected in the HTML code window, open the Script Outline window by clicking the Script Outline tab at the bottom of the Toolbox window. Figure 7-5 shows the Script Outline window for our HTML file.

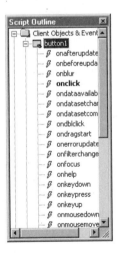

Figure 7-5. *The Script Outline window.*

Of the four folders in the Script Outline window, we are interested only in the two that relate to client objects and scripts. "Client" refers to the computers that will be downloading our Web page. The Client Objects & Events folder contains all the HTML components that we have added to our page plus the *Document* and *Window* objects. The *Window* object contains the *Document* object, and the *Document* object, in turn, contains any objects that we place on the page. In our case, the *Document* object contains the three buttons and the applet named *HouseDisplay*.

The Client Scripts folder is currently empty because we haven't added any scripts yet.

The names of the *HTML* objects (in our case *button1*, *button2*, and *button3*) as they appear in the Script Outline window come from the name property value in the HTML Properties window. The value of the name property, in turn, comes from the value assigned to the NAME attribute of the <BUTTON> tag in the HTML file. It is easy to get the name property confused with the (Id) property. The (Id) property value appears in the HTML Outline window, while the name property value appears in the Script Outline window.

Writing JScript

Let's add a script to *button1* that causes an image file to be rendered in the applet display area when the button is clicked. Start by expanding the list to the left of *button1* in the Script Outline window. A list of all the events associated with *button1* appears. This is shown in Figure 7-6.

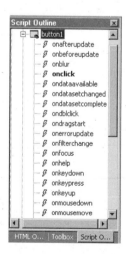

Figure 7-6.   *The Script Outline window lists events for HTML components.*

With this list displayed in the Script Outline window, we can see all the events associated with HTML buttons. This is similar to the events associated with WFC controls. A JScript function can be associated with any, all, or none of these events. Such a JScript function is analogous to an event handler in Java.

Find the Onclick event and double-click it. When you do, the HTML code window changes, and in it appears the following code:

```
<SCRIPT ID=clientEventHandlersJS LANGUAGE=javascript>
<!--

function button1_onclick()
{

}

//-->
</SCRIPT>
```

What you see here is the <SCRIPT> tag being placed into your HTML file along with the skeleton of the event handler for handling a Click event for *button1*. Notice that the value given to the LANGUAGE attribute is *javascript*. Remember that JScript is a variant of JavaScript. The "<!--" starts an HTML comment and "-->" ends it. The HTML comment markers are placed in the file to hide HMTL scripting code from older browsers that do not support scripts. The script area is closed by the </SCRIPT> tag.

With Visual J++ inserting the surrounding syntax for us, all we have to do to handle this event is place a call to one of our applet's *public* methods between the curly braces ({ }).

This JScript function is then called when the user of our Web page clicks the *button1* button. First, however, we must determine the name of the applet object created based on our applet class. We examine the <APPLET> tag that we inserted earlier, and we see the NAME attribute is set to *housedisplay*. This is the name of the instance of our applet (that is, the object of class *HouseDisplay*), and it allows us to access our applet as we would any other object. (Note that if the NAME attribute in the <APPLET> tag were to be removed, the element would show up as "<APPLET>" in the HTML Outline window.) As you will recall from our applet code, there is a *public* method called *setDisplay*. Because the method is *public*, we can call it from within the JScript code. The *setDisplay* method takes a parameter of type *int*, representing the house image that should be displayed. We can put in *1*, *2*, or *3* as the parameter value, or we can reference the *public* static final int member variables in our applet. Our event handler for *button1* looks like this:

```
function button1_onclick()
{
    housedisplay.setDisplay(housedisplay.house1)
}
```

Run the project in Internet Explorer. When the Web page comes up, click the button labeled City View House, and you will see the house image displayed. Close Internet Explorer, and return to the Visual J++ environment.

Now that we have run our project, from here on we can use Quick View to approximate its operation in a Web page. Click the Quick View tab from the HTML code window, and then click the City View House button, and you will see the City View House image rendered again.

In addition to rendering images, our applet can also display messages. Still working with *button1*, let's script a call to the method *setMessage* for the Onmouseover event of *button1*. In the Script Outline window, expand the folder for *button1*, find onmouseover, and double-click it. A skeleton of the *button1_mouseover* function appears in the script area of the HTML page. Add a call to the *setMessage* method as you see in the following code:

```
function button1_onmouseover()
{
    housedisplay.setMessage("Our flagship. Sweeping view of the City."
+        " Priced to move.")
}
```

Click the Quick View tab, and test *button1*. It should now show a text message when you move the mouse over it, and display an image when you click it. Nice job! You have now successfully scripted your applet using two different JScript events. There's a lot more to JScript and HTML than we can cover here, but this is about all there is to making the connection between Java and JScript.

Incidentally, if you want to see the connection between events and buttons in the HTML code, examine the <INPUT> tag for *button1*. You will see that the following attributes and values were added to this tag:

```
LANGUAGE=javascript onclick="return button1_onclick()"
   onmouseover="return button1_onmouseover()"
```

These should be removed if you decide that you don't need these events handled anymore.

Scripting applets is deceptively simple compared with the power it gives Web page developers. HTML developers do not even need to know Java in order to customize our applets and use them in Web pages. It would also be easy to simplify our *HouseDisplay* applet (for example, to remove the text messages) and then use it on any Web page where a set of images needs to be stored and displayed.

If you thought this example just begged for the use of arrays, you have a good point. Arrays are covered in Chapter 8.

Lab 7-2: Scripting the HouseOfHouses Web Page

Lab overview

In this lab, you will practice:

- Associating events in HTML with JScript functions.

- Using *public* methods and member variables from an applet in JScript code.

Scripting an applet is a matter of connecting JScript event handlers with the *public* methods of an applet object. We'll use Visual J++ to do just that in this laboratory exercise.

> **Lab setup**
>
> 1. If you have been following along with the example in the book, you can skip to the lab instructions.
>
> 2. If not, start Visual J++ and open the HouseOfHouses starter project (Chapter07\Lab7-2\HouseOfHouses.sln).

Lab instructions

1. Using the Script Outline window, add an event handler to the Onload event of *window*. The *Window* object is in the Client Objects & Events folder of the Script Outline window. Expand the list underneath the *Window* object, and double-click Onload. As before, a skeleton of the event handler will be provided for you. Add the following code to the JScript function as shown:

```
function window_onload()
{
    housedisplay.setMessage("Move the mouse over a button "+
        "for a description. Click a button to see"+
        "a picture.");
}
```

2. Add an event handler to the Onclick event of *button2*. The function causes the clicking of *button2* to display the image file associated with *housedisplay.house2*.

3. Associate an event handler with the Onmouseover event of *button2*. The function should display this message in the applet display area:

   "Cute 1 Bedroom. A perfect starter for the new family."

4. Repeat step 2 for *button3*, this time displaying *housedisplay.house3*.

5. Repeat step 3 for *button3*. This time the message should be:

   "A Lakeside Beauty with all the extras. Perfect retirement home."

6. Run the project to test your work. You can compare your work to the solution located in Chapter07\Sol7-2\HouseOfHouses.sln.

Optional lab enhancement

Here is an optional enhancement for you to try.

■ Try removing one or more of the <PARAM> tags for the HTML source code, and run the project again. Does the Web page behave as expected with the <PARAM> tags missing?

Saving Information

So far, we have been working with information on forms. You have learned how to display information to the user, collect information from the user, and verify that the information the user has given conforms to a predefined set of expectations. However, you have not yet learned how to store any of this information for later use. That is the topic of this chapter.

In this chapter, you'll learn about:

- *Arrays*, a type in Java used for handling multiple objects as a single object.

- Files, and how to read from and write to files using Visual J++.

- Lists, a WFC utility class that gives us more flexibility than arrays.

You will get practice using:

- Arrays

- Lists

- Files

- Interfaces

- The *ArraySorter* class

OTE Programmers often use databases for information storage and manipulation. The Standard Edition of Visual J++ does not provide direct support for databases. In Appendix D, you'll find a brief description of how to use the Component Object Model (COM) to work with a Microsoft Access database.

Working with Arrays

In this section, we'll introduce a different data type, the *array*. An array is an object that lets you manipuate a set of objects as a single unit. All the objects in the array must share the same data type. That's a little abstract; let's look at a concrete example.

Think of an ordinary phone list in a card-file format. A phone list is a good candidate for an array because all the data in it is of the same kind (names, addresses, and phone numbers). In the card file, you have a number of cards, each very similar to the others. They all have the same types of information on them, and they're easiest to use if the format of the information is similar on all the cards. The card file—all of the cards together with something that holds them together—is the array.

Each piece of data in an array is called an *element*. In the card file example, each card in the card file is one element in the array. Each element in the array has a number, or *index*, associated with it. To access a given element in the array, you use the index for that element.

As an example, let's try creating a card file in Java. To start, we create the *FileCard* class to represent a single file card:

```
class FileCard
{
    String name;
    String phoneNumber;
}
```

 OTE We could make this class more complete by including other pieces of information, such as the address or alternate phone numbers for work, home, fax, and so forth. This is a simple example.

Then we might try declaring several *FileCard* references to work with a number of different *FileCard* objects:

```
FileCard mom;
FileCard work;
FileCard cinema;
FileCard elvisPresley;
FileCard groceryStore;
```

However, that's not the way a card file works. And, it isn't the way an array works either. You can't just say

```
groceryStore.phoneNumber
```

and get the phone number of your local market. In a card file, you get the phone number for a grocery store by leafing through the card file and finding the card—that is, by determining the location of the card in the card file. In an array, you use an index (location) to access the element (card). As in the card file, you know that you have the card for the grocery store by looking at the *name* member variable.

The actual file cards in a card file are identified only by their location in the card file. The same is true in the array. Let's update our example to better reflect this:

```
FileCard arrayElement0; // Mom
FileCard arrayElement1; // Work
FileCard arrayElement2; // Cinema
FileCard arrayElement3; // Elvis Presley
FileCard arrayElement4; // Grocery Store
```

Then, to find out that *arrayElement0* is the file card for Mom, we look at its *name* member variable. And, by looking at the *name* member variable for all the cards, we can find the one for Elvis, *arrayElement3*.

 OTE The index value for arrays in Java starts at zero (0). That's why this example uses the names *arrayElement0, arrayElement1,* and so forth.

In the lab for this section, you will convert a simple phone list using individual *FileCard* references to use an array.

Declaring Arrays

Java arrays are objects. Like other kinds of objects, we access an array using a reference. The question now is what kind of reference is it? It's an *array* reference. To declare a reference, we need the reference type and name. Let's look at a familiar example of creating a reference:

```
String firstName;
```

In this example, the reference type is *String*. The name of the reference is *firstName*.

So, what does an *array* type look like? The type of an array is based on the type of the elements in the array. The type is created by adding braces [ ] after the name of the *element* type. Remember, all the elements in the array are of the same type.

Let's look at some examples. Here is the declaration for an array of *String* elements.

```
String[] daysOfTheWeek;
```

Like other reference declarations, this creates only the reference to an object. There's no *array* object yet. We'll create the array object in the next section. This array will hold the names of the seven days of the week. This is the example for this section. We'll build the example, little by little, over the course of this section. To see the code for the whole example, open the solution in Chapter08\Days\DayOfTheWeek.sln.

This example uses a familiar class, *String*. We can also create arrays of other classes or arrays of any one of the built-in types. Here is the declaration for an array of Boolean values:

```
boolean[] booleanArray;
```

And here is the declaration for an array of floating-point values:

```
float[] floatArray;
```

In addition, you can use an *array* type as the basis for another array type. In other words, you can create an array of arrays:

```
int[][] integerMatrix;
```

Here, *integerMatrix* is an array of arrays of integers. You can think of it as a two-dimensional array.

Creating Arrays

Declaring a reference for any class simply gives you a means to work with objects of that type. If you need a new object for your reference, you must explicitly create that object. As you did to create other kinds of objects, you use the keyword *new*. Constructors provide you a way to set values for the new object. In fact, sometimes you've had to provide information to create the object. Creating an array is no different. When you create an *array* object, you must give the number of elements in the array. This is called the *length* of the array.

To create an array object

■   Use the keyword *new* followed by the *element* type, and then the length of the array enclosed within braces.

Here is a bit more code from the DayOfTheWeek example:

```
String[] daysOfTheWeek;
...
daysOfTheWeek = new String[7];
```

Since the array *daysOfTheWeek* needs to hold the names of the seven days of the week, the *array* object was created with a length of seven; that is, space for seven elements.

Now we have an array of seven *String* references with a default value of *null*. It is almost as if we had written:

```
String daysOfTheWeek0;
String daysOfTheWeek1;
String daysOfTheWeek2;
String daysOfTheWeek3;
String daysOfTheWeek4;
String daysOfTheWeek5;
String daysOfTheWeek6;
```

Remember, at this point our *array* object contains seven *String* references, not seven *String* objects.

You can also create an array with specific initial values by providing a list of these values for the elements and enclosing them in braces after the array type. Here is an example of creating an array of five integers with initial values:

```
int[] listOfValues;
listOfValues = new int[] { 1, 2, 3, 4, 5 };
```

Notice that here the length of the array is determined by the number of values in the list, not a number given within the braces.

Accessing Array Elements

So, how do you get to the elements in an array?

To access an element of an array

■   Use the array reference followed by the index value within braces.

Here is the initialization code for the array from our example:

```
String[] daysOfTheWeek;
daysOfTheWeek = new String[7];
daysOfTheWeek[0] = "Sunday";
daysOfTheWeek[1] = "Monday";
daysOfTheWeek[2] = "Tuesday";
daysOfTheWeek[3] = "Wednesday";
daysOfTheWeek[4] = "Thursday";
daysOfTheWeek[5] = "Friday";
daysOfTheWeek[6] = "Saturday";
```

If you do not include the square braces, you are referring to the whole array.

Each element in the array *daysOfTheWeek* is a *String* reference. Here we assigned a *String* object to each of the seven *String* references. Remember that a value enclosed in quotation marks is a *String* object. Before this, each element had the value *null*.

Arrays as Objects

An array in Java is an object based on a specific class. The class is derived from an existing Java data type. A class defines what you can do with objects of that type.

You have already seen some of the specific things you can do with array classes:

- How to declare *array* references (no different than for any other type)

- How to create array objects by using the keyword *new* and specifying the length of the *array* object

- How to access individual elements of an array by means of an index value within square braces

You have also seen that these array index values are integers, starting with 0 (zero).

You can do other things with an *array* object. To get the length of an *array* object, use the *length* member variable. The *length* variable of an *array* object is read-only; that is, you can read the value, but not update it. For example, here's how to get the length of our *daysOfTheWeek* array:

```
String[] daysOfTheWeek;
daysOfTheWeek = new String[7];
...
if(input >= 0 & input < daysOfTheWeek.length)
{
    msg = "That's " + daysOfTheWeek[input] + ".";
}
else
{
    msg = "Value out of range. Values between 0 and 6 only.";
}
```

Lab 8-1: Improving a Phone List

Lab overview

In this lab, you will work with an application that displays names and phone numbers. Right now, it uses ten separate member variables to store the names and phone numbers. You will modify it to use an array rather than the separate member variables.

You will practice:

■   Declaring an array.

■   Creating an array object.

■   Working with the elements in that array object.

> ### Lab setup
>
> 1. Start Visual J++.
> 2. Open the PhoneList starter project (Chapter08\Lab8-1\ PhoneList.sln).

Lab instructions

1. Declare an array to hold the phone list.

    ■   Replace the 10 individual card declarations with the declaration of a single array. Name the array *cardFile*.

    ■   Replace the declaration of *currentCard* with *currentIndex*. Its data type is *int*. It holds the index value of the current *FileCard* object—that is, the one that is displayed on the form.

2. Create the array to hold the phone list.

    ■   Before the statements that create the *FileCard* objects, add a statement to create the array with 10 elements.

    ■   Modify statements that create the *FileCard* objects, to assign them into the array elements.

    ■   Set *currentIndex* to indicate the first element in the array.

3. Modify the event handlers for the Previous and Next buttons to use the array index.

   ▤ Find the event handlers for the Previous button.

   ▤ Modify the logic to select the previous *FileCard*. Use *currentIndex*. (The new code should be significantly shorter than the existing code.)

   ▤ Repeat for the Next button.

4. Modify the *saveData* and *setUI* methods to use *currentIndex*.

5. Modify the checks for the beginning and end of the phone list to use the array index.

   ▤ Modify the *setUI* method to check for the beginning of the array to enable and disable the Previous button. Use *currentIndex*.

   ▤ Modify the *setUI* method to check for the end of the array to enable and disable the Next button.

6. Test your application. You can check your work against the solution in Chapter08\Sol8-1\PhoneList.sln.

Optional lab enhancement

Here is an optional enhancement that you can add to this lab.

■ Create separate fields for first and last names. Add a Label control to the form that will display the complete name, using one of the following two formats: FIRST LAST or LAST, FIRST. Provide two menu items to let the user select the format for the complete name.

Next steps

This is pretty cool, but the application creates the elements in the array using names and phone numbers that are hard-coded in the application. Any changes you make to the elements in the array won't appear the next time you run the program. In the next section, you will learn how to use files to store values between runs of the program.

Working with Files

In this section, we work with files. Using file input and output, our application can store a user's changes to the phone list so the user will see these changes reflected each time the phone list application is run.

File I/O

The terms *input* and *output* refer to how information is brought into and out of an application. You saw some examples of this in the DayOfTheWeek code we worked on earlier in the chapter. The Edit control for data entry is named *edtInput*; the Label control for display is named *lblOutput*. *File input* refers to information an application is *reading* from a file; *file output* refers to information the application is *writing* to (or storing in) a file. These terms are usually combined and shortened to *file I/O*.

The *File* Class

As with everything else in Java, to read from and write to files you will use a class. The I/O classes provided with Visual J++ are in the WFC package com.ms.wfc.io.

The most important of the I/O classes is *File*. The *File* class provides methods for opening files on disk to read and write to them. The superclass of the *File* class is *DataStream*. The *DataStream* class provides methods for reading and writing to various data formats and, because the *File* class extends *DataStream*, *File* inherits these public methods of *DataStream*.

 OTE   There are other I/O libraries. This section discusses only the I/O capabilities provided with the WFC library.

Opening a File

Let's use another example to look at how to work with files in Java. In this example, you will use the file HALL_OF_FAME.SCORES to keep track of the high scores for a game you have written. In Visual J++, open the HiScores project, located in Chapter08\HiScores\HiScores.sln.

Before you can read from or write to a file, you need a *File* object. The *File* object in your application provides methods for reading information from or writing information to a file. It gives you access to a file on your computer's hard drive, but it is not really the file. The physical file is an area on your computer's hard disk you can use for storage. (The file could be on a floppy disk or elsewhere, such as on a network, but for this discussion, let's just say it's on the hard disk.) All the sample programs you have been creating are stored in the computer in files.

For your application to access a physical file, the *File* object in your application first needs to be associated with that physical file through the process of *opening* the file.

In WFC, you can open a file in two ways: with a *File* constructor, or using either the *open* or *create* static methods in the *File* class.

Opening with static methods

Using the two *static* methods is the easiest way to open a file. For reading or writing to an existing file, use the *File.open* method, providing the filename. To open a file for writing new data, use the *File.create* method, providing the filename.

Opening with a constructor

While the *File* constructor offers more flexibility, it's also somewhat complex. You can open a file with specific options by using the constructor with its two parameters, a *String* filename and the options for opening the file.

Table 8-1 lists some of the more common options for opening a file. These options are declared as static final member variables of *File*. (Notice that they are similar to the button set codes for the *MessageBox* class explained in Chapter 3.)

Option	Description
File.READ	Open to read from the file
File.WRITE	Open to write to the file
File.OPEN	Only open the file if it exists already (error if it doesn't)
File.CREATE	Create a file (overwrite if it already exists)
File.CREATE_NEW	Only create a new file (error if it already exists)
File.OPEN_OR_CREATE	Open if the file exists, or create if it doesn't

Table 8-1. *File constructor options for opening a file.*

Some of the options in Table 8-1 report errors, called *exceptions*. You will learn about exceptions in Chapter 9.

The static method *File.open* opens only existing files. It is exactly like using the constructor with the options *File.OPEN*, *File.READ*, and *File.WRITE*.

The static method *File.create* overwrites the file if it exists. This is just like using the constructor with the options *File.CREATE*, *File.READ*, and *File.WRITE*.

You must use the constructor format if you want to specify options for opening a file other than the filename. For example, if you want to open a file whether it exists on the disk or not, you must use the constructor with the *File.OPEN_OR_CREATE* option.

Some examples

Here are some examples of opening the file HALL_OF_FAME.SCORES for reading and writing. The first two come from the HiScores example.

- Using the static method *open*:

```
File fileScores;
static final String FILENAME = "HALL_OF_FAME.SCORES";
fileScores = File.open(FILENAME);
```

- Using the static method *create*:

```
File fileScores;
static final String FILENAME = "HALL_OF_FAME.SCORES";
fileScores = File.create(FILENAME);
```

- Using the constructor:

```
File fileScores;
static final String FILENAME = "HALL_OF_FAME.SCORES";
fileScores = new File(FILENAME,
    File.OPEN_OR_CREATE | File.READ | File.WRITE);
```

Now that you have an open file, you can start reading from and writing to your file.

Writing to a File

To write to a file, use one of the *write* methods of the *DataStream* class. Here they are:

```
public void writeByte(byte value);
public void writeShort(short value);
public void writeInt(int value);
public void writeLong(long value);
public void writeChar(char value);
public void writeBoolean(boolean value);
public void writeFloat(float value);
public void writeDouble(double value);
public void writeString(String value);
```

Let's take a look at how to use some of these methods for our HALL_OF_FAME.SCORES file. For example, at the end of the game, to write out the high score and the name of the player, you first create a new empty file:

```
File fileScores;
static final String FILENAME = "HALL_OF_FAME.SCORES";
fileScores = File.create(FILENAME);
```

Then you write out the names and scores of the top three players:

```
fileScores.writeString(name[0]);
fileScores.writeInt(score[0]);
fileScores.writeString(name[1]);
fileScores.writeInt(score[1]);
fileScores.writeString(name[2]);
fileScores.writeInt(score[2]);
```

OTE The information is stored in the file in a way that makes it easy for the computer to work with that data. If you were to open the HALL_OF_FAME.SCORES file using Notepad, it is very likely that you wouldn't recognize your information. You could probably find the names, since they are stored as a series of characters, but the score values would be very hard to decipher.

Next we will use methods in the *DataStream* class to read this information.

Reading from a File

To read from a file, use one of the *read* methods of *DataStream*. For example:

```
public byte readByte();
public short readShort();
public int readInt();
public long readLong();
public char readChar();
public boolean readBoolean();
public float readFloat();
public double readDouble();
public String readString();
```

Now we can take our file HALL_OF_FAME.SCORES and use it in the next game to determine whether the score for this player is high enough to make him one of the top three. To open an existing file, we use the static method *open*.

The *open* method reports an error if the file does not exist, so before trying to open it, we need to verify the file's existence. To check whether a file exists, call the *File.exists* method:

```
static final String FILENAME = "HALL_OF_FAME.SCORES";
if(File.exists(FILENAME))
{
        File fileScores;
        fileScores = File.open(FILENAME);
        name[0] = fileScores.readString();
        score[0] = fileScores.readInt();
        ...
}
else
{
        name[0] = "None yet";
```

```
            score[0] = 0;
            ...
}
```

 OTE   It is very important that you read the information from the file in the same order that it was written to the file.

Closing a File

It is very important to close files after you have opened them, because in general, any changes you make to a file don't become permanent until the file is closed. Closing a file when you're done with it also ensures that anyone else who needs to access the file can do so.

To close a file, call the *close* method. The typical example of file I/O includes opening the file, reading to or writing to it, and then closing it:

```
static final String FILENAME = "HALL_OF_FAME.SCORES";
File fileScores;
fileScores = File.open(FILENAME);
fileScores.writeString(name[0]);
fileScores.writeInt(score[0]);
...
fileScores.close();
```

Repetitive Actions—A Simple Loop

Often the information in a file is repetitive, as is the case in our HALL_OF_FAME.SCORES example. We can repeat the code to read a name and a score three times, as in this example:

```
static final int SIZE = 3;
String[] name = new String[SIZE];
int[] score = new int[SIZE];
static final String FILENAME = "HALL_OF_FAME.SCORES";
File fileScores;

fileScores = File.open(FILENAME);
name[0] = fileScores.readString();
score[0] = fileScores.readInt();
name[1] = fileScores.readString();
score[1] = fileScores.readInt();
name[2] = fileScores.readString();
score[2] = fileScores.readInt();
fileScores.close();
```

While this approach works, it's rather tedious. It's also error-prone, because there are more opportunities to mistype code; in the above example, typing *score[2]* instead of *score[1]* would load the wrong information into the array.

Notice that the six lines of reading the files can be divided into three pairs of lines that vary only in the array index. We can handle this repetition more efficiently through a technique called *looping*. Looping allows a programmer to execute one or more lines of code as many times as necessary to perform a specific task.

Java provides several ways to loop through code. One of them is the simple *while* statement, or *while* loop. The *while* loop looks like an *if* statement (without the *else* part). In fact, they are very similar in that they both evaluate a Boolean expression and perform some action if the expression is true.

```
while( trueFalseCheck )
{
    // stuff-to-do
}
if( trueFalseCheck )
{
    // stuff-to-do
}
```

The difference is that in a *while* loop, after the stuff-to-do is done, the program returns to the *while* part and evaluates the condition again. If it is still *true*, the block is performed. It keeps looping like this until the condition evaluates to *false*.

Let's rewrite the example above using a *while* loop to read the three names and scores from the file:

```
static final int SIZE = 3;
String[] name = new String[SIZE];
int[] score = new int[SIZE];
static final String FILENAME = "HALL_OF_FAME.SCORES";
File fileScores;

fileScores = File.open(FILENAME);

int index = 0;
while(index < SIZE)
{
        name[index] = fileScores.readString();
        score[index] = fileScores.readInt();
        index = index + 1;
}
```

IMPORTANT   You must remember to change the index—otherwise the program will keep looping...forever. This kind of programming error is called an *infinite loop*.

Here, if you forget to increment *index*, the loop would not be infinite. Instead, the information in the file eventually runs out. When it does, the next *readString* raises an exception. You will learn more about exceptions in Chapter 9. The preferred programming practice, however, is to avoid exceptions whenever you can.

Lab 8-2: Updating the Saved Phone List

In this lab, you will continue refining the phone list application. You'll add support for storing the names in a file, so the changes the user makes to the names and phone numbers persist between uses of the application.

Lab overview

In this lab, you will practice:

■ Opening a file.

■ Reading information from a file.

■ Writing information to a file.

Lab setup

1. Start Visual J++.

2. Open the PhoneList starter project (Chapter08\Lab8-2\
   PhoneList.sln).

Lab instructions

1. Note the data file MYLIST.PHONE. This data file has the
   following structure with:

   - The number of entries in the phone list.

   - The individual entries (each entry is two strings: the name and
     the phone number).

2. At the top of the file, add an *import* statement for the *com.ms.wfc.io*
   package.

3. Add a declaration for a *File* class. Name the reference *phoneListFile*.

   - Add the reference as a member variable of the *PhoneList* class.

   - Notice the final static string, *FILENAME*.

4. In the constructor, replace the code that initializes the *FileCard*
   objects to use values from the phone list file.

   - Open the file for reading. Use the static, *File.open* method.

   - Read the size of the array from the data file.

   - Create the array, using the size you read from the file.

   - Create the elements of the array, initializing them with values
     you read from the file. Use a *while* loop to repeat this action for
     each element in the array.

   - Close the file.

5. In the handler for the Closing event, add code to store files into the phone list file.

   ▦ Call *saveData* to save the values from the form.

   ▦ Open the file for writing, using the static *File.create* method.

   ▦ Write the size of the array from the data file.

   ▦ Write the values of the FileCard elements to the file. Use a *while* loop to repeat this action for each element in the array.

   ▦ Close the file.

6. Test your application. You can check your work against Chapter08\Sol8-2\PhoneList.sln.

Optional lab enhancements

Here are some suggestions for enhancements that you can add to this lab.

■ Use a form to prompt the user to save changes at application exit.

■ Let the user specify the name of the data file. Provide several "standard" files from which to choose.

■ Add menu items on the File menu to let the user open and close the file.

Next steps

Arrays give us the ability to work with a number of independent items as a single unit. However, they are rather rigid, because the number of elements in the array is fixed. In the next section, you will find out about lists.

Working with Lists

The WFC library contains several very powerful utility classes, which can be found in the *com.ms.wfc.util* package. One of the utility classes is the *List* class.

Lists are like arrays, in that they allow us to work with a number of objects as a single unit. The individual units in a list are called *items*. In addition, lists have the advantage of being able to grow and shrink as needed.

Let's look at some basic ways to work with a list by creating a simple shopping list application. To follow along with the code for this example, open the ShoppingList solution, in Chapter08\Shopping1\ ShoppingList.sln.

 OTE There are other interesting and useful classes in the WFC Util package. You can browse through the documentation for this package to find out about other utility classes.

Creating a List

When you create a list, you can choose to create either an empty list or a list with initial values. Here we'll create an empty list. When you create an empty list, you can give it two pieces of information:

- How big the list will be initially
- How much space to add when the list needs to grow

You can think of the list as a set of pages on which you jot down the groceries for the shopping list. When you create a list, you can specify much space you want in the list. You can also specify how big a sheet is— that is, when the list grows, how big the new piece of paper for the list is.

When you use the *List* constructor with no parameters, you create an empty list with default values. If you don't specify an initial size, the list starts out with space for 10 items. To create an empty list with an initial size and a "grow size," use the *List* constructor with two parameters. If you don't specify a grow size, the list will double in size each time it needs to grow.

For the shopping list, let's create an initial size of 15 and a grow size of 5:

```
import com.ms.wfc.util.*;

List shoppingList;
shoppingList = new List(15, 5);
```

Right now, the *shoppingList* object is empty, but it has space for 15 items. When we add a sixteenth item to *shoppingList*, it grows by 5 items, so it will have space for 20 items.

Adding to a List

When you're ready to add an item to a list, use the *addItem* method:

```
public void addItem(Object item);
```

 OTE The *addItem* method takes an object as a parameter. In Chapter 4, you learned that each object in Java has an "Is-A" relationship to the *java.lang.Object* class, since all classes are subclasses of *java.lang.Object*.

For example, here's the code to add a new *String* item to *shoppingList*.

```
shoppingList.addItem(edtInput.getText());
```

Looking at an Item in a List

When you get an item from a list, you use an index, just as you do with arrays.

To get an item from a list, use the *getItem* method:

```
public Object getItem(int index);
```

In the following example, we're getting the third item from our *shoppingList* object. We use the *getItem* method with an index of 2, because the first item of every list has an index value of 0 (zero). We call the *toString* method of *java.lang.Object* to get a *String* reference for the call to *setText*.

```
Object item;
item = shoppingList.getItem(2);
edtInput.setText(item.toString());
```

The return type of *getItem* is *java.lang.Object*. In order to manipulate this item in a specific way, you first need to *typecast* (change its type) to the appropriate class.

Here is an example of the typecast. This is the typical way to handle the objects you get from a list. If you aren't certain about the actual type of the object, you can use *instanceof* to check. If the typecast can't happen, the operation throws a *ClassCastException*. You will learn more about typecasting and exceptions in Chapter 9.

```
String item
item = (String)shoppingList.getItem(2);
edtInput.setText(item);
```

Removing an Item from a List

Use the *removeItem* method to remove an item from a list:

```
public Object removeItem(int index);
public boolean removeItem(Object item);
```

For example, here is the code to remove the third item from *shoppingList*:

```
shoppingList.removeItem(2);
```

In this case, we are not interested in the object that is being removed, probably because the user has already purchased that item on the shopping list. So, we ignore the return value from the *removeItem* method.

Lab 8-3: Making the Phone List Dynamic

Now you can update the phone list application to use the WFC *List* class rather than an array. The *List* class supports adding and removing items, so the user will be able to add and delete phone numbers.

Lab overview

In this lab, you will practice:

■ Creating a list.

■ Adding elements to a list.

■ Deleting elements from a list.

Lab setup

1. Start Visual J++.

2. Open the PhoneList starter project in Chapter08\ Lab8-3\PhoneList.sln.

3. If you'd like to use your own data for the labs, copy MYLIST.PHONE from the previous project.

Lab instructions

1. At the top of the file, add an *import* statement for the *com.ms.wfc.util* package.

2. Declare a *List* reference to hold the phone list.

   ■ Find the declaration of the array.

   ■ Replace it with the declaration of a *List* reference.

3. In the constructor, create the *List* object and fill it with data from the file.

   ■ Change the statement that creates the array to one that creates a *List* object.

   ■ Find the statement that assigns the *FileCard* object to an array element. Modify it to add the new *FileCard* object to the *List* object.

4. Update *saveData* to use the list.

   ■ In *saveData*, declare a *FileCard* reference. Set it equal to the item in the list indicated by *currentIndex*.

   ■ Store the values from the form in the *FileCard* object.

   ■ Make similar updates to *setUI*. Use the *getSize* method of the *List* class to get the number of items in the list.

   ■ Make a similar update to the Click event handler for *btnNext*.

5. In the *Closing* event handler, save the values in the list to a file.

   ■ Modify the statement that writes the size of the phone list.

   ■ Find the statements that write the *FileCard* name and phone number. Modify them to use values from the *List*.

   Hint: You may find it helpful to create two local variables: an *int* to hold the number of items of the list and a *FileCard* to access the individual items in the list.

6. Implement adding a new file card.

   ■ Add a handler for the Add button.

   ■ In this handler, create a new *FileCard* object, add it to the list, set *currentIndex* to access the new *FileCard* object, and call *setUI* to update the user interface.

   Hint: Use the *findIndex* method of the *List* class to get the location of an object within the list.

7. Implement deleting a file card.

   ■ Add a handler for the Delete button.

   ■ In this handler, remove the current *FileCard* object from the list. If the list is empty, add a blank *FileCard* object and set *currentIndex* to access the new card. Otherwise, update *currentIndex* to access the next card in the list. Call *setUI* to update the user interface.

   Hint: Unless you were at the end of the list, *currentIndex* is still a valid index value in the list.

8. Test your application. You can check your work against the solution in Chapter08\Sol8-3\PhoneList.sln.

Here are some suggestions for enhancements that you can add to this lab.

■ Before removing the object from the list, ask users if they really want to delete the current file card from the list.

■ Provide a Copy Entry function that creates a new entry with the name and phone number taken from the current entry.

Next steps

The user can now add and remove phone numbers from the phone list. But finding things in the list is still difficult. Shortly, we'll learn how to sort a group of objects. To do this, we'll need to learn something about interfaces.

Interfaces

Lists give you a great deal of flexibility. However, it can be difficult to find an item in a list after adding and removing many items. As with a real card file, you have to keep the cards in some sort of order if you want to find things quickly. If the entries aren't in some logical order, you'll have to look at each entry to find what you need.

Now, there aren't any utility classes for sorting a list. However, the *com.ms.wfc.util.ArraySorter* utility class sorts arrays. And there are ways to convert between arrays and lists. However, to use *ArraySorter*, you need to know about interfaces. In this section, we'll find out more about interfaces. In the next section, we'll find out about converting between lists and arrays.

What is an Interface?

An interface is a lot like a class. In fact, if you look at a very simple class and a simple interface, you'll see only one keyword difference:

```
public class SimpleClass
{
}

public interface SimpleInterface
{
}
```

Like a class, a compiled interface exists in a .class file. Also, an interface can have member variables and methods within it, though there are some restrictions on these, as we will see later in this chapter. In WFC, all interface names have an initial capital "I," which stands for "interface."

What's the difference between an interface and a class? An *interface* describes a behavior that a class implements. Interfaces are similar to the mechanisms of inheritance (subclass and superclass) with two significant differences:

■ Where a class *extends* exactly one other class, with interfaces, a class *implements* as many or as few interfaces as needed.

■ With inheritance, a class inherits the implementation of methods from its superclass; the subclass has the option to *override* the implementation of the superclass. The methods of an interface have no implementation; so the implementing class must *implement* each of the methods in the interface.

This is starting to sound a little mystical. Let's just take a look at the kinds of members an interface can have.

Members of an Interface

Like a class, an interface can have two kinds of members: member variables and methods. These members are very similar to the ones in classes, but with some differences, due to the nature of an interface. Remember that an interface has no implementation associated with it, but rather, it defines a set of actions—a behavior—for some other class.

 OTE   A discussion of the technical reasons for the following characteristics of methods and member variables in interfaces is beyond the scope of this book.

Methods in interfaces

Interfaces define behavior, so the primary members of interfaces are methods. The syntax of a method in an interface consists of the return type, the name of the method, the parameters, and a semicolon:

```
int increment(int x);
```

This method is *public* and *abstract*, even though the keywords are not present. By definition, all the methods of an interface are *public* and *abstract*.

 OTE   *Abstract* methods do not include a *body*, the implementation code that appears between the braces **{ }**, but they are terminated by a semicolon.

The current convention is to omit the *abstract* keyword from the method declaration in an interface.

Member variables in interfaces

Like interface methods, the member variables in an interface have a number of modifiers. By definition, all member variables in an interface are *public*, static, and final.

In an interface, this line of code:

```
int STEP = 5;
```

is the same as this one:

```
public static final int STEP = 5;
```

The current convention is to include all interface modifiers. Also by convention, the name of a static final member variable is all uppercase.

Final member variables cannot change value; they must be initialized. Static member variables can be accessed using the name of the interface; they are not associated with a particular instance.

An interface example

Let's look at a basic interface that simply increments numbers, using the members you have seen so far. Following the WFC naming convention, the interface name is *IIncrement*.

```
public interface IIncrement
{
        public int increment(int x);
        public static final int STEP = 5;
}
```

To see the code for this example, open the Chapter08\Incrementer\ Incrementer.sln project.

The *implements* Keyword

Now, what can you do with our basic interface? You cannot create instances directly from this interface, but you can create a class that implements this interface. To implement an interface in a class, use the *implements* keyword. Here's an example of a class that implements the *IIncrement* interface:

```
public class Adder implements IIncrement
{
     ...
}
```

For this class to compile, it must implement all the methods in the interface. In this case, there is only one: *increment*. To implement the *increment* method, let's use the *STEP* member variable. Because it is static, it is accessible using the name of the interface:

```
public class Adder implements IIncrement
{
        public int increment(int x)
        {
                return x + IIncrement.STEP;
        }
}
```

The *Adder* class implements *IIncrement*, so the members of *IIncrement* are members of *Adder*. This means that *STEP* can be accessed directly:

```
public class Adder implements IIncrement
{
        public int increment(int x)
        {
                return x + STEP;
        }
}
```

Other classes can implement this interface, as well:

```
public class SingleStep implements IIncrement
{
        public int increment(int x)
        {
                return x + 1;
        }
}
```

You can create a reference to *IIncrement* and have it access either an Adder object or a *SingleStep* object:

```
IIncrement incr1 = new Adder();
IIncrement incr2 = new SingleStep();
```

The "Acts-Like-A" Relationship

So far, we could just as well have used inheritance instead of defining an *IIncrement* interface. The value of interfaces is this: any class can implement any interface. *Adder* does not have to be a subclass of *IIncrement*; it can be a form:

```
public class AdderForm extends Form implements IIncrement
{
        public int increment(int x)
        {
                return x + STEP;
        }
        ...
}
```

AdderForm "Is-A" form; that is, it is a subclass of *Form*. *AdderForm* inherits "formness" from its superclass, *com.ms.wfc.ui.Form*. *AdderForm* also "Acts-Like-A" *IIncrement* (or "Acts-Like-An," but that's not the name of the relationship).

Any class you write can implement *IIncrement*. Any class, then, "Acts-Like-A" *IIncrement*. Or, to say it in a more code-based way, any class that implements an interface can be accessed by a reference to that interface.

In our example code, then, sometimes the *IIncrement* reference accesses the form:

```
public class AdderForm extends Form implements IIncrement
{
        IIncrement incr;
        ...
        {
                incr = this;
        }
}
```

and sometimes the *IIncrement* reference accesses an instance of *SingleStep*:

```
IIncrement incr;
SingleStep ss = new SingleStep();
...
{
        incr = ss;
}
```

Converting Between Lists and Arrays

Now that you know about interfaces, we can sort an array using *com.ms.wfc.util.ArraySorter*. Before we start, however, you need to know one more thing: how to convert between lists and arrays.

For our example, we will sort *shoppingList* to help us find things in the list. To see the code for this example, open the Chapter08\Shopping2\ShoppingList.sln project.

Getting an Array from a List

Before we can use the *ArraySorter* class, we need an array containing the values in the list. To create such an array, we use the *getAllItems* method:

```
public Object[] getAllItems();
```

This is how our *shoppingList* example looks:

```
Object[] array;
array = shoppingList.getAllItems();
```

Sorting an Array

Let's take a look at how we can use the *ArraySorter* class. The simplest way is to use the static method *sort*:

```
public static void sort(Object[] items, IComparer comp);
```

The first parameter is the array that you want to sort. The second parameter is an object that implements the *IComparer* interface. Here is the declaration for the *IComparer* interface:

```
public interface IComparer
{
        public int compare(Object a, Object b);
}
```

The *compare* method returns an integer. Table 8-2 summarizes the return values of *compare*.

Return Value	Description
0 (zero)	Both values are the same (a == b)
Negative	First value is less than second (a < b)
Positive	First value is greater than second (a > b)

Table 8-2. *Return values for* IComparer.compare.

So, to sort an array, you need a class that implements *IComparer*, a class that can compare two objects. This class is instantiated only for sorting; we don't use instances of this class for anything else. It is called a *helper* class.

Here is an example of a comparison class for *shoppingList*:

```
class StringComparer implements IComparer
{
        public int compare(Object a, Object b)
        {
                String paramA;
                paramA = a.toString();
                return paramA.compare(b.toString());
        }
}
```

 OTE This implementation uses the *toString* method of *Object* to get string representations of the two parameters. Often, you need to typecast the objects to make the comparison.

This implementation uses the *compare* method of *String*. This method returns a value appropriate for the *compare* method of *IComparer*. Often, you need to write more code to compare the values.

Here is the code that sorts *shoppingList*:

```
Object[] array;
array = shoppingList.getAllItems();
ArraySorter.sort(array, new StringComparer());
```

Now let's look at an example of another class that implements *IComparer*.

```
class IntComparer implements IComparer
{
        public int compare(Object a, Object b)
        {
                Integer paramA = (Integer)a;
                Integer paramB = (Integer)b;

                int x = paramA.intValue();
                int y = paramB.intValue();
                return x - y;
        }
}
```

Creating a List from an Array

We can create a list from an array by using the *List* constructor that takes an array parameter.

```
public List(Object[] itemsT);
```

Here's the code to create a version of *shoppingList* with the sorted values:

```
Object[] array;
array = ShoppingList.getAllItems();
ArraySorter.sort(array, new StringComparer());
ShoppingList = new List(array);
```

Lab 8-4: Sorting the Phone List

In this lab, you will continue to work on the phone list application, adding sort capabilities to the application so that the user can sort the list by name.

Lab overview

In this lab, you will practice:

■ Creating a comparison method.

■ Sorting a list.

Lab setup

1. Start Visual J++.

2. Open the PhoneList starter project (Chapter08\
   Lab8-4\PhoneList.sln).

3. If you'd like to use your own data for this lab, copy
   MYLIST.PHONE from the previous project.

Lab instructions

1. Create a helper class that implements *IComparer*.

   ▨ Add a class named *FileCardSorter* to your project.

   ▨ In *FileCardSorter*, implement *IComparer*.

   ▨ Use the Class Outline to add a stub for the *compare* method.
   Implement this method.

2. Add a Click event handler for the Sort button.

   ▨ In the handler, create an array from the data in the list.

   ▨ Use *ArraySorter* to sort the array.

   ▨ Store the sorted array in the phone list.

   ▨ Set *currentIndex* to access the first item in the list.

   ▨ Call *setUI* to update the user interface.

3. Test your application. You can check your work against the project
   in Chapter08\Sol8-4\PhoneList.sln.

Optional lab enhancements

Here are some optional enhancements that you can add to this lab:

■ Add menu items to let the user sort by name or phone number.

■ If you included the earlier enhancement separating the name into
first and last names, let the user sort by first name or by last name.

Animation in Applets

This is the third applet chapter in this book. Chapter 6 covered the basics of creating and displaying an applet. In Chapter 7, you learned about ways to communicate with your applet, using the <PARAM> tag and scripting. Now you will learn how to create applets that display animated images.

An animated image is really just a series of still images displayed in rapid succession. The human mind fills in gaps in the series to create the illusion of smooth movement. To produce this effect, you first need to learn about threads and exceptions in Java.

In this chapter, you will learn about:

■ Multithreading in Java

■ Exceptions in Java

■ Animation in an applet

You will create:

■ An applet that acts as a metronome

■ An applet that displays an animated image

Multithreading

All of the applications you have written so far in this book have had a single flow-of-control, or *thread*, that controlled everything the application did. The applications progress in an orderly manner, calling from method to method. Often they wait for the user to do something, but the applications themselves do only one thing at a time.

It is possible to create applications with more than one thread. These applications are called *multithreaded*. You can consider the threads as being completely independent.

Most of us use computers with only a single CPU; the machine can't do more than one thing at a time. But it's possible to think of the machine as doing more than one thing at a time. For example, while you are waiting for a Web page to download, you can continue writing a thank-you letter for a birthday gift. These are two separate applications, but they are sharing the CPU. This is very much like multithreading, except that true multithreading happens within a single application. For example, you can use the word processor application to print one thank-you letter, to Aunt Claire, while you're also using it to work on another thank-you letter, to your mom.

Event Handlers in the AWT

In an applet, there is one main thread, which calls only four methods: *init*, *start*, *stop*, and *destroy*. All event handlers, such as *action*, *mouseDown*, and *keyDown*, are called from other threads. The AWT creates a new thread for each handler.

To achieve an animated effect, you need to display many different images. It might be tempting to use an event handler to manage the animation (since it has its own thread). But this isn't a good idea. You should create a new thread to manage the display of multiple images.

The *java.lang.Thread* Class

For the applications and applets you have created so far, the VM for Java has created threads for you. For an application or applet to programmatically do several things independently, you need to create a thread. All the threads in a Java application use the *java.lang.Thread* class. In this section, the seven most important methods in the *Thread* class are summarized.

The *start* and *run* methods

The primary *Thread* methods are *start* and *run*:

```
public void start();
public void run();
```

Typically, a class that extends *Thread* overrides the *run* method. In this method, you put in the code you want the *Thread* object to perform. So, if you want your thread to set a value, you write something like this:

```
class Stuff
{
    int myValue = 0;

    class MyThread extends Thread
    {
        public void run()
        {
            myValue = 5;
        }
    }

    public Stuff()
    {
        Thread t = new MyThread();
    }
}
```

The value of *myValue* after you create a Stuff object is 0. The *MyThread* object has been created, but it isn't doing anything. To get the thread started, call the *start* method:

```
class Stuff
{
    int myValue = 0;

    class MyThread extends Thread
    {
        public void run()
        {
            myValue = 5;
        }
    }

    public Stuff()
    {
        Thread t = new MyThread();
        t.start();
    }
}
```

When the *start* method is called, the *Thread* object, in this case *t*, gets a flow-of-control created by the VM for Java. This flow-of-control performs the statements in the *run* method. When the *run* method completes, the VM for Java cleans up the thread and marks it for garbage collection.

The *suspend* and *resume* methods

The *suspend* method pauses the flow-of-control for the given *Thread* object; the *resume* method starts up the flow-of-control again:

```
public void suspend();
public void resume();
```

The *suspend* method can be called by the thread itself or by some other thread. Often, it is called by some other thread—for example, an event handler for a button click. Let's say that one thread manages the animation. In response to a button click event that calls *suspend*, the animation pauses until some other thread calls the *resume* method (possibly another click event handler). There is no way the animation thread can call the *resume* method; it's suspended, unable to do anything.

The *sleep* method

The *sleep* method pauses the flow-of-control for the given number of milliseconds:

```
public static void sleep(long millis) throws InterruptedException;
```

The *sleep* method has some interesting syntax.

First, the *sleep* method is *static*. It can be called without a specific *Thread* object. Calls to *Thread.sleep* cause the calling thread to sleep, even if there is no reference to that *Thread* object in the application. So, in any method, you can call the *sleep* method.

Second, the sleep method has an exception associated with it. The exception is *InterruptedException*. The *throws* keyword marks this association. You will learn about exceptions in "Exception Handling," later in this chapter.

The *interrupt* and *stop* methods

The *interrupt* method wakes up a sleeping thread:

```
public void interrupt();
```

If some thread is paused because of a call to *sleep*, a call to the *interrupt* method raises the *InterruptedException* to force the premature return from the call to *sleep*.

The *stop* method halts the thread. It raises the *ThreadDeath* error:

```
public void stop();
```

You will learn more about errors later in this chapter.

Synchronization

Multithreaded applications have some special considerations. The most important of these concern sharing.

Let's consider the word processor example again. Let's say you did write that letter to Aunt Claire, and you sent it to the printer using a background thread. Now, instead of writing a new letter to your mom, you decide to send her an edited version of the letter you wrote to Aunt Claire, changing some details. You don't want the background thread to use whatever is in the editing window, because you're changing it to become a thank-you letter to your mom. The two threads need to act independently. They also need to avoid a collision. The word processor handles this by creating a copy of the contents of the editing window for background printing.

If you have multiple threads that are updating the same values, or if you have different threads updating and using the same values, you can use the *synchronized* keyword to avoid collisions.

The *synchronized* keyword is a modifier for methods. When a *synchronized* method is called, the VM for Java blocks any calls to other *synchronized* methods on that object until the first call is completed. So, if you have multiple member variables that need to stay in sync, you can create *accessor* methods to handle synchronization.

For example, let's say you had three member variables to represent dimension. You can create *accessor* methods to manage these values:

```
class Box
{
    private int dimensions[] = new int[3];

    public void setDimensions(int x, int y, int z)
    {
        dimensions[0] = x;
        dimensions[1] = y;
        dimensions[2] = z;
    }
    public int[] getDimensions()
    {
        int retValue = new int[3];
        retValue[0] = dimensions[0];
        retValue[1] = dimensions[1];
        retValue[2] = dimensions[2];
        return retValue
    }
}
```

You can see that it would be bad to have a call to *getDimensions* interrupted by a call to *setDimensions*.

Thread 1	Thread 2
Box myBox = new Box();	
MyBox.setDimensions(2, 3, 4);	
int dims;	
dims = getDimensions();	myBox.setDimensions(7, 8, 9);

Let's say the call to *getDimensions* got through two statements and was interrupted by the call to *setDimensions* from Thread 2. You would end up with {*2, 8, 9*} as the value returned by *getDimensions*. This would be bad, but at least later calls to *getDimensions* would give the value {*7, 8, 9*}.

It would be even worse to have a call to *setDimensions* interrupted by a different call to *setDimensions*.

Thread 1	Thread 2
Box myBox = new Box();	
MyBox.setDimensions(2, 3, 4);	myBox.setDimensions(7, 8, 9);
int dims;	
dims = getDimensions();	

Let's say the call to *setDimensions* from Thread 1 was interrupted after two statements. The *dimensions* array would have the value {*7, 8, 4*}. All calls to *getDimensions* would return this bogus value.

By marking the *getDimensions* and *setDimensions* methods as synchronized, you can avoid this error:

```
class Box
{
    private int dimensions[] = new int[3];

    public synchronized void setDimensions(int x, int y, int z)
    {
        dimensions[0] = x;
        dimensions[1] = y;
        dimensions[2] = z;
    }
    public synchronized int[] getDimensions()
    {
        int retValue = new int[3];
        retValue[0] = dimensions[0];
        retValue[1] = dimensions[1];
        retValue[2] = dimensions[2];
        return retValue
    }
}
```

The *java.lang.Runnable* Interface

One way to create a thread is to extend *java.lang.Thread*. Another way to create a thread is to use the *java.lang.Runnable* interface.

The *Runnable* interface is very simple:

```
public interface Runnable
{
    public void run();
}
```

The *Thread* class has a constructor that takes a *Runnable* object as a parameter. Any class can implement the *Runnable* interface. To create a *Thread* object, call the *Thread* constructor with the *Runnable* object.

Here is the *Stuff* example code you saw earlier in this chapter:

```
class Stuff
{
    int myValue = 0;

    class MyThread extends Thread
    {
        public void run()
        {
            myValue = 5;
        }
    }
```

```
    public Stuff()
    {
        Thread t = new MyThread();
        t.start();
    }
}
```

Here it is using the *Runnable* interface:

```
class Stuff2 implements Runnable
{
    int myValue = 0;

    public void run()
    {
        myValue = 5;
    }

    public Stuff2()
    {
        Thread t = new Thread(this);
        t.start();
    }
}
```

Since the *Stuff2* class implements *Runnable*, it must override the *run* method. Now, the constructor for the *Thread* object gets the reference *this*. The *Thread* object *t* uses the *run* method from *this*.

Exception Handling

In programming, not everything always goes as planned. In this section, you will learn about *exceptions*. An exception is one of the ways in Java to signal that something unexpected has occurred. In response to an exception, some reparatory action may occur. So, who's signaling whom?

One component (or object) signals another component using an exception. The relationship between the two is that the one component has called a method on the other component. The calling component has some expectations about the behavior from the called component. If the called component is unable to complete the expected behavior, the called component signals the calling component using an exception.

Here is an example. Let's say you have created a *Queue* class. A queue is a first-in, first-out sort of data structure, like the line (or queue, if you're English) at the movies (or cinema, if you're English). Folks line up; whoever gets there first gets the first ticket. The later one arrives, the longer one must wait.

In a very simple example, your *Queue* class may look like this:

```
public class Queue
{
    public void add(Object o)
    {
        ...
    }
    public Object getNext()
    {
        ...
    }
    public int getCount()
    {
        ...
    }
}
```

So, other programmers can use your queue. They can create *Queue* objects, add objects to the queue, get the next object from the queue (taking from the head of the line), and check to see how many objects are in the queue.

What do you do if the queue is empty and someone calls *getNext*? You should raise an exception to alert the other programmer that there are no objects in the queue.

 OTE   This discussion of exceptions starts with the component that throws the exception. It is far more common to write exception handlers than to throw exceptions. However, exceptions are easier to understand if the discussion begins with how to throw exceptions.

Declaring Exceptions

Exceptions in Java are subclasses of *java.lang.Exception*. So, you can create a new exception class:

```
public class QueueEmptyException extends Exception
{
}
```

At the beginning of the *getNext* method, you can check the number of items in the queue. If there are no items in the queue, you can create a *QueueEmptyException* object and throw it:

```
public class Queue
{
    public void add(Object o)
    {

        ...
    }
    public Object getNext()
    {
        if(getCount() == 0)
            throw new QueueEmptyException();

        ...
    }
    public int getCount()
    {

        ...
    }
}
```

To indicate that the *getNext* method may throw this exception, you must include a *throws* clause in the method header.

 OTE Visual J++ requires that any method that might return an exception include a *throws* clause. Technically, you are allowed to throw and catch an exception within the same method, in which case the *throws* clause is not required. However, the exception mechanism is very expensive. One should never catch an exception in the method where it is explicitly thrown.

Fortunately, however, exceptions that are subclasses of *java.lang.RuntimeException* do not need to be reported in a *throws* clause. These exceptions potentially can occur in any method. It would be extremely burdensome if it were necessary to report these exceptions in a *throws* clause.

Here is the *getNext* method updated with the *throws* clause:

```
public class Queue
{
    public void add(Object o)
    {
        ...
    }
    public Object getNext() throws QueueEmptyException
    {
        if(getCount() == 0)
            throw new QueueEmptyException();
        ...
    }
    public int getCount()
    {
        ...
    }
}
```

The superclass *java.lang.Exception* has two constructors: one with no parameters and one that takes a *String* parameter.

The *String* parameter is the message for the exception. The *Exception* class has a *getMessage* method that returns the message. Handlers often call *getMessage* to get more information about the exception. To take advantage of this, you might update your *Exception* class as follows:

```
public class QueueEmptyException extends Exception
{
    public QueueEmptyException()
    {
        super("The queue is empty");
    }
}
```

Handling Exceptions

Let's consider the component of our example code that is using the *Queue* class:

```
public class Cinema
{
    Queue theLine = new Queue();

    public void sellTicket()
    {
```

```
            Object customer;
            customer = theLine.getNext();
            … // sell the ticket and record the sale using customer
    }
    …
}
```

The *getNext* method includes the *throws* clause for *QueueEmptyException*. The *sellTickets* method must handle the exception or pass it on. In the next section, you will learn how to pass on an exception. To handle the exception, use a *try-catch* block. The syntax for a *try-catch* block is as follows:

```
try
{
//     statements where an exception may be thrown
}
catch( exceptionName variableName )
{
//     statements to handle the exception
}
```

Create the *try* block around the statements where the exception may be thrown. If the exception is thrown at any point within the *try* block, the remaining statements in the *try* block are skipped. The flow-of-control jumps to find a *catch* block that matches the exception that's encountered. There can be multiple *catch* blocks for different *Exception* classes:

```
try
{
//     statements where an exception may be thrown
}
catch( exceptionName1 variableName )
{
//     statements to handle exceptionName1
}
catch( exceptionName2 variableName )
{
//     statements to handle exceptionName2
}
```

So, the *Cinema* class can be updated as follows:

```
public class Cinema
{
    Queue theLine = new Queue();

    public void sellTicket()
    {
        Object customer;
        try
        {
            customer = theLine.getNext();
            … // sell the ticket
        }
        catch(QueueEmptyException e)
        {
            StatusBar.setText("Error: " + e.getMessage());
            customer = null;
        }
        … // record the sale using customer
    }
    …
}
```

Notice that the declaration of *customer* occurs outside the *try* block. If the declaration were within the *try* block, the reference to *customer* would be unavailable for the *catch* block to set and for the "record-the-sale" portion of the code to use.

Passing Exceptions On

At times, the exception cannot be handled effectively, but instead should be passed on to another component. Here is the *Cinema* class we have been considering, revised to show an example of this:

```
public class Cinema
{
    Queue theLine = new Queue;

    public void sellTicket()
    {
        Object customer;
        customer = theLine.getNext();
        … // sell the ticket and record the sale using customer
    }
    …
}
```

And here is the *Queue* class that it uses:

```
public class Queue
{
    public void add(Object o)
    {

        …

    }
    public Object getNext() throws QueueEmptyException
    {
        if(getCount() == 0)
            throw new QueueEmptyException();

        …

    }
    public int getCount()
    {

        …

    }
}
```

Cinema.sellTickets calls *Queue.getNext*. *Queue.getNext* throws *QueueEmptyException*. So, *Cinema.sellTickets* must handle the exception or pass it on. You saw how to handle the exception in the previous section.

When a method passes the exception on to the caller, the method throws the exception to the calling object. The method must report this, using the *throws* clause in its method header:

```
public class Cinema
{
    Queue theLine = new Queue();

    public void sellTicket() throws QueueEmptyException
    {
        Object customer;
        customer = theLine.getNext();
        … // sell the ticket and record the sale using customer
    }
    …
}
```

Errors

An exception signals to a component that a called method did not complete as expected. In response to an exception, the component may take some reparatory action. Errors also signal that a called method did not complete as expected. However, with an error, there is often no reasonable reparation. An error generally signals the end of the application.

Exceptions are subclasses of *java.lang.Exception*. Errors are subclasses of *java.lang.Error*. They do share some similarities. Both *java.lang.Exception* and *java.lang.Error* are subclasses of *java.lang.Throwable*. *Throwable* is the root of all "oops" messages. Also, *Throwable* declares the *getMessage* method, and the *throw* operation takes a *Throwable* object as its parameter. So, you throw *Error* objects just as you throw *Exception* objects.

But remember that exceptions must be reported in the *throws* clause for the method. Errors do not have to be reported.

Another difference: Errors are generally unrecoverable. An example of an error is *ThreadDeath*. The *ThreadDeath* error is thrown when a thread is terminated by a call to the *stop* method. There is no way to recover from this; the thread cannot be restarted.

Lab 9-1: Creating a Metronome

In this lab, we will create a metronome applet. A metronome is a device that marks time in repeating intervals.

Lab overview

In this lab, you will practice:

- Implementing the *Runnable* interface.
- Creating a *Thread* object.
- Pausing a *Thread* object using the *sleep* method.
- Writing exception handlers.

Musicians use metronomes to set the tempo, or speed, for a piece of music. Tempo is generally measured in the number of beats per minute. So, a tempo of 60 means 60 beats per minute, or one beat per second. Typical tempo values range between 40 and 240.

Lab setup

1. Start Visual J++.
2. Open the Metronome starter project (Chapter09\Lab9-1\ Metronome.sln).

Lab instructions

1. Modify the *Metronome* class to implement *java.lang.Runnable*.

   - Add *implements Runnable* to the class header.

   - Add an override for the *run* method.

2. In the *run* method, create an infinite loop using the following construct:

   ```
   while(true)
   {
   }
   ```

3. Within the loop, cause the *Panel main* to flash using the following code:

   ```
   main.setBackground(Color.black);
   main.repaint();
   Thread.sleep(flash);
   main.setBackground(Color.white);
   main.repaint();
   Thread.sleep(interval - flash);
   ```

4. The *sleep* method throws *InterruptedException*. Handle this exception by setting up the handler within the loop, and in the *catch* block, updating the browser's status bar with the message from the exception.

5. Modify the *init* method to create a thread, using the *Runnable* interface, and to start the new thread.

6. Test the applet. Compare your work to the solution in Chapter09\ Sol9-1\Metronome.sln.

Optional lab enhancements

Here are some optional enhancements that you can make to this lab:

- Rewrite this applet as a WFC application.

- Provide multiple metronomes within a single applet or application.

Next steps

Now that you have all the pieces, you can create an applet that displays an animated image.

Writing Animation Code

In this section, we will write animation code. Actually, you already know all the pieces you need to write the actual animation code. However, before the animation can run, all the images need to be downloaded. In this section, you will learn how to do this with the *MediaTracker* class.

Downloading Images

The downloading of images is an asynchronous process. A download request is submitted when you call *getImage*. The call to *getImage* returns as soon as the request is submitted. The image downloads in the background. To monitor the download status of a set of images, use a *MediaTracker* object.

The key methods of *MediaTracker* are:

```
public void addImage(Image img, int id);
public void waitForAll() throws InterruptedException;
public void waitForID(int id) throws InterruptedException;

public boolean isErrorAny();
public boolean isErrorID(int id);

public int statusAll(boolean load);
public int statusID(int id, boolean load);
```

Once you've created a *MediaTracker* object, you can add images for it to track. Use the *addImage* method to add the image to *MediaTracker*. The *addImage* method takes two parameters: the *Image* object and an *ID*. Use the *ID* value to group related images together.

Typically, after you add all the *Image* objects to the *MediaTracker* object, you call *waitForAll* on the *MediaTracker* object. This method does not return until the download of all the images is complete. The download of an image is complete when one of the following three things has occurred:

■   The images have been successfully downloaded.

■   An error occurred in the download.

■   The download was canceled by the user.

Alternatively, you can call *waitForID* to wait for the download of a group of images to complete. The group is specified by the *ID* value passed to *addImage*.

After the download of the images is completed, you can use *isErrorAny* or *isErrorID* to check for errors during the download. To get more information about the status of a download, call *statusAll* or *statusID*. The values returned by these functions are defined by the following static final member variables of *MediaTracker*:

```
public static final int ABORTED;
public static final int COMPLETE;
public static final int ERRORED;
public static final int LOADING;
```

Here is an example of using *MediaTracker*:

```
MediaTracker tracker = new MediaTracker(this);
int i = 0;
while(i < MAX)
{
    imgList[i] = getImage(
        getDocumentBase(), BASENAME + (i + 1) + ".jpg");
    tracker.addImage(imgList[i], i);
    i ++;
}

try
{
    tracker.waitForAll();
    bAllLoaded = ! tracker.isErrorAny();
}
catch(InterruptedException e)
{
}
```

The code for this example is located in Chapter09\AnimDemo\AnimDemo.sln.

Lab 9-2: Spinning *E*

Lab overview

Here, we will modify an applet that displays a series of filenames. Rather than displaying the filenames, the modified applet will download the images associated with those filenames. If all the images are downloaded successfully, we will display them as a familiar animation, the Internet Explorer logo: a spinning letter *E*.

Lab objectives

In this lab, you will practice:

- Using a *MediaTracker* object to monitor image download.

- Creating an animated image.

Lab setup

1. Start Visual J++.

2. Open the AnimLab starter project (Chapter09\Lab9-2\ AnimLab.sln).

Lab instructions

1. Create an array of *Image* objects. Name it *imgList*.

2. Modify the *displayFile* method to display the *Image* objects, rather than the filenames.

3. In the *run* method, download the images:

   ■ Declare a *Boolean* member variable to track downloads. Name it *bAllLoaded*.

   ■ Create a *MediaTracker* object.

   ■ Call *getImage* for each *Image* object.

   ■ Call *addImage* for each *Image* object.

   ■ Wait for all the objects to be completely downloaded.

   ■ If all the images have been downloaded successfully, display the images. Otherwise, display an error message.

4. Test the modified applet. You can check your work against Chapter09\Sol9-2\AnimLab.sln.

Optional lab enhancements

Here are some enhancements that you can add to this lab:

■ Modify the applet to use parameters to specify the name of the images and the number of images.

■ Modify the applet to use a parameter to specify the number of milliseconds between images.

Packages in Java

Because all Java classes are grouped together in packages, we can't do much in Java without them.

This chapter starts out with a look at the syntax and semantics for packages in Java. It continues with a discussion about some of the packages that come with Java and Visual J++. As you may have noticed, virtually all the classes you have used in your programming are contained in these predefined packages. Using existing packages is much more common than creating new ones. However, there will be times when you need to create your own package, and the chapter ends with an example of how to do that.

In this chapter, you'll learn about:

- The relationship between packages and folders
- Intrinsic packages in Java
- The Windows Foundation Class (WFC) framework and WFC packages
- Creating your own package

You will create:

- An application that reads and writes strings to the Clipboard
- A clock application
- A utility package that includes a simple class for adding numbers

What Is a Package?

The package is the primary organizational entity for Java. A package groups related classes together logically. The package also defines one kind of access between classes. Each application has a default package that contains all the packages referenced in the code.

To declare a class as a member of a named package

- Include a *package* statement as the first line in the source code:

```
package pkgname;
```

The value for *pkgname* is the name of the package, and it must match the directory or folder name where the source code is located. Here is a *package* statement for the MyStuff package:

```
package MyStuff;
```

The *package* statement must appear at the beginning of its source code file—only blank lines and comments may come before it. The package statement applies to all the classes defined within that source code file.

Packages and the File System

Packages have an intimate relationship to the file system. This relationship is reminiscent of the tie between public classes and files.

Remember that a public class must be located in a file that shares the same name with it. That is, a public class named *MyClass* must be in the source code file MyClass.java.

Files that include a *package* statement must also be located in a folder of the same name. For example, the following lines of code imply that there is a file named MyClass.java that is found in a folder named MyStuff.

```
package MyStuff;

public class MyClass
```

The location of the class files is also important. Compiling this source code file

```
package MyStuff;

public class MyClass
{
    ...
}

class MyHelper
{
    ...
}
```

creates the two class files MyClass.class and MyHelper.class. These class files must be in a folder named MyStuff.

Package names can include multiple identifiers separated by periods. Each part of a multiple-part package name implies a separate folder. For example, the following lines of code imply that a file named MyClass.java is found in a folder named MySubPackage. Moreover, the MySubPackage folder is found in the MyStuff folder.

```
package MyStuff.MySubPackage;

public class MyClass
{
    ...
}
```

The package name indicates a specific package in a specific location. There is no special relationship between packages of the same name that are located in different folders, or between classes of the same name in different packages. In the first example above, the package name is MyStuff. In the second example, the package name is MyStuff.MySubPackage. The one package may be in a subfolder of another package, yet the classes in these packages aren't related. Similarly, there is no special relationship between the classes *MyStuff.MyClass* and *MyStuff.MySubPackage.MyClass*.

The Classpath

The classpath is a list of the folders (or directories) that together form the default package of an application. All named packages are found in subfolders of the folders on the classpath. The package folder is a subfolder of the classpath folder.

For example, let's assume that the classpath consists of the following folders:

- C:\Windows\Java\Classes
- C:\Windows\Java\Lib
- C:\MyLibrary

The class file C:\Windows\Java\Classes\Utilities.class is located directly within the default package.

Now, let's say we create a class file on the classpath by compiling the following lines of code in a file named MyClass.class:

```
package MyStuff;

public class MyClass
{
    ...
}
```

The MyStuff.MyClass file could be in any of the following folders:

- C:\Windows\Java\Classes\MyStuff
- C:\Windows\Java\Lib\MyStuff
- C:\MyLibrary\MyStuff

Additionally, most Virtual Machines (VM) for Java can use class files that are stored in ZIP, JAR, or CAB files. Any CAB, ZIP, or JAR file must be *explicitly* listed in the classpath. These compressed files can include file and folder information with many subfolders.

Let's update the classpath with these two folders:

- C:\Windows\Java\Classes\Classes.ZIP

- C:\Library\MyClasses.CAB

Now, the class file MyClass.class could appear in either Classes.ZIP or MyClasses.CAB. If it is contained in MyClasses.CAB, it is stored in the subfolder MyStuff.

Access Control

When you read about access control in Chapter 4, you learned that there were three access modifiers associated with access: *public*, *private*, and *protected*.

You also learned that there is a fourth kind of access with no associated keyword: *default access*. Items with default access are available only to other items defined within the same package. Because it assigns access to members of the same package, it is also called package access. For example, in the following code, one class and one method are *public*, and one of each has default access:

```
package MyStuff;

public class MyClass
{
    public void getMoreStuff()
    {
        ...
    }

    void doSomeMore()
    {
        ...
    }
}

class Helper
{
}
```

Therefore we can say that the following statements are true:

- Any class can define a member variable of type *MyStuff.MyClass*.

- A method in any class can define a local variable of type *MyStuff.MyClass*.

- Given a *MyStuff.MyClass* object, methods in any class can call the *getMoreStuff* method.

- Only classes in the *MyStuff* package can define a member variable of type *MyStuff.Helper*.

- Only methods in classes in the *MyStuff* package can define a local variable of type *MyStuff.Helper*.

- Given a *MyStuff.MyClass* object, only methods in classes in the *MyStuff* package can call the *doSomeMore* method.

With default or package access, the creator of a package can define classes, methods, and member variables that are accessible only to other classes within that package.

The Java Packages

Let's take a quick look at some of the packages that come with the VM for Java. The packages that are distributed as a standard part of the portable Java library start with "java." We'll examine the java.lang package in some detail and summarize the other eight packages.

The java.lang Package

The heart of the Java language is the java.lang package. This package defines the most basic classes in Java. It is so central to Java that every Java source code file has an implicit import statement for java.lang classes:

```
import java.lang.*;
```

The java.lang package contains the *Object* class. The *java.lang.Object* class is the root of the entire class hierarchy in Java. This package also defines a number of classes to work with basic types:

String	*Boolean*
Character	*Byte*
Integer	*Short*
Long	*Float*
Double	

These classes support numeric type conversions and string manipulation. We worked with these classes rather extensively in earlier chapters.

Some of the other classes defined within java.lang are listed in Table 10-1.

java.lang Class	Description
Class	Provides support for information gathered at run time—for example, the *instanceof* operator.
Math	Provides mathematical constants such as *pi* and *e*. It also supports trigonometric functions.
System	Provides access to the operating system, including the default I/O streams, environment variables, garbage collection, system time, and system properties. Many *System* methods access the methods of the *Runtime* class.
Runtime	Provides access to the operating system. Most *Runtime* methods can be accessed more easily using *java.lang.System*. One exception is the *exec* method, which starts a new process.
Thread	Works with the related *java.lang.Runnable* interface to supply multithreaded support in Java. For a review of threads, see "Multithreading" in Chapter 9.
Throwable	Is the base class for all exceptions in Java. It is the superclass for *java.lang.Exception*, *java.lang.Error*, and *java.lang.RuntimeException*. The exceptions and errors signal "unexpected" events that occurred during the running of the application. For more information about exceptions and errors, see "Exceptions and Exception Handling" in Chapter 9.

Table 10-1.   *Several important classes that are defined in the java.lang package.*

Now let's take a look at some of the other Java packages.

- java.applet—Provides support for Java applets and audio clips. For more information, see "The java.applet Package," in Chapter 6, and "Playing Sounds in an Applet" in Chapter 7.

- java.awt—Supports the Abstract Window Toolkit (AWT), the intrinsic windowing and drawing package for Java. Basic drawing capabilities are included here, such as fonts, colors, and shapes. It also supports components, such as buttons, lists, menus, and text fields, as well as layout managers for controlling the arrangement of components. The AWT is portable. (Most of the graphics I/O in this book uses WFC instead of the AWT.) Chapter 5 includes a brief discussion of the AWT.

- java.beans—Defines the applications programming interface (API) for Java Beans. Java Beans is the platform-neutral component architecture for the Java application environment.

- java.io—Defines a large number of local I/O support classes. Both byte-stream and character-stream I/O are supported. For more details, see "Working with Files" in Chapter 8.

- java.math—Supports mathematical operations for values of arbitrary precision. It contains two classes: *BigDecimal* and *BigInteger.*

- java.net—Supports both URL-based and socket-based network I/O. For more information, see Chapter 13.

- java.text—Provides classes for internationalizing applications, including support for date, numeric, and currency formats and for sorting order.

- java.util—Contains a variety of miscellaneous classes supporting data structures, random numbers, dates, time zones, and calendars.

The WFC Packages

Most of the code we have seen thus far has used the Windows Foundation Class (WFC) library, which comes with Visual J++. The WFC classes all exist in packages within com.ms.wfc.

- app—Contains classes for application support, including the *Application*, *Message*, *Window*, *Clipboard*, *DataFormat*, *Registry*, *Time*, *Timer*, and *Version* classes.

  This is an important package. We'll spend some time exploring some of the major classes in the package following this overview of the primary WFC packages.

- core—Defines core classes for WFC applications and the View Designer. They include the *Component*, *Container*, *Event*, *EventHandler*, *EventInfo*, *PropertyInfo*, *ClassInfo*, and *Enum* classes. This package also defines a number of basic editors for use in the View Designer.

- data and data.ui—Provide database access using ActiveX Data Objects (ADO).

- html—Supports Dynamic HTML (DHTML).

- io—Supports file I/O in Win32. Details are included in "Working with Files" in Chapter 8.

- ole32—Provides support for OLE drag-and-drop.

- ui—Defines the user interface components in WFC. You have been working extensively with the classes in this package each time you work with a form.

- util—Defines several utility classes for data structures. Chapter 8 introduced several utility classes for working with lists.

The WFC Application Package

The WFC application package provides access to many of the basic services needed by an application.

The *Application* Class

The *Application* class supports basic application services. We've used it in almost every lab and demo in this book, and we have used the *run* and *exit* methods in this class to start and stop applications.

This class also includes an overloaded *createThread* method.

```
public static Thread createThread(Delegate method);
public static Thread createThread(Delegate method, Object args[]);
public static Thread createThread(Delegate method, Object args[],
    int priority)
```

The *createThread* method creates a thread based on a *delegate*. A delegate is an object that refers to a specific method in some object. The use of delegates for thread creation allows a single class to create threads with varying actions. In contrast, a class extending *java.lang.Thread* or implementing *java.lang.Runnable* creates threads that perform the actions in the *run* method. A class can have only a single *run* method, so to create threads that perform different actions we need to create a new class for each set of actions.

 OTE   Delegates form the basis of the eventing model in WFC. A full discussion of delegates is outside the scope of this book. However, you can get more information about delegates at the Microsoft Web site: *http://www.microsoft.com/visualj/techmat/feature/delegates/default.htm*

To create a thread using *Application.createThread*

1. Write a method with no parameters that performs the actions you want the thread to perform.

2. Create a delegate for that method, using the MethodInvoker. For example:

```
new MethodInvoker(this.doSomething);
```

3. Call *Application.createThread* with the new delegate.

4. Start the thread.

Here is a simple example of creating a thread in response to an event. You can look at the complete project files in Chapter10\Threading\ DelegateThread.sln.

```
// This method specifies the actions for the thread.
public void doSomething()
{
    addOutput("doing something");
    for(int i = 1; i < 4; i ++)
    {
        addOutput("Number " + i);
        try
        {
            Thread.sleep(500);
        }
        catch(InterruptedException e)
        {
        }
    }
    addOutput("done");
}

// This is a helper method to handle output.
public synchronized void addOutput(String s)
{
    lbOutput.addItem(s);
}

// This is the event handler that creates the thread.
private void startThread(Object source, Event e)
{
    // Declaring the thread reference.
    Thread t;

    // Creating the thread using the delegate MethodInvoker
    t = Application.createThread(new MethodInvoker(this.doSomething));
    try
    {
        t.start();
    }
    catch(IllegalThreadStateException itse)
    {
    }
```

The *Clipboard* Class

The *Clipboard* class is a very simple class that provides access to the system Clipboard. It comprises two methods for copying data to and from the Clipboard: *setDataObject* and *getDataObject*. The *setDataObject* method can take any type of object. The *getDataObject* method returns an *IdataObject* interface.

To place data on the Clipboard

■ Call *setDataObject*.

```
public static void setDataObject(Object data);
public static void setDataObject(Object data, boolean copy);
```

The single-parameter version calls the two-parameter version with *false* as the value of the second parameter. This does not copy the data to the Clipboard—only a reference to the data is placed on the Clipboard. When the single-parameter version is used, at the end of the application, the data on the Clipboard is cleared.

To retrieve data from the Clipboard

■ Call *getDataObject*.

```
public static IDataObject getDataObject();
```

The *IDataObject* Interface and the *DataObject* Class

The *IDataObject* interface handles uniform data transfer (UDT), which is the basis for data transfer in OLE and ActiveX. It is used with the Clipboard and OLE drag-and-drop. Here is the definition of the *IDataObject* interface:

```
public interface IDataObject
{
    public Object getData(String format);
    public Object getData(Class format);

    public void setData(String format, Object data);
    public void setData(Class format, Object data);
    public void setData(Object data);

    public boolean getDataPresent(String format);
    public boolean getDataPresent(Class format);

    public String[] getFormats();
}
```

The *Class* parameter is a class defined in *java.lang.Class*. The *String* parameter is a value defined in the *DataFormats* class.

You can support multiple Clipboard formats with a *DataObject* object. The *DataObject* class implements the *IdataObject* interface. Call *setData* for each Clipboard format you want to supply.

To specify the format for retrieved Clipboard data, call *getData*, giving the Clipboard format you want. And to check for a specific format for retrieved Clipboard data, call *getDataPresent*, again giving the Clipboard format you want.

The *DataFormats* Class

The *DataFormats* class defines *String* constants for the standard Clipboard formats, and some new formats for WFC classes. Here's a list of the static final *String* member variables of the *DataFormats* class:

> *CF_TEXT*
> *CF_UNICODETEXT*
> *CF_DIB*
> *CF_BITMAP*
> *CF_ENHMETAFILE*
> *CF_METAFILEPICT*
> *CF_SYLK*
> *CF_DIF*
> *CF_TIFF*
> *CF_OEMTEXT*
> *CF_PALETTE*
> *CF_PENDATA*
> *CF_RIFF*
> *CF_WAVE*
> *CF_HDROP*
> *CF_LOCALE*
> *CF_HTML*
> *CF_RTFTEXT*
> *CF_CSV*
> *CF_STRINGCLASS*
> *CF_WFCOBJECT*

Lab 10-1: Manipulating Clipboard Strings

In this lab, we will create an application that reads and writes strings to the Clipboard.

Lab overview

You will practice:

- Working with the Clipboard.
- Checking data formats.

Lab setup

- Start Visual J++.

Lab instructions

1. Create a Windows Application project. Name it *ClipboardStrings*.

2. On the form, add an Edit control and two Button controls:

   - Name the Edit control *edtClipboard*.

   - Name one Button control *btnGetData*, and set its Text property to *Get Data*.

   - Name the other Button control *btnSetData*, and set its Text property to *Set Data*.

3. In the Click event handler for *btnGetData*, do the following:

   - Get the data object from the Clipboard.

   - If the data object has *String* data, update *edtClipboard* with the string data.

   - If the data object does not have *String* data, display a message to that effect in *edtClipboard*.

4. In the Click event handler for *btnSetData*, set the Clipboard to the text in *edtClipboard*.

5. Test the application.

- Copy text to the Clipboard using Notepad.

- Get the Clipboard data using the application.

- Set the Clipboard data using the application.

- Paste the Clipboard data into Notepad.

- Copy an image to the Clipboard using Paint.

- Get the Clipboard data using the application. You should get the error message.

You can compare your work to the solution located in Chapter10\ Sol10-1\ClipboardStrings.sln.

Optional lab enhancements

Here are some optional enhancements for you to try:

- Add a method that disables the Get button if the data on the Clipboard is not a string. Call this method from a *Timer* event handler.

- Instead of buttons, try a menu control with menu items for the commands.

The *Time* Class

The WFC *Time* class has a number of constructors that track date and time using Win32 time. It easily handles dates before January 1, 1970. (In contrast, the *java.util.Date* class, like the C run-time library, has values that begin on January 1, 1970 and run through sometime in 2037 C.E.)

Creating *Time*

You have several ways to create a *Time* object.

To create a *Time* object with the current time

- Use the parameterless constructor:

```
public Time();
```

To create a *Time* object based on a *String* value

■ Use the *String* constructor.

```
public Time(String time);
```

To create a *Time* object with a specific date value

■ Use the three-parameter constructor:

```
public Time(int year, int month, int day);
```

To create a *Time* object with a specific date and time value

■ Use the six-parameter constructor.

```
public Time(int year, int month, int day,
    int hour, int min, int sec);
```

Checking *Time*

The *Time* class has a number of accessor or conversion methods for accessing dates and times. Here are examples of the *get*, *set*, and *format* methods.

To get a portion of the *Time* value

■ Use one of these accessor methods.

```
public int getYear();
public int getMonth();
public int getDay();
public int getHour();
public int getMinute();
public int getSecond();
public int getMillis();

public int getDayOfWeek();
public int getDayOfYear();
public Time getDate();
public Time getTimeOfDay();
```

To set the date or time portion of a *Time* object

■ Use one of these accessor methods.

```
public Time setDate(Time date);
public Time setTimeOfDay(Time timeOfDay);
```

To format the *Time* value for *String* output

■ Use one of these conversion methods.

```
    public String formatShortTime();
public String formatLongTime();
public String formatShortDate();
public String formatLongDate();
```

The output types from each method are listed in the following table.

Method	Output Type
formatShortTime	hours and minutes
formatLongTime	hours, minutes, and seconds
formatShortDate	month, day, and year (for example, 10/5/97)
formatLongDate	*String* dates (for example, Sunday, October 05, 1997)

Updating *Time*

A *Time* object can be updated using a number of *add* methods:

To change a *Time* value

■ Use one of these *add* methods.

```
public Time addYears(int interval);
public Time addMonths(int interval);
public Time addDays(int interval);
public Time addHours(int interval);
public Time addMinutes(int interval);
public Time addSeconds(int interval);
public Time addMillis(int interval);
```

These methods add whole units to the *Time* value. To add fractional days to the *Time* value, use this overload of *addDays*:

```
public Time addDays(double interval);
```

The *Timer* Class

The *Timer* class creates a Windows timer. The timer fires an event at regular intervals. The intervals are specified in milliseconds.

To work with a *Timer* object on a form

1. Place a Timer control on the form.

2. Set the timer properties in the Properties window. Note that the interval property contains the number of milliseconds between timer events.

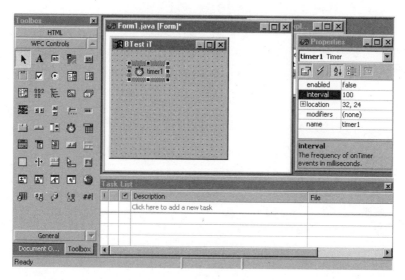

Figure 10-1.   *A timer control on a form with the timer properties displayed.*

Here is the default constructor for timer1 in Figure 10-1.

```
private void timer1_timer(Object source, Event e)
    {

    }
```

To start the timer

- Call the *start* method.

  —or—

- Set the enabled property to *true*.

To stop the timer

- Call the *stop* method.

  —or—

- Set the enabled property to *false*.

Lab 10-2: Building Your Own WFC Clock

This lab gives you an opportunity to create a digital clock using WFC.

Lab overview

You will practice:

- Using a *Timer* object.

- Creating a *Time* object to get the current time.

Lab setup

- Start Visual J++.

Lab instructions

1. Create a new Windows Application project, and name it *DigitalClock*.

2. On the form, place a label, and name it *lblTime*. Set the text to *99:99:99*, and adjust the font and size to make a pleasing display.

3. Place a Timer control on the form. Set the interval to *500* (milliseconds)—half a second.

   Notice that the enabled property is *false* by default.

4. Create a method named *showTime* that does the following:

   - Creates a *Time* object with the current time

   - Formats the *Time* object to show the time, including seconds

   - Updates *lblTime* with the formatted time value

5. Have the constructor for the form start the timer and call *showTime* to update the initial display.

6. Create a handler for the timer event, and have it call *showTime*.

   Test your application. You can compare your work to the solution located in Chapter10\Sol10-2\DigitalClock.sln.

Optional lab enhancements

Here are some optional enhancements for you to try:

- Add a menu that includes commands for modifying the display format.

- Add handlers to the form so that the date is displayed when the form is clicked. Revert to displaying the time when the mouse button is clicked again. Alternatively, revert to displaying the time when the mouse button is released.

Creating Your Own Packages

In this section, you will learn how to create packages using Visual J++. You will also learn how to add folders to the classpath for a project.

Creating a New Package

Visual J++ uses a directory-based project system. That is, every project includes all the files in the project folder. You can verify this by actually viewing all the files within a project: on the Project Explorer toolbar, select Show All Files. Compare this list of files to the one shown by Windows Explorer.

The Project Explorer window is also where you create a folder within a project. Right-click either a project or a project item, and then choose New Folder. In the Add Package/Folder dialog box, enter the name for the folder. To have the folder act as a Java package, the name must conform to Java naming conventions. You can learn more about Java names in the "Identifiers and Naming Conventions" section in Chapter 3.

When you right-click a project item, the new folder will be a peer of the selected item. When you start with a project or folder, your new folder will be within the project or item you selected.

To create source files within a folder, right-click the folder and select Add. Any source files you create in a subfolder will automatically contain the appropriate package statement.

Adding Folders to the Classpath

The project and solution mechanism of Visual J++ supports creating a solution that contains multiple projects. The projects in a solution can be either new or existing projects.

During development, you might have multiple projects for each component of a solution. Within the context of creating packages, you could have different projects for each package you create.

Within one solution, all the project folders are included on the classpath. So, there are no special actions necessary for accessing the classes defined in the other projects of the solution. On the other hand, once you have some projects that are relatively stable, it may not make as much sense to include those projects in each solution that uses the classes. There are two ways to approach this:

- Install the packages on the classpath for the development machine.

- Include the desired packages on the classpath for the projects or solutions that use them.

Both approaches have some merit. Installing the packages on the development machine classpath means that those classes will be uniformly available. This is the likely configuration on the users' machines. However, with this arrangement it's difficult to continue developing the original packages or alternative versions of the packages.

When you keep the packages in the classpath for the projects or solutions that use them, you retain the flexibility to support packages that are still in flux. However, you must set the classpath for each project that uses the desired package.

To add a folder to the classpath for a project:

1. From the View menu, choose Project Properties.

2. In the Project Properties dialog box, click Classpath.

3. Click Add, and enter the desired folder.

Lab 10-3: Writing Your Own Package

Try your hand at creating a very basic package with a utility class; it adds two numbers together.

Lab overview

You will practice:

■ Creating a package in Visual J++.

Lab setup

■ Start Visual J++.

Lab instructions

1. Create a new project, and name it *CreateAdder*.

2. Add a new folder to this project, and name it *MyUtilities*.

3. In the new folder, add a new class: *Adder*.

4. In *Adder*, add an *add* method with *public* access that simply returns the sum of two parameters.

5. Test the *Adder* class:

   ▦ Create a form that takes two numbers and adds them.

   ▦ Implement the *Click* event handler to use *MyUtilities.Adder*.

6. You can compare your work to the solution located in Chapter10\Sol10-3\CreateAdder.sln.

Optional lab enhancements

Here are some optional enhancements for you to try:

■ Create the test application in a different project within the same solution.

■ Create a command-line version of the test application.

Lab 10-4: Using Your Package with Another Solution

Lab overview

You will practice:

- Adding folders to the classpath.

- Copying existing files into projects.

Lab setup

- Start Visual J++.

You will use the MyUtility package you created in Lab 10-3 to access the *Adder* class from another solution. If you created two projects within the same solution, both project folders are on the classpath.

Lab instructions

1. Create a new project in a new solution, and name it *TestAdder*.

2. Copy the test form from CreateAdder to the new project:

   - Right-click the TestAdder project in the Project Explorer, and then choose Add.

   - In the Add Item dialog box, click Existing.

   - Navigate to CreateAdder, and select the test form.

3. Try to build the project.

   The build should fail, because the package *MyUtilities* is not on the classpath.

4. Add the CreateAdder folder to the project classpath.

5. Try to build the project again.

   The build should now succeed.

6. Test the application. You can compare your work to the solution files in Chapter10\Sol10-4\TestAdder.sln.

Console Applications

This chapter could really be called "Applications." Many of the things you'll learn here will be just as useful for creating Windows applications as they are for command-line-based applications, because you're going to learn more about how applications work in Java generally. We'll also tie up some loose ends here. The Visual J++ entry point for this material is the Console Application template.

In this chapter, you'll learn about:

- Console I/O

- The *main* method

- Flow control

- Loops

You will get a chance to practice using:

- Command-line parameters

- Command-line switches

- The *for*, *do*, and *switch* statements

What Is Different About Console Applications?

Console applications do not have a graphical user interface. That is, they don't do Windows. All input and output appears on a command line or on a printout, and there is nothing for a mouse to click.

Using the Console Application Template

The easiest way to create a console application to use the Console Application template provided as part of Visual J++.

To create a console application

1. From the File menu, choose New Project.

2. In the left pane of the New Project dialog box, select the Visual J++ Project/Application subfolder.

3. In the right pane, select Console Application, and type the name for the new project.

4. Click Open to create the new project.

The console application we just created includes Class1.java. When you open Class1.java, you'll see the following.

```
/**
 * This class can take a variable number of parameters on the command
 * line. Program execution begins with the main() method. The class
 * constructor is not invoked unless an object of type 'Class1'
 * created in the main() method.
 */
public class Class1
{
    /**
     * The main entry point for the application.
     *
     * @param args Array of parameters passed to the application
     * via the command line.
     */
    public static void main (String[] args)
    {
        // TODO: Add initialization code here
    }
}
```

The only code in this class is the *main* method. It is this method that makes this code an application. When we look at other applications, we see a *main* method in them as well.

The *main* Method

All applications have a *main* method. This method describes what should happen when the application runs.

```
public static void main (String args[])
{
    // stuff-to-do
}
```

Notice the main method is *public*, *static*, and *void* (returns nothing). Let's look at the characteristics of the *main* method. (The parameter is discussed in the next section.)

- *static*—At the very beginning of running an application, nothing exists for that application, just the Virtual Machine for Java (VM). The VM can call a *static* method without needing an instance of the class. *Static* methods exist outside an object, and can be accessed by any object.

- *public*—Obviously, the VM needs to have access to the *main* method. Since the VM is external to this class, the method must be *public* so that external entities may access this method.

- *void*—The VM is not really designed to handle values being returned. If there is a run-time error, an exception will be raised. So, there is no need to return a value that the VM will ignore.

Windows applications

In the Windows Application template, the *main* method looks like this:

```
public static void main (String args[])
{
    Application.run(new Form1());
}
```

This *main* method creates an instance of the form and hand it to the *Application.run* method. *Application.run* hooks up this form to the Windows operating system.

Console applications

In the Console Application template, the *main* method looks like this:

```
public static void main (String[] args)
{
    // TODO: Add initialization code here
}
```

By default, it does nothing. It's a *tabula rasa* waiting for you to enter commands.

 NOTE The Windows Application template uses "main(String args[])," while the Console Application template uses "main (String args[])." Java is flexible in handling the space before the parameter list.

Command-Line Parameters

Here is that simplest example of the *main* method again:

```
public static void main (String args[])
{
    // stuff-to-do
}
```

The parameter is an array of *String* objects. Here is another way of writing this method:

```
public static void main (String[] args)
{
    // stuff-to-do
}
```

The *args* parameter holds additional information that is given to the application when it begins. You may wonder how the application gets additional information. To understand this, let's look at how a Java application is run.

Running a Java application

When you run a Java application, you need to access the VM for Java and hand it a class. You have two commands for running applications from the command line: WJVIEW and JVIEW. With *WJVIEW*, the command prompt is immediately available again. With *JVIEW*, the command prompt is not available until the Java application completes.

To run a Java application with no parameters

1. At the command prompt, set the current directory to the directory that contains the class file.

   It is very important that the class file be on the classpath. The classpath includes the current working directory.

2. At the command prompt, type the command *WJVIEW*, followed by the name of the class. For example:

   ```
   WJVIEW MyClass
   ```

   —or—

   Type the command *JVIEW*, followed by the name of the class. For example:

   ```
   JVIEW MyClass
   ```

 OTE   Java is case-sensitive, while DOS is not.

To supply parameters to the Java application, include them on the command line following the name of the class. For example, if you want to print the words "This is a test," you can use the following command:

```
WJVIEW Form1 This is a test
```

Here we have four parameters, each of which contains a separate word: *This*, *is*, *a*, and *test*.

To supply a parameter that includes spaces, simply enclose the parameter within quotation marks. For example, the following command line passes two parameters to the *main* method:

```
WJVIEW Form1 "This is a test." "It is only a test."
```

In this case, the two *args* parameters are *This is a test.* and *It is only a test.*

OTE   The name of the class at the command prompt should use the same case as the name of the class in the Java file. Using the wrong case may work, but it is not guaranteed to do so. The wjview command is not case sensitive.

Setting the Launch File

We just saw how to run a Java application from the command line. We also saw how to supply command-line parameters to the application. Well, you can do the same thing when you run your own application from the Visual J++ environment. This is called setting the launch file. You can do this with or without parameters.

In a project, there may be several different files that could start up the project. For example, you may have multiple Java files that include a *public static void* method named *main* that takes an array of *Strings* as its parameter. Any forms you have that were added using the Form template include this method. So, if you have multiple forms in your project, any one of those forms could be the main form for the project.

Here's another example: if you have a project that is a Web site, there may be multiple HTML files in the project. Any one of those HTML files could be the *launch file*, the typical initial entry point into that Web site.

When you're running the application manually, you explicitly type in the name of the class with the *main* method or type in the name of the "main" HTML file. You have the same option when you are working within the IDE.

To set the launch file for a project without parameters

1. In the Project Explorer window, right-click the desired project, and from the pop-up menu, choose *<PROJECT>* Properties, where *<PROJECT>* is the name of the project you want.

2. In the Project Properties dialog box, click the Launch tab.

3. Select the Default radio button, and from the drop-down list, select the start-up file from the list of Java files. Each of the Java files in the list contains a callable *main* method or HTML files.

4. Click OK.

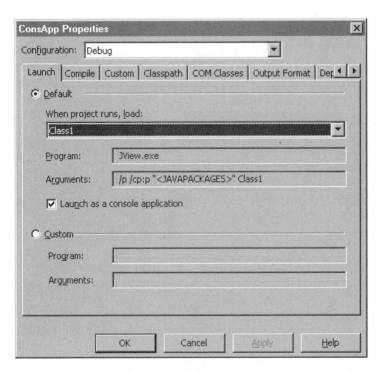

Figure 11-1.   *Setting a parameterless launch file.*

Now, what do you do if you want to supply parameters? Just before you click that OK button in the Project Properties dialog box (step 4 in the preceding procedure), click the Custom radio button. You'll see in Figure 11-2 that the Program and Arguments settings for Default are copied to the Program and Arguments settings for Custom. Next, in the arguments edit box, enter the parameters for the application. These arguments will be used when this project is run, either with or without debugging.

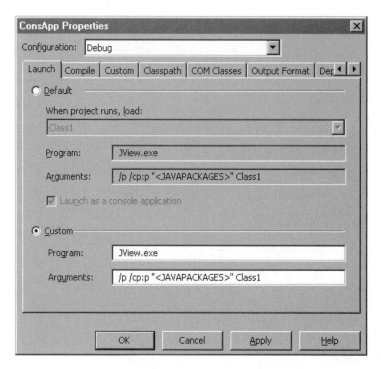

Figure 11-2. *Setting a launch file with two parameters.*

You may well have a solution with more than one project in it. If so, when the solution is started, the launch file for the start-up project is run. To set the start-up project, right-click the project in Project Explorer, and then choose Set as StartUp Project.

Lab 11-1: Running an Application from the Command Line

In this lab, you will create an application that echoes command-line parameters.

Lab overview

In this lab, you will practice:

■ Accessing the command-line parameters in a Java application.

■ Running an application from the command line.

■ Setting the IDE to provide command-line parameters.

Lab instructions

1. Create a new Windows Application project called ListParameters.

2. Name the form *ListParameters.java*.

3. Add a ListBox control to the form, and name it *lbParams*.

4. In the *main* method, fill *lbParams* with the parameter values in *args*.

5. Build the project.

6. Open a Command Prompt window. Navigate to the *ListParameters* folder.

7. Run the application from the command line, supplying various parameters. Note the parameters in the list box. Try using quotation marks to create parameters with embedded spaces.

8. Run the application from the IDE, supplying various parameters.

9. Try this again, using a ListView control instead of a ListBox control. Number the parameters.

10. You can check your work against the solution in Chapter11\ Sol11-1\ListParams.sln.

Next steps

Parameters are used to handle command-line flags for applications. These flags are typically preceded by a hyphen (-) or slash (/). In the next section, we'll update this application with a command-line flag that permits the list of parameters to be sent to a console window.

Console I/O

In the previous section, we learned that a console application does not have a graphical user interface. In fact, a console application uses the name "console" because its I/O is like an old-fashioned console or terminal, containing no graphics, just lines of text.

When you select a Java file as the launch file, the Launch As A Console Application check box becomes available in the Launch tab of the Project Properties dialog box. When the check box is selected and the application is run, an MS-DOS prompt window appears, displaying output and prompting for user input.

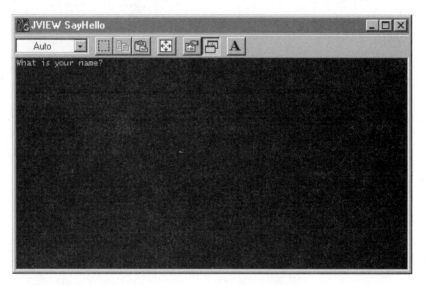

Figure 11-3.   *A console application running in a DOS window.*

If the application tries to perform console I/O without a console window, the exception com.ms.wfc.io.WinIOException is raised.

Console I/O Methods

Console (text) I/O is supported by the *com.ms.wfc.io* package. Its two primary interfaces are *IReader* and *IWriter*. This package also includes classes that implement these interfaces.

Reading strings

Let's start by considering the "I" side of console I/O, reading console input.

■ *IReader* interface—Provides simple access to characters and strings.

```
public interface IReader
{
    public void close();
    public int peek();
    public int read();
    public int read(char[] buffer, int index, int count);
    public String readLine();
}
```

You might have noticed that there is no way to specify what you are reading from. The class that implements IReader must provide an *open* method or a constructor to do that.

■ *Reader* class—Implements the *IReader* interface. Provides support for reading characters and lines from a buffer. It is the superclass of *TextReader* and *StringReader*.

■ *TextReader* class—Associates the *Reader* buffer with a file or other byte stream. *TextReader* has two constructors:

  ▪ One associates the *Reader* buffer with the byte stream. This constructor takes an *IByteStream* parameter, such as a *com.ms.wfc.io.File* object.

  ▪ The other constructor uses a *String* parameter as a filename to open a file for reading and associates the *Reader* buffer with the opened file.

■ *StringReader* class—Associates the *Reader* buffer with a string. It has a constructor that takes a *String* parameter.

Writing strings

Now, let's look at the "O" side of console I/O, writing to the console.

■ *IWriter* interface—Provides simple access to converting the "standard" types to strings and writing them. Notice the many overloaded functions.

```
public interface IWriter
{
    public void close();
    public void flush();
    public void write(char value);
    public void write(char[] buffer);
    public void write(char[] buffer, int index, int count);
    public void write(boolean value);
    public void write(int value);
    public void write(long value);
    public void write(float value);
    public void write(double value);
    public void write(String value);
    public void write(Object value);
    public void writeLine();
    public void writeLine(char value);
    public void writeLine(char[] buffer);
    public void writeLine(char[] buffer, int index, int
    count);
    public void writeLine(boolean value);
    public void writeLine(int value);
    public void writeLine(long value);
    public void writeLine(float value);
    public void writeLine(double value);
    public void writeLine(String value);
    public void writeLine(Object value);
}
```

The *IWriter* interface describes a number of methods. It is reasonable to do this when writing out textual representations of data. However, it is not practical to provide this sort of rich support for reading. The problem, when reading, is that you cannot make assumptions about the accuracy of the information. The best choice is to read a string and use parse methods to try to interpret the string as a numerical or Boolean value.

- The *Writer* class—Implements the *IWriter* interface, and provides support for writing to a buffer. It also handles conversion to *String* representations of values. It is the superclass of *TextWriter* and *StringWriter*.

- *TextWriter* class—Associates the *Writer* buffer with a file or other byte stream. *TextWriter* has two constructors:

- One takes an *IByteStream* parameter, such as a *com.ms.wfc.io.File* object, and associates the *Writer* buffer with the byte stream.

- The other uses a *String* parameter as a filename to create a file for writing and associates the *Writer* buffer with the newly created file.

■ *StringWriter* class—Associates the *Writer* buffer with a *StringBuffer* object. *StringWriter* has two constructors:

- One takes a *StringBuffer* parameter. The *getStringBuffer* method returns the associated string buffer.

- The other is a zero-parameter constructor that creates a new *StringBuffer*. The *getStringBuffer* method returns the associated string buffer.

The Text class

The *com.ms.wfc.io.Text* class provides simple access to reading and writing to the console.

```
public final class Text
{
    public static final TextReader in;
    public static final TextWriter out;
    public static final TextWriter err;

    private Text() {
    }

    static {
        in = new TextReader(File.openStandardInput());
        out = new TextWriter(File.openStandardOutput());
        out.setAutoFlush(true);
        err = new TextWriter(File.openStandardError());
        err.setAutoFlush(true);
    }
}
```

The member variables *in*, *out*, and *err* are associated with standard input, standard output, and standard error. Here is an example of using *in* and *out* to read from and write to the console window:

```
import com.ms.wfc.io.*;

public class SayHello
{
    public static void main(String[] args)
    {
        Text.out.write("What is your name? ");
        String name = Text.in.readLine();
        Text.out.write("Hello ");
        Text.out.writeLine(name);
        Text.out.write("Press <enter> to end this application");
        name = Text.in.readLine();
    }
}
```

The code for this example is located in Chapter11-1\ConsoleIO\ConsoleIO.sln.

Lab 11-2: Using Console I/O

In this lab, you will update the application to alternately list the parameters using console I/O.

Lab overview

In this lab, you will practice how to:

- Interpret command-line flags.

- Use console I/O methods.

Lab setup

There is no setup for this lab if you work from your existing solution to Lab 11-1. However, you might want to begin with the provided starting code for Lab 11-2, as it includes helpful TODO comments.

1. Start Visual J++.

2. Open the ListParams project (Lab11-1\ListParams.sln).

Lab instructions

1. Add a method named *writeArgsToConsole* with this format:

   ```
   void writeArgsToConsole(String[] args);
   ```

2. In the new method, do the following:

   - Open standard output.

   - Write the values of parameters to standard output, one per line.

3. Find the *main* method in this application.

4. In the *main* method, check the first command-line parameter.

   If it is */c*, call *writeArgsToConsole* with the command-line parameters. Remove the flag */c* from the list.

   If the first command-line parameter is not */c*, display the window version from Lab 11-1.

5. Run the application both with and without the */c* flag.

6. Check your work against the solution in Chapter11\Sol11-2\ ListParams.sln.

Optional lab enhancements

Here are some optional enhancements for you to try:

- Include error checking for unrecognized command-line flags.

- Include a */help* command-line switch that explains the command-line flags and parameters.

More Flow of Control

You have seen various types of statements for flow of control. In this section, we'll take a look at the other flow-of-control statements in the Java language.

The *switch* and *break* Statements

The *switch* statement is, perhaps, the statement in the Java language most likely to give you trouble. The *switch* statement supports branching based on a discrete value. This concept is probably familiar to you from other programming languages: the *switch* statement in Visual Basic and the *case* statement in Pascal are similar.

The *switch* statement looks like this:

```
switch( discrete-expression )
{
case value1 :
    // stuff-to-do
    break;
case value2 :
    // stuff-to-do
    break;
default:
    // stuff-to-do
}
// stuff-after-the-switch
```

The *switch* statement starts with the keyword *switch*, followed by a discrete expression within parentheses. The expression can be of any of the following types:

    int

    short

    long

    char

    byte

A block follows. The *block* statement contains *case* labels. Each *case* label is the keyword *case*, followed by a value of the appropriate type and a colon. The flow of control jumps to the *case* label that matches the discrete expression. The statements following the *case* label are performed. The *break* statement causes the flow of control to jump to the end of the *switch* statement. At the end of the block, you can include a *default* label. The *default* label will match any value that does not have a *case* label. The *default* label is optional.

Let's take a look at an example from the Days project, located in Chapter11\Days\TwelveDays.sln.

```
String ordinal;
switch(nDayNumber)
{
case 1:
    ordinal = "first";
    break;
case 2:
    ordinal = "second";
    break;
case 3:
    ordinal = "third";
    break;
case 4:
    ordinal = "fourth";
    break;

case 5:
    ordinal = "fifth";
    break;
case 6:
    ordinal = "sixth";
    break;
case 7:
    ordinal = "seventh";
    break;
case 8:
    ordinal = "eighth";
    break;
case 9:
    ordinal = "ninth";
    break;
case 10:
    ordinal = "tenth";
    break;
case 11:
    ordinal = "eleventh";
    break;
case 12:
    ordinal = "twelfth";
    break;
default:
    ordinal = "oops";
}
```

It is critically important to include the *break* statements in the *switch* statement. In the next section, you will see more clearly how the *break* statement changes the behavior of the *switch* statement.

The *switch* Statement and Fall-Through

The *break* statement is very important to the *switch* statement. The flow of control does not automatically jump to the end of the *switch* statement when another *case* label is encountered. In fact, the way to get multiple values associated with a single set of statements is to place multiple *case* labels on the statement. For example, the values 4 through 12 would cause the same statements to be executed in the switch statement that follows:

```
switch(nDayNumber)
{
case 1:
    output.write("1st");
    break;
case 2:
    output.write("2nd");
    break;
case 3:
    output.write("3rd");
    break;
case 4:
case 5:
case 6:
case 7:
case 8:
case 9:
case 10:
case 11:
case 12:
    output.write(nDayNumber);
    output.write("th");
    break;
}
```

There are nine *case* labels for the "th" branch (case 4 through case 12). They all apply to the same three statements:

- output.write(nDayNumber);

- output.write("th");

- break;

Sometimes this behavior is called *fall-through* because the flow of control "falls through" to the next case.

Here is another example of fall-through.

```
switch(nDayNumber)
{
case 12:
    output.writeLine("  Twelve drummers drumming,");
    sleep(3 * pulse);
case 11:
    output.writeLine("  Eleven pipers piping,");
    sleep(3 * pulse);
case 10:
    output.writeLine("  Ten lords a-leaping,");
    sleep(3 * pulse);
case 9:
    output.writeLine("  Nine ladies dancing,");
    sleep(3 * pulse);
case 8:
    output.writeLine("  Eight maids a-milking,");
    sleep(3 * pulse);
case 7:
    output.writeLine("  Seven swans a-swimming,");
    sleep(3 * pulse);
case 6:
    output.writeLine("  Six geese a-laying,");
    sleep(3 * pulse);
case 5:
    output.writeLine("  Five gold rings,");

    sleep(8 * pulse);
case 4:
    output.writeLine("  Four calling birds,");
    sleep(3 * pulse);
case 3:
    output.writeLine("  Three French hens,");
    sleep(3 * pulse);
case 2:
    output.writeLine("  Two turtle doves,");
    sleep(3 * pulse);
case 1:
    output.writeLine("  And a partridge in a pear tree.");
    sleep(8 * pulse);
}
```

Other Looping Statements

There are several styles of loop constructs available in Java: "test at the top," "test at the bottom," and "counted." We'll go over each in turn and then compare them.

Test at the top

In Chapter 8, we learned about the *while* loop, which uses this format:

```
while( true-false-check )
{
    // stuff-to-do
}
// stuff-after-the-loop
```

This simple loop has the check at the beginning of each iteration. If *true-false-check* is true, the application does *stuff-to-do* and loops back to the top to check again. When *true-false-check* is false, the application moves on to *stuff-after-the-loop*.

Test at the bottom

The *do* loop in Java is very similar to the *while* loop:

```
do
{
    // stuff-to-do
} while( true-false-check );
// stuff-after-the-loop
```

This simple loop has the check at the *end* of each iteration. The application does *stuff-to-do* and then performs the check. If *true-false-check* is true, the application loops back, does *stuff-to-do*, and checks again. If it is false, the application continues with *stuff-after-the-loop*.

 OTE The do loop does stuff-to-do at least once. In the while loop, if true-false-check starts out false, stuff-to-do is skipped completely.

Counted

The *for* loop is somewhat more complex than the other two loops. Technically, the *for* loop can be used in many ways. The simplest and most common way to use the *for* loop is as a counted loop:

```
for( initialization ; true-false-check ; update )
{
    // stuff-to-do
}
// stuff-after-the-loop
```

In the *for* loop, as in the *while* loop, the check occurs before *stuff-to-do*. However, *initialization* occurs before *true-false-check* the first time. After *stuff-do-to*, *update* occurs before the next *true-false-check*. As we're beginning to see, this is a bit complicated. An example should make it clearer; here is a *for* loop that counts from 0 to 9:

```
output.writeLine("Starting to count");
for(int nCounter = 0; nCounter < 10; nCounter ++)
{
    output.writeLine(nCounter);
}
output.writeLine("All done.");
```

After writing out "Starting to count", the *for* loop starts. The first thing that happens is *initialization*:

```
int nCounter = 0
```

A temporary variable named *nCounter* is created. It has the initial value 0. The next thing that happens is *true-false-check*:

```
nCounter < 10
```

This is true, so the *stuff-to-do* is performed:

```
output.writeLine(nCounter);
```

After *stuff-to-do*, we continue with *update*:

```
nCounter ++
```

Now *nCounter* is updated from 0 to 1. And *true-false-check* is evaluated:

```
nCounter < 10
```

And so we continue with *stuff-to-do*. Eventually, *nCounter* is 9, and *stuff-to-do* prints out "9." When *update* happens, *nCounter* becomes 10. The check fails:

```
nCounter < 10
```

And the application continues with *stuff-after-the-loop*:

```
output.writeLine("All done.");
```

 OTE The declaration of *nCounter* was within the *for* loop. At the end of the loop, *nCounter* was no longer available. This is different from the *for* loop in C++.

Comparing loop examples

Here is the example of counting from 0 to 9, using the *for* loop again.

```
output.writeLine("Starting to count");
for(int nCounter = 0; nCounter < 10; nCounter ++)
{
    output.writeLine(nCounter);
}
output.writeLine("All done.");
```

Here is a *while* loop, also counting from 0 to 9.

```
output.writeLine("Starting to count");
int nCounter = 0;
while(nCounter < 10)
{
    output.writeLine(nCounter);
    nCounter ++;
}
output.writeLine("All done.");
```

Notice that the declaration of *nCounter* is outside the *while* loop. Also, the *update* (nCounter++) is inside the braces of the loop. In this case, *nCounter* does not disappear at the end of the loop.

And here is a *do* loop, counting from 0 to 9:

```
output.writeLine("Starting to count");
int nCounter = 0;
do
{
    output.writeLine(nCounter);
    nCounter ++;
} while(nCounter < 10);
output.writeLine("All done.");
```

As with the *while* loop, *nCounter* is declared outside the loop. It continues to be available after the loop is done.

Lab 11-3: Observing a Console Application: The Twelve Days of Christmas

This is a simple lab to acquaint you with the behavior of the *switch* statement. In this lab, we'll examine a simple console application that gives the words to the song "The Twelve Days of Christmas."

Lab overview

In this lab, you will:

■ see examples of the **switch** statement

Lab setup

1. Start Visual J++.
2. Open the TwelveDays project (Lab11-3\TwelveDays.sln).

Lab instructions

1. Examine the code in this application, noting the *startVerse* and *listGifts* methods.

    The application has a number of *sleep* statements. These statements pause the output so that it will synchronize with someone singing the song. The pause is based on the member variable *pulse* that gives the number of milliseconds per beat. It is set to 500, so each beat is half a second.

2. Run the application. Notice the behavior of the two *switch* statements.

3. See what happens when you remove *break* statements to the *switch* statement in *startVerse*.

4. See what happens when you remove *break* statements to the *switch* statement in *listGifts*.

5. Rewrite the code using a different looping statement.

6. You can compare your work to the solution located in Chapter11\ Sol11-3\TwelveDays.sln.

Using External Components in WFC

Microsoft Windows provides a rich environment for programming. The WFC (Windows Foundation Class) library makes most of that environment available to you when you program in Java, but not all of it.

You can access other resources in Windows in several ways. You can use the Component Object Model (COM), the communications framework for the majority of Windows applications. For example, Microsoft Visual J++ is made up of many different pieces that communicate with each other using COM. COM also lets your application interact with other applications, such as Microsoft Word and Microsoft Excel. COM gives you access to many prebuilt components in Windows.

At the other end of the spectrum is the Win32 application programming interface (API), a set of low-level functions that underlies every Windows program. J/Direct makes these low-level functions available to your application.

In this chapter, you will learn how to:

■ Use J/Direct to call API functions

■ Add components to the toolbox for use in the Designer

■ Use COM components

In this chapter, you will get a chance to:

■ Create an application that plays different system sounds

You will create several versions of this application using the technologies you will learn about in this chapter.

Working with the Win32 API

The Win32 API is the basis for all applications written for 32-bit Windows. This is a common API for Windows 95, Windows 98, Windows NT, and subsequent operating systems. The Win32 API is based in the Windows API for classic 16-bit Windows. Many of the functions and structures of the API can be traced back to Windows 1.0 or Windows 3.1. The API is very flexible, but somewhat complicated. Many programmers use libraries, application frameworks, and tools to simplify creating Windows applications. However, these frameworks might not support all the rich features of the API.

WFC is written using the Win32 API. All the WFC forms and controls that you've used in this book are built on top of the Win32 windowing scheme. Other application frameworks in Visual Studio include:

■ MFC in Visual C++.

■ Ruby forms in Visual Basic.

The common operations are handled by the framework. This frees you up to work on application-specific features. However, sometimes you'll want to do something not supported by the framework.

Using the J/Direct Call Builder

J/Direct lets you declare a native method and call it from a single source file; all type conversions are handled by the Virtual Machine (VM) for Java. Using J/Direct, Java applications can easily access the full range of Win32 API system functionality or any existing dynamic link library (DLL) written for Win32.

Let's look at an example. The *MessageBox* class and its *show* methods are related to the Win32 *MessageBox* function. Here is the overloaded *show* method of *com.ms.wfc.ui.MessageBox*:

```
public static int show(String text, String caption, int style);
public static int show(String text, String caption);
public static int show(String text);
```

The second and third versions call the first version with some default values for the parameters.

Here is the prototype for the Win32 *MessageBox* function, taken from the Windows header file for programming in C or C++:

```
WINUSERAPI int WINAPI MessageBox(
    HWND hWnd, LPCSTR lpText, LPCSTR lpCaption, UINT uType);
```

You can see how the parameters of the first version of *show* correspond to this C function. J/Direct gives you direct access to this function. It uses special tags in the JavaDoc comment for the method:

```
/**
 * @dll.import("USER32", auto)
 */
public static native int MessageBox(
    int hWnd, String lpText, String lpCaption, int uType);
```

The JavaDoc comment tag indicates that the function is the USER32 DLL and that the types for the parameters follow automatic mapping. To help you create these import declarations, Visual J++ includes the J/Direct Call Builder, a tool window that you can dock to the sides of the Integrated Design Environment (IDE) and tab with other tool windows. The J/Direct Call Builder supports adding declarations for API functions to your project.

To open the J/Direct Call Builder

1. From the View menu, choose Other Windows.

2. From the Other Windows menu, choose J/Direct Call Builder. The J/Direct Call Builder appears.

Figure 12-1. *The J/Direct Call Builder window.*

Typically, we use the J/Direct Call Builder to add access to functions from the Win32 API. This adds method declarations to a class. By default, the methods are added to the public class *Win32* in the default package. The J/Direct Call Builder creates this class (and file) if they do not exist already. You can also use the J/Direct Call Builder to add declarations for constants (static final member variables) and structures (nested classes).

To add declarations for Win32 API resources to your project

1. Open the J/Direct Call Builder.

2. Select the items to import. Use the Shift key to select contiguous items. Use the Ctrl key to select noncontiguous items.

3. Select the target for the copy operation. The default target is the class *Win32* in the default package.

4. Click Copy To Target.

To find items in the J/Direct Call Builder, type the beginning of the item name in the Find edit control.

Let's create a demo that calls the Win32 *MessageBox* function. This demo simply calls the function with some text supplied by the user in a WFC form. *MessageBox* asks whether the user wants to continue and presents Yes and No buttons. The code for this example is in located in Chapter12\ MessageBox\MessageBox.sln.

Here are the contents of Win32.java after you import the *MessageBox* function and some related constants:

```
public class Win32
{
    /**
     * @dll.import("USER32", auto)
     */
    public static native int MessageBox(
        int hWnd, String lpText, String lpCaption, int uType);
    public static final int MB_YESNO = 0x00000004;
    public static final int IDNO = 7;
    public static final int IDYES = 6;
}
```

Here is the event-handler method that calls *MessageBox*:

```
private void btnShow_click(Object source, Event e)
{
    String msg;
    msg = edtMessage.getText() + "\n\nDo you want to continue?";
    int response;
    response = Win32.MessageBox(
        this.getHandle(), msg, edtCaption.getText(), Win32.MB_YESNO);
    if(response == Win32.IDNO)
    {
        Application.exit();
    }
}
```

> **NOTE** You can easily do this using *MessageBox.show*. The demo simply demonstrates how to use J/Direct and the J/Direct Call Builder.

Lab 12-1: *MessageBeep*

In this lab, we will create an application that plays system sounds, using the Win32 API call *MessageBeep*. *MessageBeep* takes a single parameter: the sound to be played. The values (listed below) are associated with *MessageBox* flags that we saw in the demo. They are also associated with the listed Windows sounds.

- MB_OK - Default Sound

- MB_ICONERROR - Critical Stop

- MB_ICONQUESTION - Question

- MB_ICONEXCLAMATION - Exclamation

- MB_ICONASTERISK - Asterisk

Set these sounds using the Sounds icon on the Control Panel:

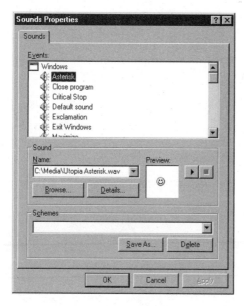

Figure 12-2. *The Sounds Properties dialog box.*

Lab overview

You will practice:

- Using J/Direct to access the Win32 API

- Using the J/Direct Call Builder

Lab setup

1. Start Visual J++.
2. Create a new Windows Application project named Jdirect.

Lab instructions

1. Create the following user interface for your application:

2. Use the J/Direct Call Builder to add declarations to your application. Add the declarations to Win32.java. These are the declarations:

MessageBeep

MB_OK

MB_ICONERROR

MB_ICONQUESTION

MB_ICONEXCLAMATION

MB_ICONASTERISK

3. In the click handlers for the buttons, call *MessageBeep* using the appropriate parameter.

4. Test your application. You can compareyour work to the solution located in Chapter12\Sol12-1\JDirectBeep.sln.

Optional lab enhancements

Here are some optional enhancements for you to try:

■ Modify the user interface to use a list box to select the sound. Add a Play button.

■ Modify the list box to play the sound in response to a double click.

Next steps

Using the Win32 API gives us the freedom to use any features of Windows. However, programming at the API level is quite complex. Programmers often use prebuilt libraries, frameworks, and components. In the next section, you'll learn about using additional controls in your WFC applications.

Working with Additional Controls

The Win32 API provides low-level access to Windows. It is common to use components that package the power of the API. Controls package the API into components that are easier to use. So far, all the controls that we've placed on WFC forms are from the com.ms.wfc.ui package. These controls are included in the basic WFC framework. WFC also supports other controls.

In this section, you'll learn about using other controls in WFC forms: ActiveX controls and other WFC controls.

Adding an ActiveX Control to the Toolbox

ActiveX controls provide component-level support for an extraordinary range of applications and functions. They are among the primary building blocks in Visual Basic applications. They are also referred to as *OLE Controls* or *OCXs*.

Let's create a simple application that uses an ActiveX control. For this example, we'll use the Masked Edit control. The code for this example is located in Chapter12\UseActiveX\UseActiveX.sln. If the Masked Edit control is not registered on your system, this demo won't work. You'll need to register the file MSMASK32.OCX for the project.

To register an ActiveX control and add it to the toolbox

1. From the Tools menu, choose Customize Toolbox.

2. In the Customize Toolbox dialog box, select the ActiveX Controls tab.

3. In the ActiveX Control pane, click Browse.

4. In the Browse dialog box, navigate to the file. Click Open to select the control file and close the dialog box.

5. Click OK.

If the ActiveX control is already registered, there's a simpler way to add it to the toolbox:

1. From the Tools menu, choose Customize Toolbox.

2. In the Customize Toolbox dialog box, select the ActiveX Controls tab.

3. In the list of controls, select the control to add to the toolbox by selecting the check box next to the item.

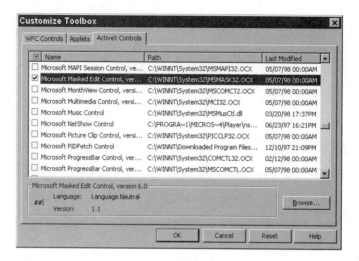

4. Click OK.

After you add the ActiveX control to the toolbox, you can add it to WFC forms as you would any other control. For example, you can use a numeric mask for a phone number edit box.

Adding the control to the project generates wrapper classes for the control. The Project Explorer window is updated with the new classes. For more on wrapper classes, see "COM Wrapper Classes," later in this chapter.

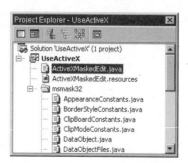

These wrapper classes make the properties, methods, and events of the ActiveX control available in Java. You can set properties and create event handlers using the Properties window.

IntelliSense provides autocompletion for method calls.

In essence, you can't distinguish between WFC controls and ActiveX controls in your application.

Adding a WFC Control to the Toolbox

In addition to supporting ActiveX controls, Visual J++ supports adding new WFC controls to the toolbox.

To add a WFC control to the toolbox

1. From the Tools menu, choose Customize Toolbox.

2. In the Customize Toolbox dialog box, select the WFC Controls tab.

3. In the list of controls, select the control to add to the toolbox.

4. Click OK.

 OTE   The WFC control must be on the classpath to be available.

Once you add the WFC control to the toolbox, you can use it as you would any other control in the toolbox.

Lab 12-2: WFC *MessageBeep*

In this lab, we will use a WFC control to play *MessageBeep*. In Lab 12-1, we created the *MessageBeep* control. In this lab, the control project is part of the Visual J++ solution, so the new control will be on the classpath. At other times, we might have to add a package to the classpath to make the control available. For more information on this, see "Adding Directories to the Classpath" in Chapter 10.

Lab overview

You will practice:

- Adding a new control to the toolbox

- Using a custom WFC control

Lab setup

1. Start Visual J++.

2. Open the NewControl project located in Chapter12\Lab12-2\ NewControl.sln.

Lab instructions

1. Expand *BeeperControl* in the Project Explorer window.

2. Open Beeper.java in Designer View.

3. Create the following user interface in the form:

Beeper control

Listbox

4. Add a handler for the Click event of the Play button. This handler calls the *play* method of Beeper.

5. Add a handler for the *played* event of the Beeper. This handler logs the played event in the list box. The log message should indicate the event and the current value of the Choice property.

6. Add a handler for the changed event of the Beeper. This handler logs the Change event in the list box. Make the log message analogous to the one added by the *played* handler.

7. Add a handler for the Click event of the Clear button. This handler clears the contents of the list box.

8. Test your application. You can compare your work to the solution in Chapter12\Sol12-2\NewControl.sln.

Optional lab enhancements

Here are some optional enhancements for you to try:

■ Add buttons to this form to select the sound.

■ Add another WFC Beeper control to the form.

Next steps

ActiveX controls and WFC controls can support a lot of complex processing. The typical way to use these controls is to add them to a form using the Designer. However, many other components are not form-based. In the next section, we'll learn about using non-form-based COM components.

Using COM Components

COM is a model and binary standard for component interaction. It is the communication layer in OLE, ActiveX, and automation. COM objects form the basis for a growing number of Windows applications. In fact, Visual J++ 6.0 is composed of a number of separate components that use COM to communicate.

COM and Java

COM is a binary standard for component communications, so the mechanism used to access COM objects must be uniform across programming languages and platforms. To handle this, COM uses COM interfaces and coclasses. There are some stunning parallels between the structure of COM with COM interfaces and coclasses, and the structure of Java.

 OTE   This section presents some of the basics of working with COM objects. Much of the information is not directly applicable to Visual J++. However, it is provided as background material.

COM interfaces and coclasses

A COM interface is essential, like a Java interface. It is a list of functions and methods. No implementation information is associated with the functions in a COM interface. For more information on interfaces in Java, see "Interfaces" in Chapter 8.

A coclass is a component object class. The coclass is the creatable entity in COM. It implements one or more COM interfaces. A coclass is like a Java class that implements one or more interfaces.

Creating an object

To create a COM object, we use the coclass. Creating a COM object returns an interface pointer to the new object. In Java terms, this is an interface reference. This is analogous to the *new* operator in Java.

Accessing an object

Once we have an interface pointer to a COM object, we use that interface pointer to access the object. Unlike in Java, we cannot use a reference to the class to access the COM object. This is very important.

The life of a COM object

A COM object remains until no one can use it—that is, until no one has a reference to the object. This is called *reference counting*. In COM, reference counting uses the methods *AddRef* and *Release*. To increment the reference count of a COM object, we call *AddRef*. To decrement the reference count of a COM object, call *Release*.

Creating a COM object sets its reference count to one. When the reference count of a COM object becomes zero, the object is destroyed.

In Java, reference counting is handled by the VM. The VM tracks all the assignments and parameter passing associated with each Java object. When no more references to an object remain, the object is available for garbage collection. For more information on reference counting and garbage collection in Java, see "References to Objects" in Chapter 4.

Multiple interfaces

A COM object can implement multiple COM interfaces. In fact, this is the norm, as we'll see. To get a pointer to a different interface, we call *QueryInterface*.

In Java, an object can implement multiple interfaces. Type casting is used to get a different reference type to an object. For more information on type casting, see "Type Casting" in Chapter 9.

The *IUnknown* interface

The three functions you've just learned about form the basis of every COM object. They are grouped together in the COM interface *IUnknown*, which is the root of all COM interfaces. At a minimum, a COM object must implement *IUnknown*. *IUnknown* does not provide support for anything except reference counting and accessing other COM interfaces. It is equivalent to *java.lang.Object*, the ultimate superclass in Java; so, every Java object Is-A *java.lang.Object*. The *java.lang.Object* class supports a bit more than *IUnknown*, but not much. For more information on *java.lang.Object*, see "The *java.lang.Object* Class" in Chapter 4.

Finding classes and interfaces

In COM, all the coclasses and COM interfaces are registered in the system registry. If the coclass or COM interface is not in the registry, the COM object cannot be used. (The registry is the database that contains configuration information about your system: the hardware, the software, and your individual user settings. To view the registry, use REGEDIT.EXE.)

To register a self-registering COM object, use the REGSVR32 program and pass the filename of the control as a command-line parameter. In Windows 95, REGSVR32 is in the SYSTEM subdirectory of your Windows installation directory. In Windows NT, it is in the SYSTEM32 subdirectory of your Windows installation directory.

 OTE   Do not make changes while you are viewing the registry. REGEDIT makes live changes in the registry. You cannot undo or exit without saving changes. A compromised registry can make your system unusable or even unbootable.

The VM finds Java classes using the classpath. For more information on the classpath, see "The Classpath" in Chapter 10.

COM Wrapper Classes

As we've just seen, COM objects are created using coclasses and accessed using COM interfaces. The Java VM has built-in support for working with COM objects. To work with COM objects, we simply need a Java way to refer to the coclasses and COM interfaces. We refer to coclasses and COM interfaces using special Java classes that the VM recognizes as wrappers for coclasses and COM interfaces.

Adding wrapper classes

To register a COM component and add wrapper classes to your project:

1. From the Project menu, choose Add COM Wrapper.

2. In the COM Wrappers dialog box, click Browse.

3. In the Select COM Component dialog box, navigate to the file. Click Open to select the component file and close the dialog box.

4. Click OK.

If the COM component is already registered, it is a bit simpler to get wrapper classes:

1. From the Project menu, choose Add COM Wrapper.

2. In the COM Wrappers dialog box, select the component from the list of COM components by selecting its check box.

3. Click OK.

The wrapper classes are added to the current project and placed in a package. The package name is derived from the filename of the COM component. Since Java is case sensitive, the convention for the package name is all lowercase.

Adding an ActiveX control to your form also generates COM wrapper classes. Here is the Project Explorer showing the wrapper classes for the Masked Edit control:

The Masked Edit control is in the file MSMASK32.OCX, so the package is msmask32.

Using wrapper classes

When we add wrapper classes for a COM component, we get both Java classes and Java interfaces. The classes correspond to coclasses, and the interfaces correspond to COM interfaces.

For the wrapper classes, you must use the class to create the object. We typically use the interfaces to access the object. For example, we use the wrapper classes *COMClass* and *COMInterface* as follows:

```
COMInterface pInf;
pInf = new COMClass();
pInf.foo();
```

The reference to the object is the interface type, *COMInterface*. The class *COMClass* is used to create the COM object. Any access to the object uses the interface reference.

To access a COM object using a different COM interface, we cast the reference to the desired wrapper interface.

Lab 12-3: COM *MessageBeep*

In this lab, we'll create another application to play *MessageBeep* sounds. This time we'll use a COM object to call the Win32 API. This COM object was written in Visual Basic. If you have Visual Basic installed on your system, you can look at the project that created this COM DLL in Chapter12\VBObject.

The COM object exports two methods: *GetString* and *PlaySound*. It also exports the enumerated type *BeeperEnum*.

Lab overview

You will practice:

- Adding COM wrapper classes to your project
- Creating a COM object using a wrapper class for the coclass
- Accessing a COM object using the wrapper class for the interface

Lab setup

1. Register the VbBeeper.dll file. Follow the instructions located in Chapter12\Lab12-3\RegisterDLL.txt.

2. Start Visual J++.

3. Open the COMBeeper project located in Chapter12\Lab12-3\COMBeeper.sln.

Lab instructions

1. Create COM wrapper classes for *VBBeeper*. If *VBBeeper* is not in the list of COM classes, you can use the Browse button to register the component as you create Java wrappers. This creates the local package *vbbeeper*, which contains three classes: *Control*, *_Control*, and *BeeperEnum*. *Control* is the coclass. *_Control* is the interface for the coclass. *BeeperEnum* is a parameter type for the beeper values.

2. Add a member variable to hold the reference to the COM object. Its type is *vbbeeper._Control*, the interface class for *vbbeeper*. Name the member variable *ctl*.

3. Add an *int* array member variable to associate items in the list box with *BeeperEnum* values. Name the array *values*. Make it five elements long.

4. In the constructor for the form, create a *vbbeeper.Control* object. Assign it to the member variable. Use the values of *vbbeeper.BeeperEnum* and the *Control* object to fill the list box. Associate the entry in the list box with the *BeeperEnum* value, using the *values* array. The values in *BeeperEnum* are *DefaultBeep*, *ErrorBeep*, *QuestionBeep*, *ExclamationBeep*, and *AsteriskBeep*.

Here is some sample code for this operation:

```
String str;
int val;
int idx;

val = vbbeeper.BeeperEnum.DefaultBeep;
str = ctl.GetString(val);
idx = lstBeeps.addItem(str);
values[idx] = val;
```

5. Add a handler for the Click event of the Play button. This handler calls the *PlaySound* method of the *VBBeeper* object. For the parameter for *PlaySound*, use the *values* array indexed by the value of the *selectedIndex* property for the list box.

6. Test your application. You can compare your work to the solution in Chapter12\Sol12-3\COMBeeper.sln.

Optional lab enhancements

Here are some optional enhancements for you to try:

■ Add a double-click handler for the list box. This will play the selected sound.

■ Replace the list box with a drop-down list. A drop-down list is a combo box whose style is set to *Dropdownlist*.

Next steps

In this chapter, we have learned about using components. In the next chapter, we'll learn about creating WFC components and about creating Web applications using WFC and DHTML.

Chapter 13

Portable I/O

This chapter covers the portable I/O packages, java.io and java.net. These packages give a Java program access to files and to the network. WFC (Windows Foundation Class) also includes a file I/O package, com.ms.wfc.io. You learned about the WFC I/O package in Chapter 8. The java.io package provides the same type of functionality as the WFC I/O package, but it uses a different approach. Learning about java.io will make learning about java.net easier.

In this chapter, you'll learn about:

- The java.io classes for working with files
- The java.net package for accessing network resources

You will get a chance to:

- Create an application that reads from a local file and display its contents
- Create an application that reads from a file on the network and displays its contents

---

 OTE   Do not mix WFC I/O and java.io operations. They are two separate file I/O packages from two different sources.

Working with Files

The java.io package supports I/O to streams. A stream is an ordered set of bytes. It's easy to see how files are streams. As we'll see later in this chapter, other types of streams also use the methods and classes of java.io.

The java.io classes can be categorized in several ways. Not surprisingly, there are input classes and output classes. You can also subdivide the java.io classes based on the type of stream, binary or text—that is, byte streams or character streams. (Remember that the char data type in Java is 2 bytes wide.) There are also abstract classes that serve as a common superclass for related classes. You'll find major parallels between the binary-stream and character-stream classes.

In this chapter, we'll discuss the underlying abstract classes, the binary I/O classes, and then the text I/O classes.

Abstract Input Classes

The foundation of binary input in java.io is the abstract class *java.io.InputStream*. The foundation of text input in java.io is the abstract class *java.io.Reader*. These two abstract classes define the basic methods of byte-oriented and character-oriented input.

 OTE   For simplicity, we'll use the term *atom* to describe a byte or a character rather than repeat the phrase "byte or character" over and over.

Reading from a stream

To get bytes of data from an *InputStream*, we call one of the *read* methods:

```
public int read() throws IOException;
public int read(byte[] b) throws IOException;
public int read(byte[] b, int offset, int len) throws IOException;
```

To read characters from a *Reader*, we call one if its *read* methods:

```
public int read() throws IOException;
public int read(char[] b) throws IOException;
public int read(char[] b, int offset, int len) throws IOException;
```

The zero-parameter version reads a single atom and returns the numerical value of the atom read. The one-parameter and three-parameter versions read an array of atoms from the input stream and return the number of atoms read into the array parameter. All of these methods return −1 after the end-of-file marker has been encountered.

Closing a stream

To close an *InputStream* or a *Reader*, we call the *close* method:

```
public void close() throws IOException;
```

Note that the *close* method for both the *InputStream* and *Reader* classes looks the same.

The *close* method closes the associated stream and frees any associated system resources. Needless to say, you shouldn't use a stream after you call *close*.

Discarding atoms from a stream

To discard a number of bytes from an *InputStream* or to discard a number of characters from a *Reader*, we call the *skip* method:

```
public long skip(long n) throws IOException;
```

Note that the *skip* method for both the *InputStream* and *Reader* classes looks the same.

The *skip* method discards the specified number of atoms from the stream.

Abstract Output Classes

The foundation of binary output in java.io is the abstract class *java.io.OutputStream*. The foundation of character input in java.io is the abstract class *java.io.Writer*. These two abstract classes define the basic methods of byte-oriented and character-oriented output.

Writing to a stream

To write bytes to an *OutputStream*, we call one of these *write* methods:

```
public void write(int b) throws IOException;
public void write(byte[] b) throws IOException;
public void write(byte[] b, int offset, int len) throws IOException;
```

To write characters to a *Writer*, we call one of these *write* methods:

```
public void write(int c) throws IOException;
public void write(char[] b) throws IOException;
public void write(char[] b, int offset, int len) throws IOException;
public void write(String str) throws IOException;
public void write(String str, int offset, int len) throws IOException;
```

The *int* parameter version writes a single atom value. The other single-parameter version writes a set of atoms (an array of atoms or a string). The three-parameter version writes only a portion of a set of atoms.

Closing a stream

To close an *OutputStream* or a *Writer*, you call the *close* method:

```
public void close() throws IOException;
```

 OTE The *close* method for both the *OutputStream* and the *Writer* look the same.

The *close* method closes the associated stream and frees any associated system resources. For an *OutputStream*, this method also flushes the stream. Needless to say, you shouldn't use a stream after you call *close*.

Flushing the buffer associated with a stream

To force output of the buffer associated with an *OutputStream* or a Writer, you call the *flush* method:

```
public void flush() throws IOException;
```

 OTE The *flush* method for both the *OutputStream* and the *Writer* look the same.

The *flush* method forces buffered output to be written to the stream.

Binary Input Classes

The nonabstract subclasses of *InputStream* are *java.io.DataInputStream* and *java.io.FileInputStream*. The *java.io.DataInputStream* class extends *InputStream*. It provides methods to read common data types. Here are some of the more important methods:

```
public DataInputStream(InputStream in);

public final boolean readBoolean() throws IOException;
public final byte readByte() throws IOException;
public final char readChar() throws IOException;
public final short readShort() throws IOException;
public final int readInt() throws IOException;
public final long readLong() throws IOException;
public final float readFloat() throws IOException;
public final double readDouble() throws IOException;
public final String readUTF() throws IOException;
```

There are three things to note here:

■ The constructor for *DataInputStream* takes an *InputStream*.

■ The method *readUTF* is the *String* method.

■ The *DataInputStream* methods are *final*—they cannot be overridden.

The *java.io.FileInputStream* class extends *InputStream*. It associates an input stream with a file. Here are two of the more important ones:

```
public FileInputStream(String name) throws FileNotFoundException;
public FileInputStream(File file) throws FileNotFoundException;
```

The first version of the constructor takes a *String* parameter—the name of the file. The second version takes a *java.io.File* object. You'll learn more about the *File* class later in this chapter.

An example

Here's an example of reading values from a binary file:

```
FileInputStream fisInput = new FileInputStream(fileInput);
DataInputStream disInput = new DataInputStream(fisInput);
String strValue = disInput.readUTF();
int nValue = disInput.readInt();
float fValue = disInput.readFloat();
boolean bValue = disInput.readBoolean();
```

The *FileInputStream* class is used to open the file. This object is an *InputStream*, so it is used to create a *DataInputStream* to read the values of specific types. The code for this example is in the Demo13-1 project for Chapter 13.

 OTE   This code doesn't include any exception handlers, so it's easier to see how to use the I/O methods. To see an example that includes the exception handlers, see the Demo13-1 project for Chapter 13.

Binary Output Classes

The nonabstract subclasses of *OutputStream* are *java.io.DataOutputStream* and *java.io.FileOutputStream*. The *java.io.DataOutputStream* class extends *OutputStream*. It provides methods to write common data types. Here are some of the more important methods:

```
public DataOutputStream(OutputStream out);

public final void writeBoolean(boolean v) throws IOException;
public final void writeByte(int v) throws IOException;
public final void writeChar(int v) throws IOException;
public final void writeShort(int v) throws IOException;
public final void writeInt(int v) throws IOException;
public final void writeLong(long v) throws IOException;
public final void writeFloat(float v) throws IOException;
public final void writeDouble(double v) throws IOException;
public final void writeUTF(String s) throws IOException;
```

This class provides for conversion between the byte stream and common data types. Notice that the constructor for *DataOutputStream* takes an *OutputStream*.

The *java.io.FileOutputStream* class also extends *OutputStream*. It associates an output stream with a file. Here are three of the more important ones:

```
public FileOutputStream(String name) throws IOException;
public FileOutputStream(String name, boolean append)
    throws IOException;
public FileOutputStream(File file) throws IOException;
```

The first version of the constructor takes a *String* parameter—the name of the file. The second version takes the filename and a flag indicates whether to append to the end of the file or not. The third version takes a *java.io.File* object. You'll learn more about the *File* class later.

An example

Here's an example of writing values from a binary file:

```
FileOutputStream fosOutput = new FileOutputStream(fileOutput);
DataOutputStream dosOutput = new DataOutputStream(fosOutput);
dosOutput.writeUTF(strValue);
dosOutput.writeInt(nValue);
dosOutput.writeFloat(fValue);
dosOutput.writeBoolean(bValue);
```

The code for this example is also in the Demo13-1 project for Chapter 13.

Textual Input Classes

The nonabstract subclasses of *Reader* are *java.io.InputStreamReader* and *java.io.FileReader.*

To associate a *Reader* with an *InputStream*, we use the *java.io.InputStreamReader* class. *InputStreamReader* extends *Reader* so that all of the methods of *Reader* are available. The most important constructor is:

```
public InputStreamReader(InputStream in);
```

The *java.io.FileReader* class extends *InputStreamReader*. You use this class to associate the *FileReader* with the given file. Here are two of the more important constructors.

```
public FileReader(String name) throws FileNotFoundException;
public FileReader(File file) throws FileNotFoundException;
```

An example

Here's an example of reading 25 characters from a file:

```
FileReader fileInput = new FileReader( filename );
char[] buffer = new char[25];
int nNumberOfCharactersRead;
nNumberOfCharactersRead = fileInput.read(buffer);
if(nNumberOfCharactersRead < 25)
{
```

Text Output Classes

The nonabstract subclasses of *Writer* are *java.io.OutputStreamWriter* and *FileWriter*.

To associate *Writer* with an *OutputStream*, we use the *java.io.OutputStreamWriter* class. *OutputStreamWriter* extends *Writer* so that all of the methods of *Writer* are available. The most important constructor in the class is:

```
public OutputStreamWriter(OutputStream out);
```

The *java.io.FileWriter* class extends *OutputStreamWriter*. The constructors associate the *FileWriter* with the given file. The two most important constructors are shown below:

```
public FileWriter(String name) throws IOException;
public FileWriter(File file) throws IOException;
```

An example

Here's an example of a writing string to a text file:

```
FileWriter fileOutput = new FileWriter( filename );
fileOutput.write(edtTextForOutput.getText());
```

You can also use the *java.io.PrintStream* class to extend *OutputStream*. It creates binary output, and it includes many overrides to convert the common types to their *String* representations. Here are the important methods of *PrintStream*:

```
public PrintStream(OutputStream out);
public PrintStream(OutputStream out, boolean autoFlush);

public void print(boolean b);
public void print(char c);
public void print(int i);
public void print(long l);
public void print(float f);
public void print(double d);
public void print(char[] s);
public void print(String s);
public void print(Object o);
```

```
public void println();
public void println(boolean b);
public void println(char c);
public void println(int i);
public void println(long l);
public void println(float f);
public void println(double d);
public void println(char[] s);
public void println(String s);
public void println(Object o);
```

These methods are self-explanatory. You might wonder, though, about the absence of methods for the *byte* and *short* types. These types are automatically converted to *int*. This conversion is safe because *int* has more precision that either *byte* or *short*. The next section shows an example of using a *PrintStream* object.

The *java.lang.System* Class and Standard I/O

Three streams are defined in the *java.lang.System* class. They are all *public*, static, and final:

```
public static final InputStream in;
public static final PrintStream out;
public static final PrintStream err;
```

These streams access the standard input, standard output, and standard error streams for the application. This is analogous to the *WFC Text* class. To learn more about the *WFC Text* class, see Chapter 11.

Here is the java.io version of Hello World:

```
public class SayHello
{
    public static void main(String[] args)
    {
        System.out.println("Hello, World!");
    }
}
```

Here is the WFC version:

```
import com.ms.wfc.io.Text;
public class SayHello
{
    public static void main(String[] args)
    {
        Text.out.writeLine("Hello, World!");
    }
}
```

Note that both versions write the same line of output, "Hello, World!".

The *java.io.File* Class

The *java.io.File* class provides access to files and the file system. Here are some of the more interesting and important methods of the *File* class:

```
public File(String path);
public File(String path, String name);
public File(File dir, String name);

public boolean canRead();
public boolean canWrite();
public boolean isFile();
public boolean isDirectory();
public boolean exists();
public long length();
public long lastModified();

public String getName();
public String getPath();
public String getParent();

public boolean mkdir();
public boolean mkdirs();

public boolean delete();
public boolean renameTo(File name);
```

Most of these methods are self-explanatory. However, note that there are no methods to create or open files. To create a file, we use *FileOutputStream* or *FileWriter*. To open a file, we use *FileInputStream*, *FileOutputStream*, *FileReader*, or *FileWriter*.

The *getParent* method returns the directory in which the file is found. The *mkdir* method takes the filename as a directory name and creates that directory. The *mkdirs* method creates intermediate directories in the path as needed.

An example

Here's an example that uses the *File* class to check for the existence of a file before overwriting it:

```
File fileOutput = new File(cbNames.getText());
if(fileOutput.exists())
{
    if(MessageBox.show(
        "File exists. Overwrite it?",
        "File Error",
        MessageBox.YESNO) == MessageBox.IDNO)
    {
        return;
    }
}
```

The code for this example is in the Demo13-1 project for Chapter 13.

Lab 13-1: Reading a File from Disk

In this lab, we will add code to a simple application so that it will open a text file for reading and display the contents of the file in an edit control.

Lab overview

In this lab, you will practice:

■ Opening a file using the java.io package.

■ Reading from a file using the java.io package.

Lab setup

1. Start Visual J++.

2. Open the FileReader project (Chapter13\Lab13-1\ FileReader.sln).

Lab instructions

1. Add an *import* statement for the java.io package.

2. Find the *click* handler for *btnRead*.

3. In the handler, declare a reference to a *FileReader* object. Create a *FileReader* for the filename in *edtInput*.

   The constructor for *FileReader* throws *FileNotFoundException*. You must add a handler for this exception. In the *catch* block, do the following:

   - Set the *foreColor* of *edtOutput* to red.

   - Set the *backColor* of *edtOutput* to white.

   - Set the text of *edtOutput* to display an error message. The *getMessage* method of *FileNotFoundException* returns the name of the file that was not found.

   Outside the *try* block, set *edtOutput* for normal output:

   - Set the *foreColor* of *edtOutput* to the window text color.

   - Set the *backColor* of *edtOutput* to the window background color.

   - Clear *edtOutput* of text.

4. Declare a *char* array for the buffer to hold the characters read. Name it *buffer*. Make it 256 elements long.

5. Declare an *int* variable to hold the number of characters read from the file.

6. Create a loop to read from the file. Update the text property of *edtOutput* with the characters read from the file.

   Create a loop to read from the file. Recall that *read* returns −1 to indicate end-of-file. Otherwise, it returns the number of characters read into the buffer.

   Append the characters read to the end of *edtOutput*. The following *String* constructor will be helpful:

   ```
   public String(char[] buffer, int offset, int length);
   ```

The *read* method throws *IOException*. You must add a handler for this exception. If the exception is thrown, exit the loop and display an error message at the end of *edtOutput*. Set the colors of *edtOutput* to red on white to indicate the error.

7. After reading from the file, close it. The *close* method throws *IOException*. You must add a handler for this exception. The *catch* block can be empty.

8. Set the focus to *edtInput* before returning from the handler.

9. Test your application. You can compare your work to the solution located in Chapter13\Sol13-1\FileReader.sln.

Here are some suggested enhancements you can add to this lab:

■ Create an alternative version of SYSEDIT. Replace *edtInput* with a drop combo. Set the contents of the drop combo to the following system files:

C:\AUTOEXEC.BAT

C:\CONFIG.SYS

C:\WINDOWS\WIN.INI

C:\WINDOWS\SYSTEM.INI

C:\WINDOWS\PROTOCOL.INI

■ Rewrite the lab using *System.in* and *System.out* for the input and output streams.

Next steps

The functionality we used here is equivalent to the functionality you learned about in Chapter 8. In the next section, you'll use many of the same classes to read network files using the java.net package.

Working with the Internet

Support for working with the Internet in Java is contained in the java.net package. The java.net package has two very interesting classes in it:

- *java.net.Socket*
- *java.net.URL*

The *java.net.Socket* Class

The *Socket* class supports communication over the network. It is a general class that can be used for any type of data transfer. It includes the methods *getInputStream* and *getOutputStream*. Once the sockets are connected, you can use these functions to access *java.io.InputStream* and *java.io.OutputStream* functionality.

The *java.net.URL* Class

The *java.net.URL* class supports the manipulation of URLs. You can use this class to download the data associated with a URL. Actually, we already used the URL class when we worked with media files in applets. The *Applet.getCodeBase* and *Applet.getDocumentBase* methods return URL references. The *Applet.getAudioClip*, *Applet.getImage*, and *Applet.play* methods take URL references as parameters.

The commonly used methods of java.net.URL are:

```
public URL(String protocol, String host, String file)
    throws MalformedURLException;
public URL(String spec) throws MalformedURLException;
public URL(URL context, String spec) throws MalformedURLException;

public String getProtocol();
public String getHost();
public String getFile();

public final InputStream openStream() throws IOException;
```

You can use these methods to access resources on the Internet. If you need more flexibility with the connection to the URL, use the following function:

```
public URLConnection openConnection() throws IOException;
```

The *java.net.URLConnection* class supports a wide variety of I/O operations. For more information about this class, see the product documentation.

Lab 13-2: Reading from the Web

In this lab, we will add code to a simple application so that it will display the stream returned by a URL. This lab is similar to Lab 13-1 earlier in this chapter. You can copy your solution to the File lab to use as a basis for this lab, or you can use the starter project files.

Lab overview

In this lab, you will practice:

- Opening network connections using a URL.

- Reading from a network connection.

Lab setup

1. Start Visual J++.
2. Open the URLReader project (Chapter 13\Lab13-2\ URLReader.sln).

Lab instructions

1. Add *import* statements for the java.io and java.net packages.

2. Find the click handler for *btnRead*.

3. In the handler, declare a reference to a URL object. Create a URL for the *text* value in *edtInput*.

   The constructor for URL throws *MalformedURLException*. You must add a handler for this exception. In the catch block, do the following:

   - Set the *foreColor* of *edtOutput* to red.

   - Set the *backColor* of *edtOutput* to white.

   - Set the text of *edtOutput* to display an error message. The *getMessage* method of *MalformedURLException* returns the URL.

Outside the *try* block, set *edtOutput* for normal output:

- Set the *foreColor* of *edtOutput* to the window text color.

- Set the *backColor* of *edtOutput* to the window background color.

- Clear *edtOutput* of text.

4. Declare a *char* array for the buffer to hold the characters read. Name it *buffer*. Make it 256 elements long.

5. Declare an *int* variable to hold the number of characters read from the URL.

6. Create a loop to read from the URL. Update the text property of *edtOutput* with the characters read from the URL.

   Create a loop to read from the URL. Remember that read returns −1 to indicate end-of-file. Otherwise, it returns the number of characters read into the buffer.

   Append the characters read to the end of *edtOutput*.

   The read method throws *IOException*. You must add a handler for this exception. If the exception is thrown, exit the loop and display an error message at the end of *edtOutput*. Set the colors of *edtOutput* to red on white to indicate the error.

7. After reading from the URL, close it. The *close* method throws *IOException*. You must add a handler for this exception. The *catch* block can be empty.

8. Set the focus to *edtInput* before returning from the handler.

9. Test your application. You can compare your work to the solution located in Chapter13\Sol13-2\URLReader.sln.

Optional lab enhancements
Here are some optional enhancements for you to try:

- Replace the *edtInput* edit control with a ComboBox control. Load the ComboBox with the URLs of some of your favorite Web sites.

- Add an HTML control to the application to display the input stream as HTML.

Appendix

Quick Syntax Comparison

This appendix provides a comparison of Java, C, C++, and Visual Basic code modules. Each module defines a coordinate type as two integer values, *x* and *y*. Each module also defines a method to add two coordinates together and a method that gives the quadrant location of a particular coordinate.

You can see how much the C++ version looks like the Java version. Structurally, the Visual Basic version is also very similar. All three of these versions are written as object-oriented modules. Individual lines of the C module look like lines of the C++ or Java module because these three languages share a similar syntax.

 OTE A well-designed module would also include other functions to manipulate coordinates.

C Version for Coordinates Module

```
// file: coordinate.h
struct Coordinate
{
        int x;
        int y;
};

struct Coordinate add(
        const struct Coordinate pt1,
        const struct Coordinate pt2);

int Quadrant(const struct Coordinate pt);

// file: coordinate.c
#include "coordinate.h"
struct Coordinate add(
        const struct Coordinate pt1,
        const struct Coordinate pt2)
{
        struct Coordinate returnValue;
        returnValue.x = pt1.x + pt2.x;
        returnValue.y = pt1.y + pt2.y;
        return returnValue;
}

int Quadrant(const struct Coordinate pt)
{
        if(pt.x >= 0) {
                if(pt.y >= 0) {
                        return 1;
                } else {
                        return 4;
                }
        } else {
                if(pt.y >= 0) {
                        return 2;
                } else {
                        return 3;
                }
        }
}
```

C++ Version for Coordinates Module

```cpp
// file: coordinate.h
class Coordinate
{
private:
        int xValue;
        int yValue;
public:
        int getX() const;
        int getY() const;
        void setX(int value);
        void setY(int value);
        Coordinate add(const Coordinate& pt2) const;
        int getQuadrant() const;
}

// file: coordinate.cpp
#include "coordinate.h"

int Coordinate::getX() const
{
        return xValue;
}

int Coordinate::getY() const
{
        return yValue;
}

void Coordinate::setX(int value)
{
        xValue = value;
}

void Coordinate::setY(int value)
{
        yValue = value;
}

Coordinate Coordinate::add(const Coordinate& pt2) const
{
        Coordinate returnValue;
        ReturnValue.xValue = this.xValue + pt2.xValue;
        ReturnValue.yValue = this.yValue + pt2.yValue;
        return returnValue;
}
```

(continued)

```
int Coordinate::Quadrant() const
{
      if(this.xValue >= 0) {
            if(this.yValue >= 0) {
                  return 1;
            } else {
                  return 4;
            }
      } else {
            if(this.yValue >= 0) {
                  return 2;
            } else {
                  return 3;
            }
      }
}
..
```

Java Version for Coordinates Module

```
// file: Coordinate.java
public class Coordinate
{
      private int xValue;
      private int yValue;

      public int getX()
      {
            return xValue;
      }

      public int getY()
      {
            return yValue;
      }

      public void setX(int value)
      {
            xValue = value;
      }

      public void setY(int value)
      {
            yValue = value;
      }

      public Coordinate add(Coordinate pt2)
      {
```

```
            Coordinate returnValue = new Coordinate();
            ReturnValue.xValue = this.xValue + pt2.yValue;
            ReturnValue.yValue = this.yValue + pt2.yValue;
            return returnValue;
     }

     public int getQuadrant()
     {
            if(this.xValue >= 0) {
                   if(this.yValue >= 0) {
                          return 1;
                   } else {
                          return 4;
                   }
            } else {
                   if(this.yValue >= 0) {
                          return 2;
                   } else {
                          return 3;
                   }
            }
     }
}
```

Visual Basic Version for Coordinates Module

```
' file: Coordinate.cls
Dim xValue As Integer
Dim yValue As Integer

Public Property Get X() As Integer
      X = xValue
End Property

Public Property Get Y() As Integer
      Y = yValue
End Property

Public Property Let X(value As Integer)
      xValue = value
End Property

Public Property Let Y(value As Integer)
      yValue = value
End Property

Public Function Add(ByVal pt2 As Coordinate) As Coordinate
      Set Add = New Coordinate
```

(continued)

```
            Add.X = Me.X + pt2.X
            Add.Y = Me.Y + pt2.Y
End Function

Public Function GetQuadrant() as Integer
        If Me.X >= 0 Then
                If Me.Y >= 0 Then
                        GetQuadrant = 1
                Else
                        GetQuadrant = 4
                End If
        Else
                If Me.Y >= 0 Then
                        GetQuadrant = 2
                Else
                        GetQuadrant = 3
                End If
        End If
End Function
```

Quick Reference to Java Syntax

Java Language Keywords

Keywords/Reserved Words

abstract	extends	multicast
boolean	false	native
break	final	new
byte	finally	null
byvalue	float	operator
case	for	outer
cast	future	package
catch	generic	private
char	goto	protected
class	if	public
const	implements	rest
continue	import	return
default	inner	short
delegate	instanceof	static
do	int	super
double	interface	switch synchronized
else	long	this

(continued)

continued

    throw

    throws

    transient

    true

    try

    var

    void

    volatile

    while

Here are a few points about the Keywords/Reserved Word list:

- This is a list of names that you can't (or shouldn't) use as identifiers, so it shows more than just the reserved words in use by the Java 1.1 language.

- The reserved words *delegate* and *multicast* are new with Visual J++ 6.0. They are defined within the Windows Foundation Class (WFC) and are used to assist in processing events.

- The reserved words *const* and *goto* are recognized by Visual J++ 6.0 (that is, they are syntax colored), but they have no special meaning in Java 1.1. Because Visual J++ recognizes these as reserved words, you cannot use them as identifiers.

- The reserved words *byvalue, cast, future, generic, inner, operator, outer, rest,* and *var* are reserved words in the Java language that also have no special meaning in Java 1.1, but are not syntax colored by Visual J++. Visual J++ allows you to use these as identifiers; however, for maximum portability and clarity, you should avoid doing so.

- The Boolean values *true* and *false* are technically not reserved words, but you can't use them as identifier names, so they look, act, and feel like reserved words.

Built-in Types

Type	Values	Variable Default
boolean	*true* and *false*	*false*
byte	integer values between *−128* and *128*	*0*
char	Unicode characters between *\u0000* and *\uFFFF*	*\u0000*
double	64-bit floating point number	*0.0*
float	32-bit floating point number	*0.0*
int	32-bit integer	*0*
long	64-bit integer	*0*
short	16-bit integer	*0*

Java Syntax Overview

The following brief overview of Java syntax provides a quick reference for the most commonly used syntax structures of the language. It is not the complete formal grammar of the Java language.

Flow of Control

do while loop (related keywords: *break* and *continue*)

```
do
    {
    loop body
    } while (boolean expression)
```

for loop (related keywords: *break* and *continue*)

```
for (initialization; boolean expression; increment)
    {
    loop body
    }
```

if (related keyword: *else*)

```
if (boolean expression)
    {
    statement(s)
    }
else
    {
    statement(s)
    }
```

switch (related keywords: *break, case,* and *default*)

```
switch (integral variable)
    {
    case integral value:
        statement(s)
        break;
    other case(s) as necessary
    default:
        statement(s)
    }
```

try block (related keywords: *catch, finally, throw,* and *throws*)

```
try
    {
    statement(s)
    }
catch (exceptionType identifier)
    {
    statement(s)
    }
other catch blocks as necessary
finally
    {
    statement(s)
    }
```

while loop (related keywords: *break* and *continue*)

```
while (boolean expression)
    {
    statement(s)
    }
```

Classes

Square braces ([ ]) indicate optional syntax.

```
[public][abstract] class ClassName
{
methods and member variables
}
```

Inheritance

```
class SubclassName [extends SuperclassName] [implements InterfaceName]
{
    methods and member variables
}
```

Interfaces

```
[public] [abstract] interface InterfaceName [extends
SuperInterfaceName]
{
    method declarations and final member variables
}
```

Packages

```
package packageName;
import packageName.className;
import packageName.*;
```

Methods

Access Methods

```
[accessModifier] returnType methodName (parameter_list)
{
    body of method
}
```

Where *accessModifier* is either *public, private, protected,* or default (package).

Threads

```
synchronized returnType methodName (parameter_list) {…}
```

Inheritance

```
[final | abstract] returnType methodName (parameter_list) {…}

returnType methodName (parameter_list)
{
    super(parameter_list);
    statement(s);
    return value;
}
```

Class Methods

```
static returnType methodName (parameter_list)
{
    statement(s)
}
```

Native Methods

```
class className
{
    native returnType methodName (parameter_list);
    static
    {
        native method initialization(s)
    }
    remainder of class definitions
}
```

Exceptions

```
returnType methodName (parameter_list) throws exceptionName
{
    statement(s)
    throw new exceptionName;
    statement(s)
}
```

Member Variables

Access

```
[accessModifier] type variableName [ = initialValue];
```

Where *accessModifier* is either *public*, *private*, *protected*, or default (package).

Behavior

```
static
final
volatile
transient
```

Typecasting, RTTI (Run-Time Type Information)

```
if (variable instanceof type)
{
    ((type)variable).method(parameterList);
    statement(s)
}
```

Programming: What's Going On?

When I was in college taking computer programming classes, I had a teaching assistant who insisted that we meticulously plan what our programs would do, how they would do it, and what the I/O would look like, before we wrote a line of code. He wouldn't help us debug our programs if we could not show him that we had done our planning ahead of time. In this same class, there was a guy who never did any planning. He just sat down in front of a computer terminal and started typing. He was pretty smart, and, fortunately for him, the assignments were simple enough that you could write them as you went along. That sums up pretty much either end of computer programming: plan, plan, plan, or wing it.

The problem with planning is that, well, if programmers could predict the future, we wouldn't be programmers, would we? Obviously though, you can't just sit down and write a program that requires thousands of lines of code, let alone hundreds of thousands, or even millions, without some planning. What we need, then, is some method of writing software that aids programmers in the way that programmers work. If you are a meticulous planner, then the method should help you plan your work without getting bogged down in the trivia of insignificant detail. If you are the type that likes to sit down and code away, then the method should allow you to get to the keyboard as soon as possible, while making it as easy as possible for you to record what you are doing, the reason why you're doing it that way, and maybe even what your next step should be.

Finding this method is not an easy task. People have been working on it for a while now, and the easy answers haven't popped up yet. Many software systems, especially large ones, have historically been developed using the "Waterfall Model." Figure C-1 shows a picture of the Waterfall Model.

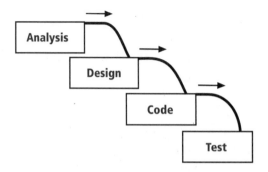

Figure C-1.   *The Waterfall Model of software development.*

It's called the Waterfall Model because you move from one stage to the next and never look back; you simply flow through the process and then you're done. The trouble with the Waterfall Model is that most people don't work this way. And, if you do try to work this way, what inevitably happens is that you make a mistake in one of the stages and you have to start all over. In fact, one of the most likely "mistakes" is that the person who asked you to write the code didn't really know exactly what he or she wanted, or has changed his or her mind.

Still, you can't just sit down and code without having some idea of what you are trying to accomplish or how you are going to accomplish it. That's where a more cyclic approach to software development comes in. Figure C-2 shows a diagram of this cyclic approach.

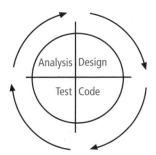

Figure C-2. *The Cyclic Model of software development.*

Notice that the stages of each model are the same. What changes is how many times we expect to visit each stage. This model is sometimes referred to as the "Design a little, Code a little, Test a little" approach.

The four stages of the model are Analysis, Design, Code, and Test. We will define below what is done in each stage, using a simple example program. For our example, let's say that someone has asked you to write a Windows-based program that calculates take-home pay. That's a pretty simple example, and maybe you could just sit down and write such a program off the top of your head. Don't focus on the example, focus on the steps we take to solve the problem, and then you can imagine how a more complex problem (like getting NASA's Pathfinder to Mars) might be solved with a similar approach.

Analysis

In the Analysis stage of a project, the task is to figure out exactly what it is that your software is supposed to do. In this stage we are full of questions. If you have a customer (the "someone" who asked you to write the program), drill this person with questions. If the customer is not sure, make suggestions. It is better to have your suggestions shot down than to have your finished program shot down. Here are some questions to consider for the customer in our take-home pay program:

- What is take-home pay?

- Who will be using this program (expert or novice users of Windows)?

- How will the program be getting its input?

- In what form do users need the output (on-screen or in a file)?

- Will users need online Help?

- Is World Wide Web access required?

- How soon is this program needed?

- Are there standards to which the program must adhere?

Your analysis should uncover the purpose of the program and what the program will do to fulfill that purpose.

Design

The Design stage consists of determining how the software is going to do what it is supposed to do. Let's say that in the Analysis stage you determined that users of every level of Windows proficiency are going to use this program to enter their hourly rate and their number of hours worked, and that on the screen should appear their expected take-home pay.

In the Design stage you decide that in order to make this happen, you will need a form with two labels, two edit boxes, and two buttons. You make a rough sketch of your form, something like Figure C-3.

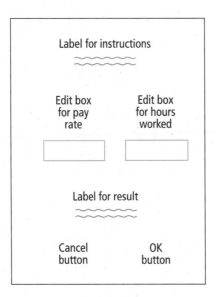

Figure C-3.   *Your rough sketch of the "Take-Home Pay" form.*

In the Analysis stage, you determined that take-home pay is equal to rate of pay per hour multiplied by the number of hours worked, minus the expected tax rate for that rate of pay, minus miscellaneous deductions. The Design stage is where you decide that in order to do this calculation you will need to:

1. Turn the text in the pay-rate edit box into a number.

2. Turn the text in the hours-worked edit box into a number.

3. Multiply those two numbers together.

4. Subtract the taxes.

5. Subtract the miscellaneous deductions.

6. Set the text in the result label equal to the result of your calculation.

Your completed design should tell you how everything that the program is designed to accomplish will be done.

Code

By the time you get to the Code stage, you should know what the software is supposed to do (Analysis) and how the software is supposed to do it (Design). The Code stage is where the Design is turned into actual source code.

For our example, we get into the Visual J++ environment; create a new project; add a form to it; and populate the form with labels, edit boxes, and buttons. Our design will express itself in the form of source code that goes into the event procedures of the WFC controls that we place on the form.

Test

You know that your code is going to work the first time, and *I* know that your code is going to work the first time, but for those Doubting Thomases out there who don't know this, we have the Test stage. Here are a few testing hints:

- Enter values at the edge of your legal range (that is, the smallest legal value and the largest legal value).

- Enter values outside your legal range. (What happens if someone puts in a negative number for hourly pay rate?)

- Enter values that don't make sense. (How much is "A" dollars?)

Does your program behave gracefully in all cases?

When you think things are working pretty well, take the program to your customer. You may find that with something to look at, the customer has some new idea about what is needed. Of course, you don't have to wait until you have a running program to get the customer involved. For example, the rough sketch of the form from the Design stage is a great thing to show the customer before you code it.

That feedback from the customer, coupled with your own hard-won experience, is the input into the next go-round of the Analysis stage. And the cycle continues until everybody has what he or she wants. Or at least that's how it works on paper.

Event-Driven Programming

Next to "object-oriented programming," "event-driven programming" is just about the hottest phrase to hit the field of software development in the 1990s. How is event-driven programming different from regular programming? Event-driven programming is all about giving control of the flow of a program to the user.

The history of computing has been a history of attempting to move control of a program's flow to its users. At one time, computers were programmed by connecting and disconnecting wires. This might be called "hardware-driven programming." If the programmer wanted to make a change to the program, the programmer had to go to the computer and modify the machine itself. The programmers had to understand in minute detail the operation of the computer—not exactly user friendly. (For their troubles, the programmers got a much-improved method of calculating trajectory tables for lobbing shells at the enemy.)

Then switches came along to make computer programming a little less hardware intensive. Later, various media (punch cards, paper tape, magnetic tape, and the like) were used to convey information to a computer. Computers no longer had to be programmed using hardware modifications, but instead were programmed through software. We might call this "media-driven programming." The media contained the instructions that determined what information was processed by the computer, and in what order it was processed.

Next, "interactive computing" came along, and for the first time the flow of a program could be modified while the program was running. But this control was limited—and to a large degree had to be foreseen—by the programmer writing the program. Before the emergence of GUIs (Graphical User Interfaces, pronounced "Gooeys"), the flow of a program was dictated by the programmer. Users were forced to go from one command prompt to the next, filling in data in exactly the way the programmer or code designer thought was best.

This really wasn't best for anybody, but it was a giant leap forward from punch cards. Previously, users simply handed their specifications to programmers, and the programmers determined how the data would be fed into the machine. Now that users were interacting with the computer directly, it meant that software developers not only had to understand what the users needed the software to do, but also the order in which the users entered their data. This order is actually arbitrary, but the software developers had to pick just one way and then code the system using that order. Users, on the other hand, had to deal with systems that were often non-intuitive and difficult to learn. What was a good setup for the mythical "average user" was often a bad fit for any particular user. But the field of interactive computing was new, and computer memory and storage was relatively small and expensive, so it was the best we could do.

As computers became faster and held more information, developers began to put more and more effort into making the computer display and accept information in a way that was accommodating to users. Prior to GUIs, most of the computational power of the computer was directed toward number crunching, and almost no effort was expended on making the presentation of the input or output easy for human beings to use. Raw pages of numbers may be exciting to some, but most people prefer graphics.

So, we made the step to event-driven programming. Now, the control of the flow of a computer program is where we wanted it all along: with the user. What does this mean to us as programmers? The I/O portion of our programs now consists of a nonsequential set of interface components that users are free (within bounds) to use in any order that makes sense. Our programs wait for the user to select a menu item, click a button, or move a scroll bar. When the user does take an action, our programs execute the appropriate block of code and then wait around for the next event. (By the way, not all events come from users. Pretty much anything outside our program can cause an event: hardware interrupts, clock timers, other software.)

Early event-driven programs had something called a "main event loop" that would loop forever, looking for events to happen. The event would come into the program and be identified as a particular kind of event: mouse click or drag, timer timeout, and so forth. The event would then be dispatched to the correct procedure to be handled. This sort of program structure was the same for every event-driven program out there. The Visual J++ environment takes care of most of these details for us, so we don't see things like the "main event loop" in our code. The environment automatically attaches event handlers to actions like the clicking of a button, for example, based on how you build your software. This frees us programmers from worrying about how the events get to us, so that we can concentrate on what we want the program to do when a particular event has occurred.

Note: Italic page numbers indicate figures, tables, or code listings.

J

About the Authors

Kevin L. Ingalls is a programmer and software engineer at Boeing in Seattle, where he works in the training department developing and teaching courses in Ada, C/C++, and Object-Oriented Technology. He lives in Kent, Washington with his wife, Misa, two daughters, Linnea and Megan, and Amelia, a Chesapeake Bay Retriever (Retriever? ha!). He and his wife enjoy exotic tropical SCUBA diving vacations, and each other.

Daniel Jinguji is a Microsoft developer working on Visual J++. He has 15 years of experience in educating and training computer programmers and often presents at computer industry events. Outside the realm of binary compatibility and software components, Dan busies himself with early music, the Roman liturgy, and sacramental catechesis.

MICROSOFT LICENSE AGREEMENT

(Book Companion CD)

IMPORTANT—READ CAREFULLY: This Microsoft End-User License Agreement ("EULA") is a legal agreement between you (either an individual or an entity) and Microsoft Corporation for the Microsoft product identified above, which includes computer software and may include associated media, printed materials, and "on-line" or electronic documentation ("SOFTWARE PRODUCT"). Any component included within the SOFTWARE PRODUCT that is accompanied by a separate End-User License Agreement shall be governed by such agreement and not the terms set forth below. By installing, copying, or otherwise using the SOFTWARE PRODUCT, you agree to be bound by the terms of this EULA. If you do not agree to the terms of this EULA, you are not authorized to install, copy, or otherwise use the SOFTWARE PRODUCT; you may, however, return the SOFTWARE PRODUCT, along with all printed materials and other items that form a part of the Microsoft product that includes the SOFTWARE PRODUCT, to the place you obtained them for a full refund.

SOFTWARE PRODUCT LICENSE

The SOFTWARE PRODUCT is protected by United States copyright laws and international copyright treaties, as well as other intellectual property laws and treaties. The SOFTWARE PRODUCT is licensed, not sold.

1. GRANT OF LICENSE. This EULA grants you the following rights:

   a. Software Product. You may install and use one copy of the SOFTWARE PRODUCT on a single computer. The primary user of the computer on which the SOFTWARE PRODUCT is installed may make a second copy for his or her exclusive use on a portable computer.

   b. Storage/Network Use. You may also store or install a copy of the SOFTWARE PRODUCT on a storage device, such as a network server, used only to install or run the SOFTWARE PRODUCT on your other computers over an internal network; however, you must acquire and dedicate a license for each separate computer on which the SOFTWARE PRODUCT is installed or run from the storage device. A license for the SOFTWARE PRODUCT may not be shared or used concurrently on different computers.

   c. License Pak. If you have acquired this EULA in a Microsoft License Pak, you may make the number of additional copies of the computer software portion of the SOFTWARE PRODUCT authorized on the printed copy of this EULA, and you may use each copy in the manner specified above. You are also entitled to make a corresponding number of secondary copies for portable computer use as specified above.

   d. Sample Code. Solely with respect to portions, if any, of the SOFTWARE PRODUCT that are identified within the SOFTWARE PRODUCT as sample code (the "SAMPLE CODE"):

      i. Use and Modification. Microsoft grants you the right to use and modify the source code version of the SAMPLE CODE, *provided* you comply with subsection (d)(iii) below. You may not distribute the SAMPLE CODE, or any modified version of the SAMPLE CODE, in source code form.

      ii. Redistributable Files. Provided you comply with subsection (d)(iii) below, Microsoft grants you a nonexclusive, royalty-free right to reproduce and distribute the object code version of the SAMPLE CODE and of any modified SAMPLE CODE, other than SAMPLE CODE (or any modified version thereof) designated as not redistributable in the Readme file that forms a part of the SOFTWARE PRODUCT (the "Non-Redistributable Sample Code"). All SAMPLE CODE other than the Non-Redistributable Sample Code is collectively referred to as the "REDISTRIBUTABLES."

      iii. Redistribution Requirements. If you redistribute the REDISTRIBUTABLES, you agree to: (i) distribute the REDISTRIBUTABLES in object code form only in conjunction with and as a part of your software application product; (ii) not use Microsoft's name, logo, or trademarks to market your software application product; (iii) include a valid copyright notice on your software application product; (iv) indemnify, hold harmless, and defend Microsoft from and against any claims or lawsuits, including attorney's fees, that arise or result from the use or distribution of your software application product; and (v) not permit further distribution of the REDISTRIBUTABLES by your end user. Contact Microsoft for the applicable royalties due and other licensing terms for all other uses and/or distribution of the REDISTRIBUTABLES.

2. DESCRIPTION OF OTHER RIGHTS AND LIMITATIONS.

   - **Limitations on Reverse Engineering, Decompilation, and Disassembly.** You may not reverse engineer, decompile, or disassemble the SOFTWARE PRODUCT, except and only to the extent that such activity is expressly permitted by applicable law notwithstanding this limitation.

   - **Separation of Components.** The SOFTWARE PRODUCT is licensed as a single product. Its component parts may not be separated for use on more than one computer.

   - **Rental.** You may not rent, lease, or lend the SOFTWARE PRODUCT.

   - **Support Services.** Microsoft may, but is not obligated to, provide you with support services related to the SOFTWARE PRODUCT ("Support Services"). Use of Support Services is governed by the Microsoft policies and programs described in the user manual, in "on-line" documentation, and/or in other Microsoft-provided materials. Any supplemental software code provided to you as part of the Support Services shall be considered part of the SOFTWARE PRODUCT and subject to the terms and conditions of this EULA.

With respect to technical information you provide to Microsoft as part of the Support Services, Microsoft may use such information for its business purposes, including for product support and development. Microsoft will not utilize such technical information in a form that personally identifies you.

- **Software Transfer.** You may permanently transfer all of your rights under this EULA, provided you retain no copies, you transfer all of the SOFTWARE PRODUCT (including all component parts, the media and printed materials, any upgrades, this EULA, and, if applicable, the Certificate of Authenticity), **and** the recipient agrees to the terms of this EULA.

- **Termination.** Without prejudice to any other rights, Microsoft may terminate this EULA if you fail to comply with the terms and conditions of this EULA. In such event, you must destroy all copies of the SOFTWARE PRODUCT and all of its component parts.

3. COPYRIGHT. All title and copyrights in and to the SOFTWARE PRODUCT (including but not limited to any images, photographs, animations, video, audio, music, text, SAMPLE CODE, REDISTRIBUTABLES, and "applets" incorporated into the SOFTWARE PRODUCT) and any copies of the SOFTWARE PRODUCT are owned by Microsoft or its suppliers. The SOFTWARE PRODUCT is protected by copyright laws and international treaty provisions. Therefore, you must treat the SOFTWARE PRODUCT like any other copyrighted material **except** that you may install the SOFTWARE PRODUCT on a single computer provided you keep the original solely for backup or archival purposes. You may not copy the printed materials accompanying the SOFTWARE PRODUCT.

4. U.S. GOVERNMENT RESTRICTED RIGHTS. The SOFTWARE PRODUCT and documentation are provided with RESTRICTED RIGHTS. Use, duplication, or disclosure by the Government is subject to restrictions as set forth in subparagraph (c)(1)(ii) of the Rights in Technical Data and Computer Software clause at DFARS 252.227-7013 or subparagraphs (c)(1) and (2) of the Commercial Computer Software—Restricted Rights at 48 CFR 52.227-19, as applicable. Manufacturer is Microsoft Corporation/One Microsoft Way/Redmond, WA 98052-6399.

5. EXPORT RESTRICTIONS. You agree that you will not export or re-export the SOFTWARE PRODUCT, any part thereof, or any process or service that is the direct product of the SOFTWARE PRODUCT (the foregoing collectively referred to as the "Restricted Components"), to any country, person, entity, or end user subject to U.S. export restrictions. You specifically agree not to export or re-export any of the Restricted Components (i) to any country to which the U.S. has embargoed or restricted the export of goods or services, which currently include, but are not necessarily limited to, Cuba, Iran, Iraq, Libya, North Korea, Sudan, and Syria, or to any national of any such country, wherever located, who intends to transmit or transport the Restricted Components back to such country; (ii) to any end user who you know or have reason to know will utilize the Restricted Components in the design, development, or production of nuclear, chemical, or biological weapons; or (iii) to any end user who has been prohibited from participating in U.S. export transactions by any federal agency of the U.S. government. You warrant and represent that neither the BXA nor any other U.S. federal agency has suspended, revoked, or denied your export privileges.

6. NOTE ON JAVA SUPPORT. THE SOFTWARE PRODUCT MAY CONTAIN SUPPORT FOR PROGRAMS WRITTEN IN JAVA. JAVA TECHNOLOGY IS NOT FAULT TOLERANT AND IS NOT DESIGNED, MANUFACTURED, OR INTENDED FOR USE OR RESALE AS ON-LINE CONTROL EQUIPMENT IN HAZARDOUS ENVIRONMENTS REQUIRING FAIL-SAFE PERFORMANCE, SUCH AS IN THE OPERATION OF NUCLEAR FACILITIES, AIRCRAFT NAVIGATION OR COMMUNI-CATION SYSTEMS, AIR TRAFFIC CONTROL, DIRECT LIFE SUPPORT MACHINES, OR WEAPONS SYSTEMS, IN WHICH THE FAILURE OF JAVA TECHNOLOGY COULD LEAD DIRECTLY TO DEATH, PERSONAL INJURY, OR SEVERE PHYSICAL OR ENVIRONMENTAL DAMAGE.

DISCLAIMER OF WARRANTY

NO WARRANTIES OR CONDITIONS. MICROSOFT EXPRESSLY DISCLAIMS ANY WARRANTY OR CONDITION FOR THE SOFTWARE PRODUCT. THE SOFTWARE PRODUCT AND ANY RELATED DOCUMENTATION IS PROVIDED "AS IS" WITHOUT WARRANTY OR CONDITION OF ANY KIND, EITHER EXPRESS OR IMPLIED, INCLUDING, WITHOUT LIMITATION, THE IMPLIED WARRANTIES OF MERCHANTABILITY, FITNESS FOR A PARTICULAR PURPOSE, OR NONINFRINGEMENT. THE ENTIRE RISK ARISING OUT OF USE OR PERFORMANCE OF THE SOFTWARE PRODUCT REMAINS WITH YOU.

LIMITATION OF LIABILITY. TO THE MAXIMUM EXTENT PERMITTED BY APPLICABLE LAW, IN NO EVENT SHALL MICROSOFT OR ITS SUPPLIERS BE LIABLE FOR ANY SPECIAL, INCIDENTAL, INDIRECT, OR CONSEQUENTIAL DAMAGES WHATSOEVER (INCLUDING, WITHOUT LIMITATION, DAMAGES FOR LOSS OF BUSINESS PROFITS, BUSINESS INTERRUP-TION, LOSS OF BUSINESS INFORMATION, OR ANY OTHER PECUNIARY LOSS) ARISING OUT OF THE USE OF OR INABIL-ITY TO USE THE SOFTWARE PRODUCT OR THE PROVISION OF OR FAILURE TO PROVIDE SUPPORT SERVICES, EVEN IF MICROSOFT HAS BEEN ADVISED OF THE POSSIBILITY OF SUCH DAMAGES. IN ANY CASE, MICROSOFT'S ENTIRE LIABILITY UNDER ANY PROVISION OF THIS EULA SHALL BE LIMITED TO THE GREATER OF THE AMOUNT ACTUALLY PAID BY YOU FOR THE SOFTWARE PRODUCT OR US$5.00; PROVIDED, HOWEVER, IF YOU HAVE ENTERED INTO A MICROSOFT SUPPORT SERVICES AGREEMENT, MICROSOFT'S ENTIRE LIABILITY REGARDING SUPPORT SERVICES SHALL BE GOVERNED BY THE TERMS OF THAT AGREEMENT. BECAUSE SOME STATES AND JURISDICTIONS DO NOT ALLOW THE EXCLUSION OR LIMITATION OF LIABILITY, THE ABOVE LIMITATION MAY NOT APPLY TO YOU.

MISCELLANEOUS

This EULA is governed by the laws of the State of Washington USA, except and only to the extent that applicable law mandates governing law of a different jurisdiction.

Should you have any questions concerning this EULA, or if you desire to contact Microsoft for any reason, please contact the Microsoft subsidiary serving your country, or write: Microsoft Sales Information Center/One Microsoft Way/Redmond, WA 98052-6399.

Register Today!

Return this
Learn Microsoft® Visual J++™ 6.0 Now
registration card today

Microsoft *Press*
mspress.microsoft.com

OWNER REGISTRATION CARD   1-57231-923-2

Learn Microsoft® Visual J++™ 6.0 Now

_____   _____   _____
FIRST NAME   MIDDLE INITIAL   LAST NAME

_____
INSTITUTION OR COMPANY NAME

_____
ADDRESS

_____

_____   _____   _____
CITY   STATE   ZIP

                                                           (   )
_____   _____
E-MAIL ADDRESS   PHONE NUMBER

U.S. and Canada addresses only. Fill in information above and mail postage-free.
Please mail only the bottom half of this page.

For information about Microsoft Press®

products, visit our Web site at

mspress.microsoft.com

Microsoft®*Press*